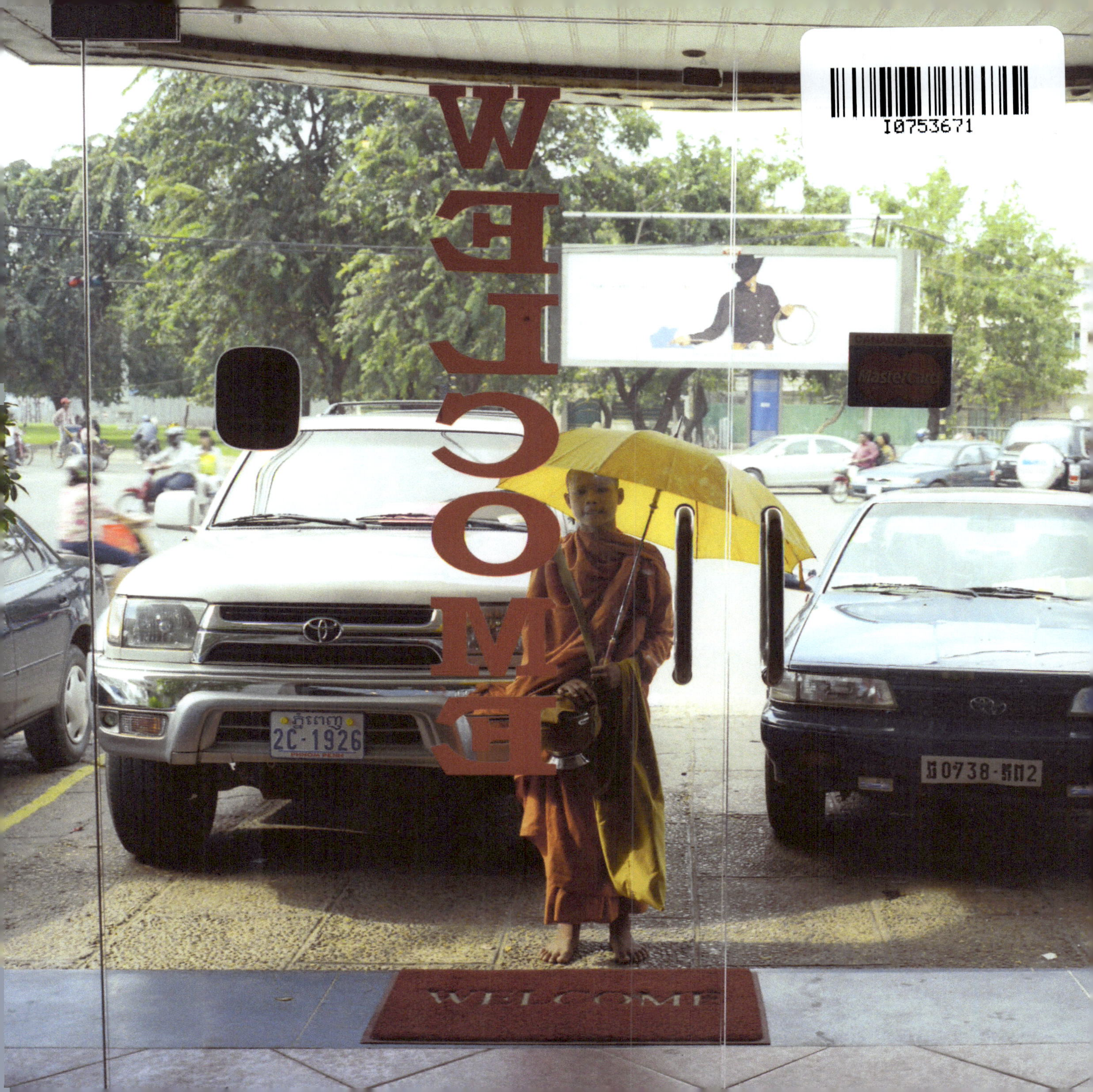

I0753671
WELCOME
2C-1926
WELCOME

ISBN 978-0-6152-4175-3

Contact:
dearcambodia@gmail.com

Printed:
Lulu Press
Morrisville, NC, U.S.A.
www.lulu.com

PHOTOGRAPHY: Mat Roe
DESIGN: Jennifer Moody

Special Thanks to:
Leonard & Gladys, P & S & F, and to all my friends–past and present–who call Cambodia their home.

Dear
CAMBODIA
A pictorial love letter to a country

CONTENTS

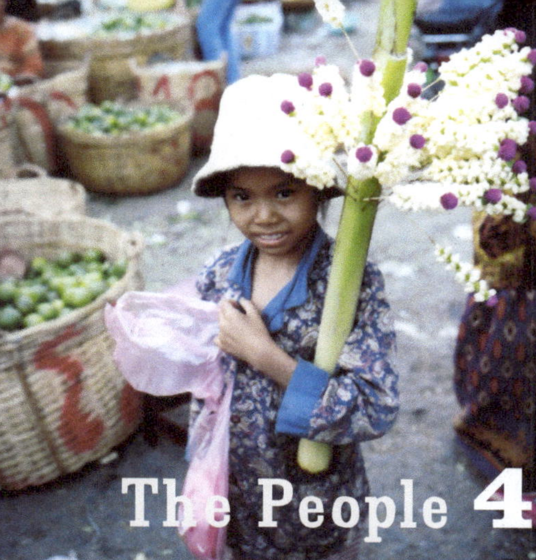

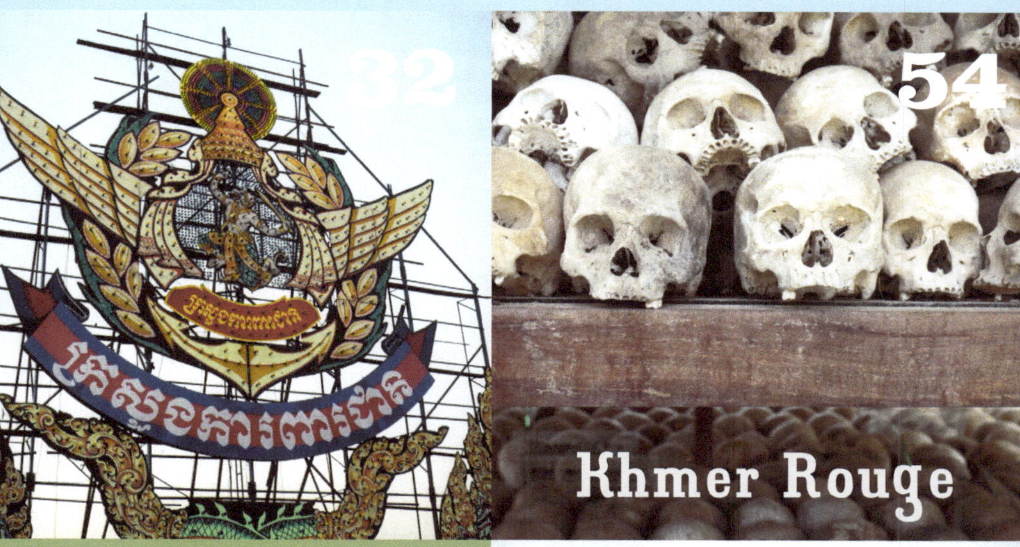

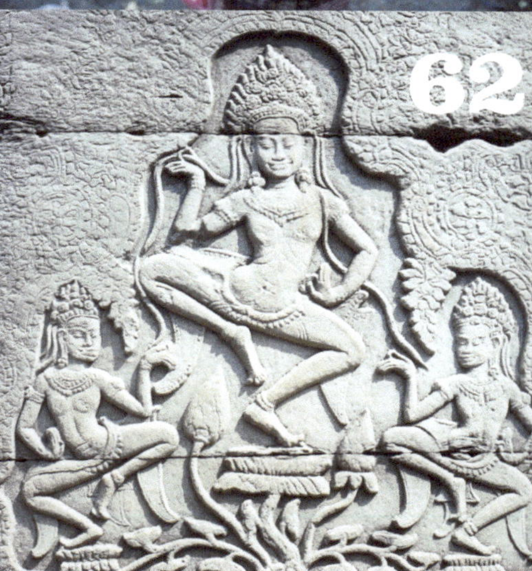

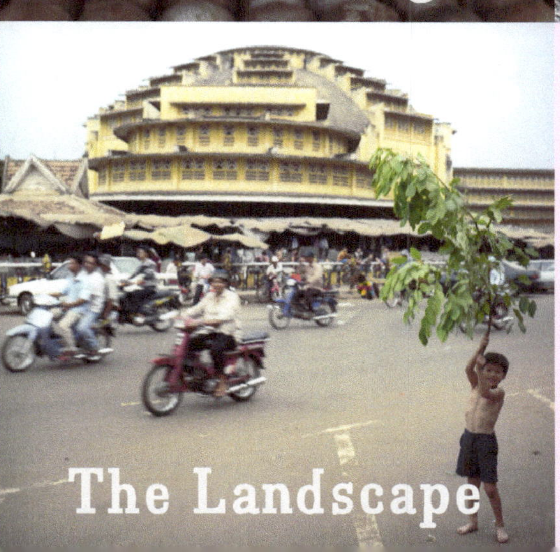

Photography by Mat Roe

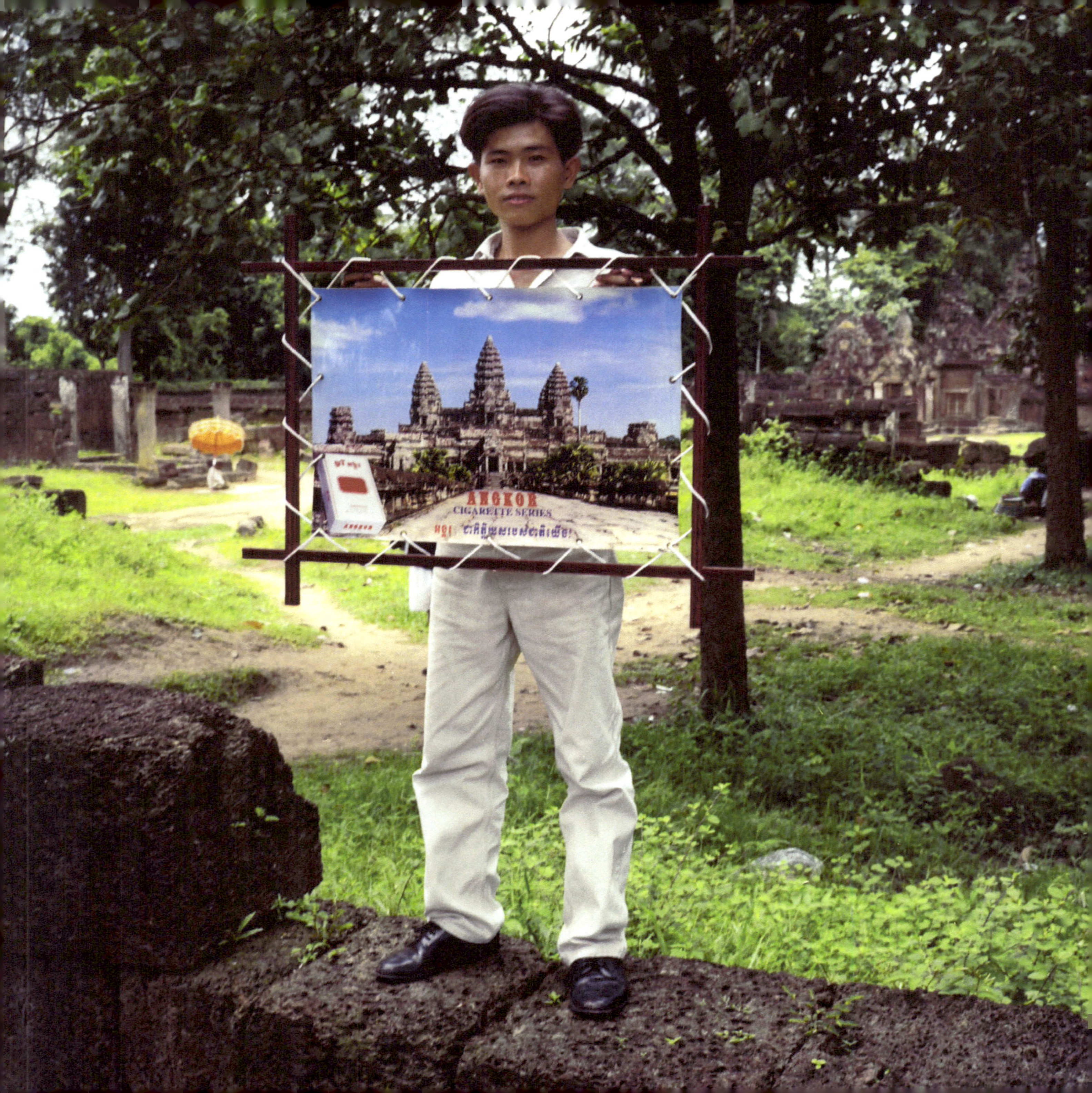
ANGKOR
CIGARETTE SERIES
ANGKOR

PEOPLE

in your country are so resilient with such charm and kindness. I have had eye-opening experiences teaching me much about your manners and culture. Your country makes it easy not to feel homesick for the U.S., but I am often homesick for Cambodia! From the farmers to the monks to the families, I have so much gratitude for my friends and the complete strangers who have all helped me explore Cambodia.

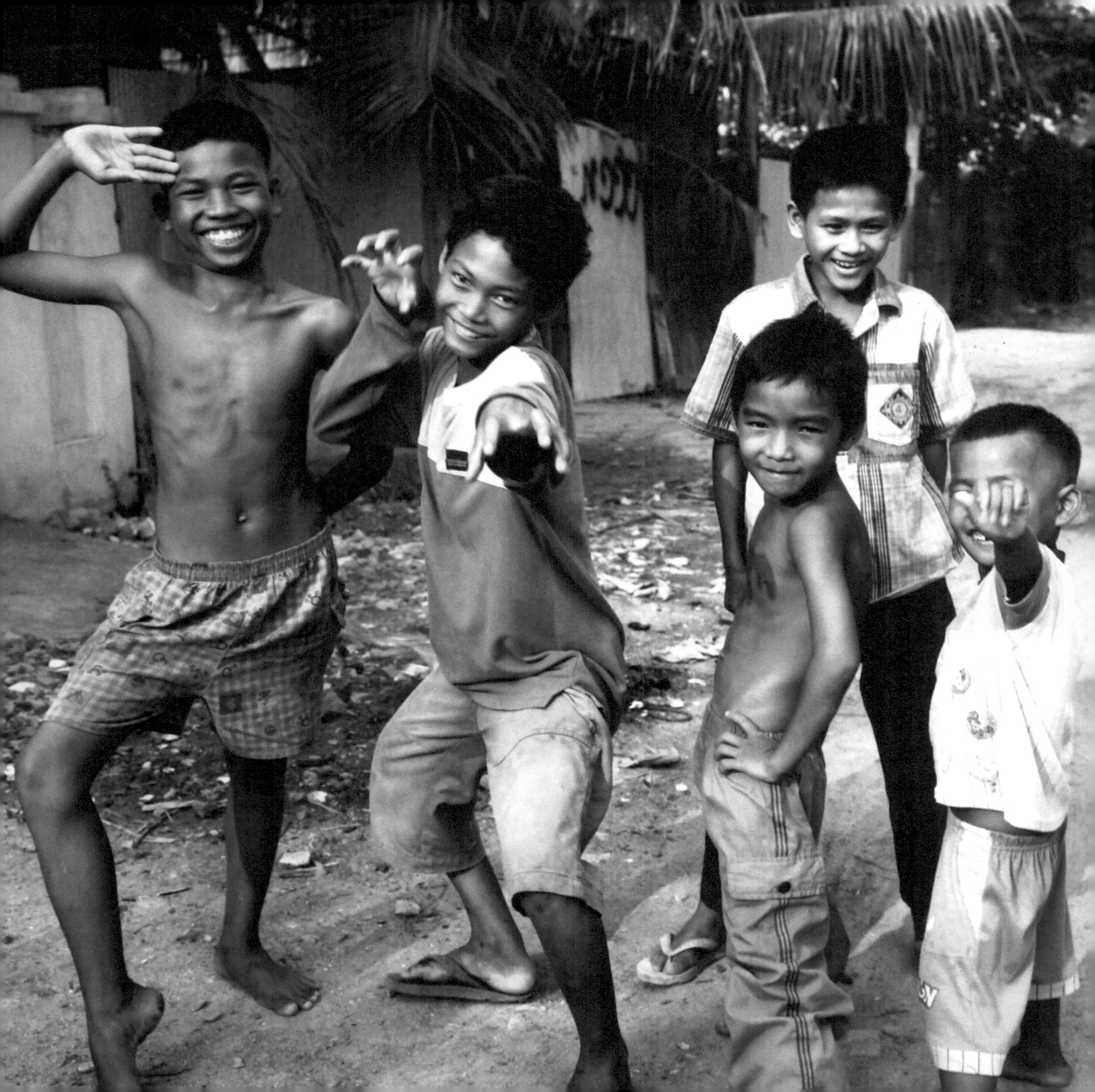

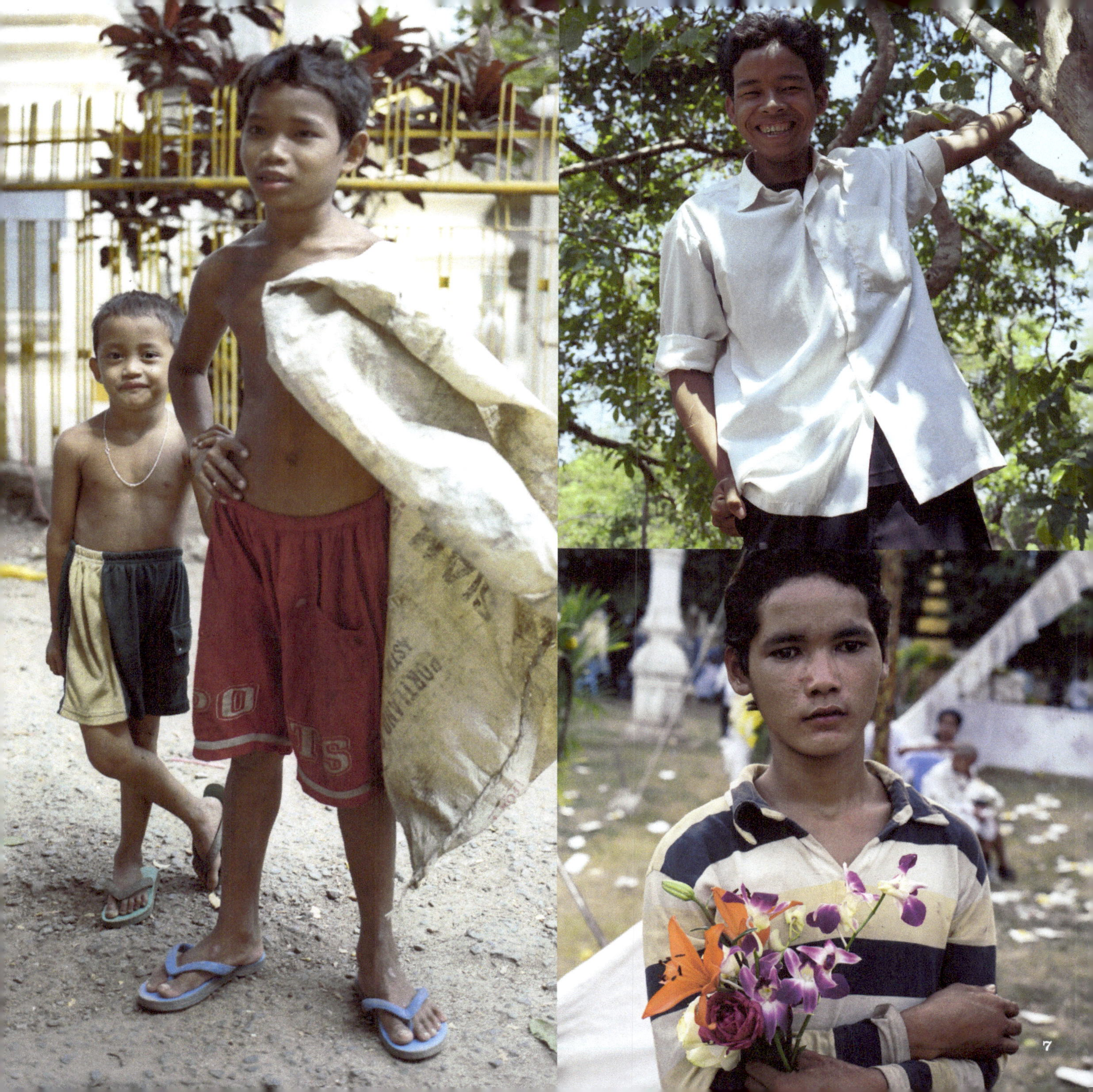

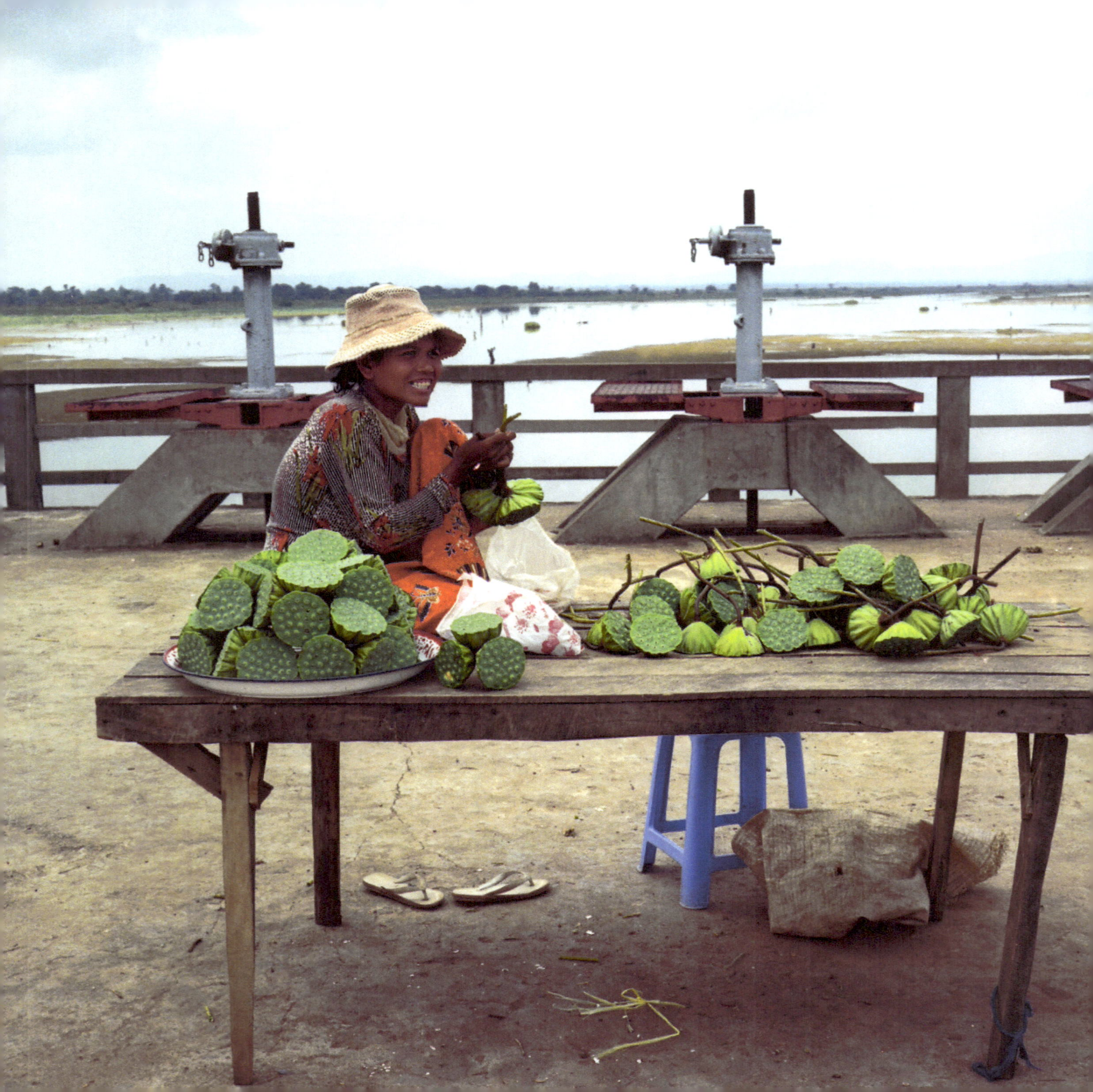

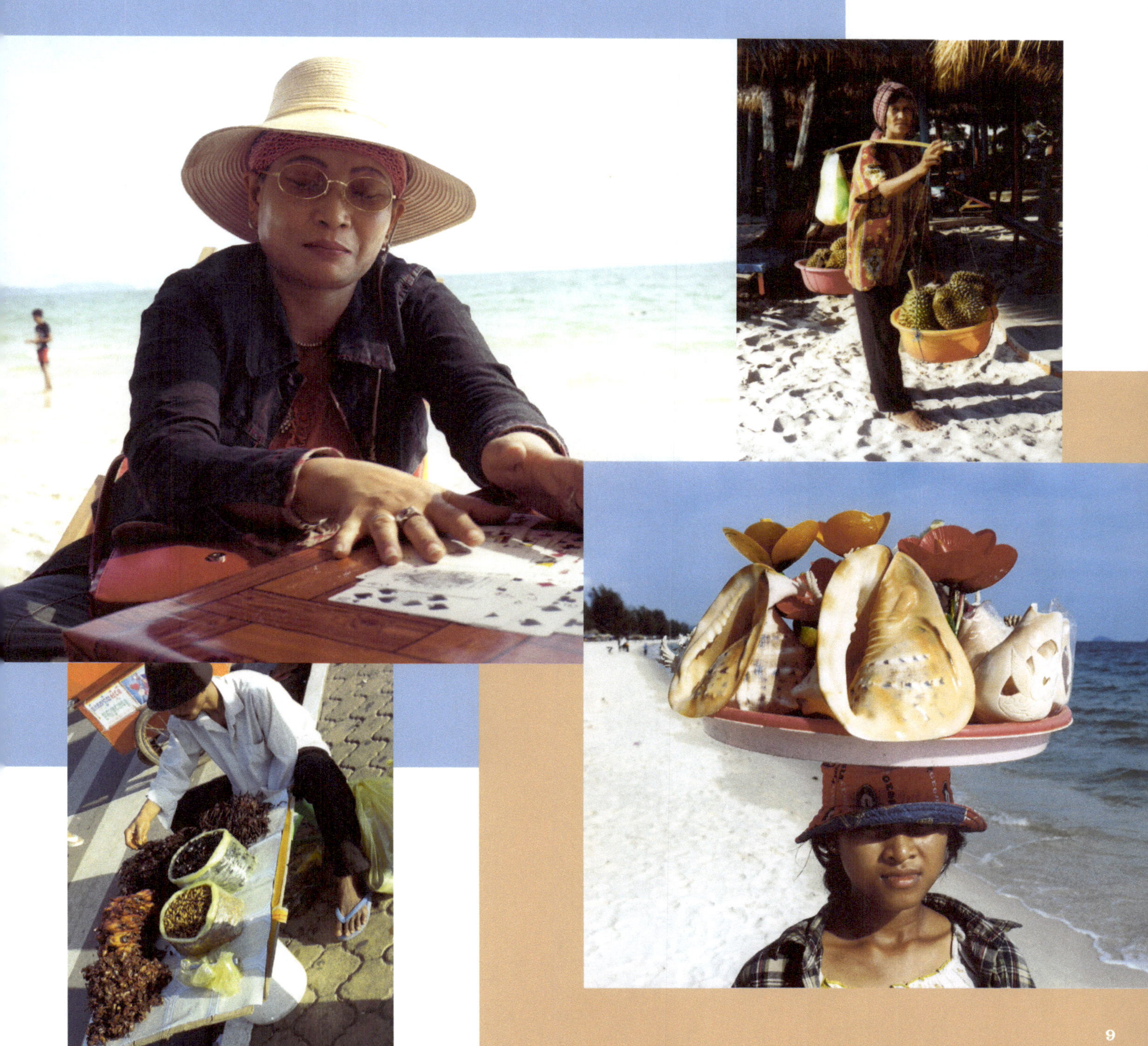

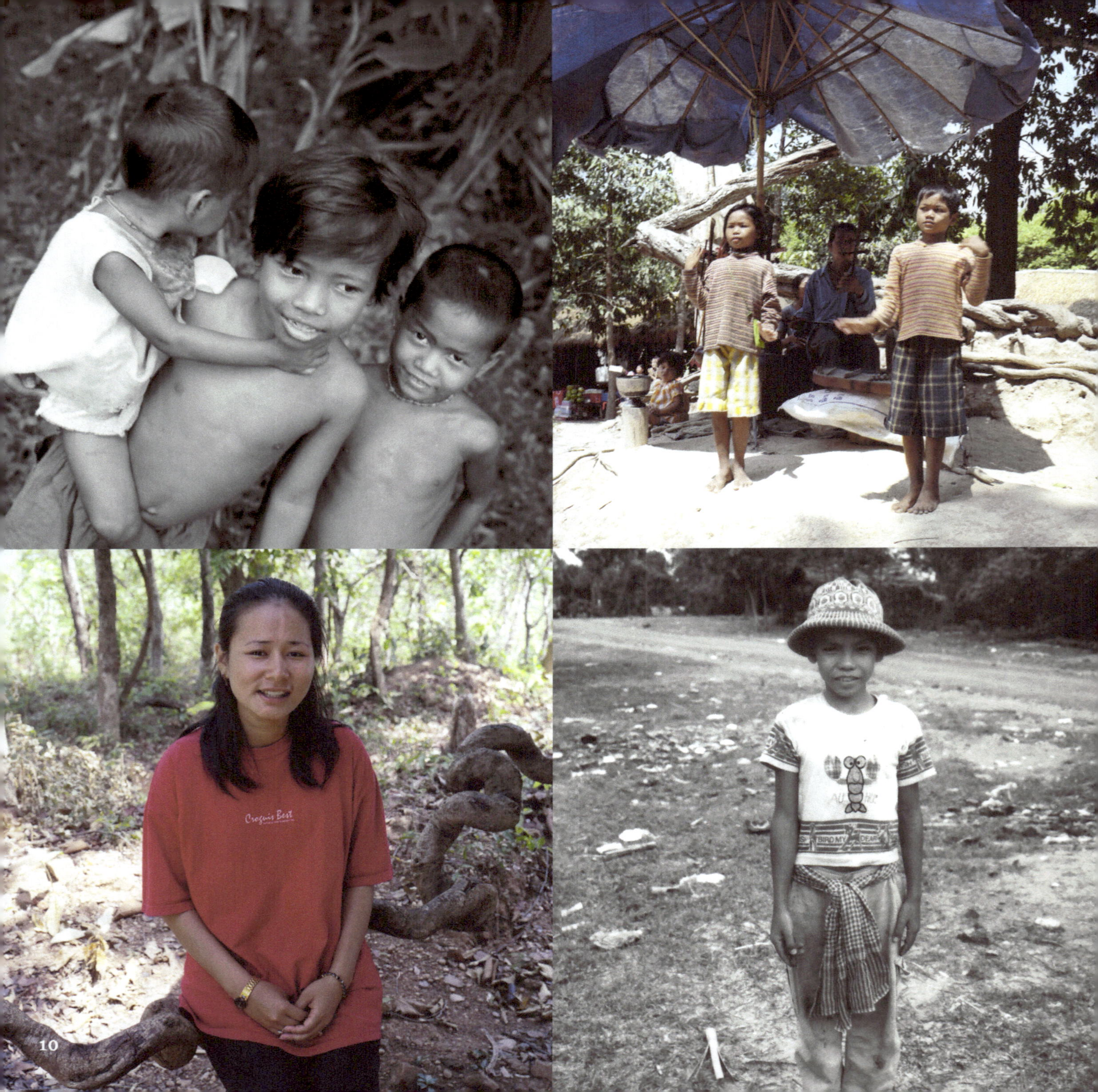
Croquis Best

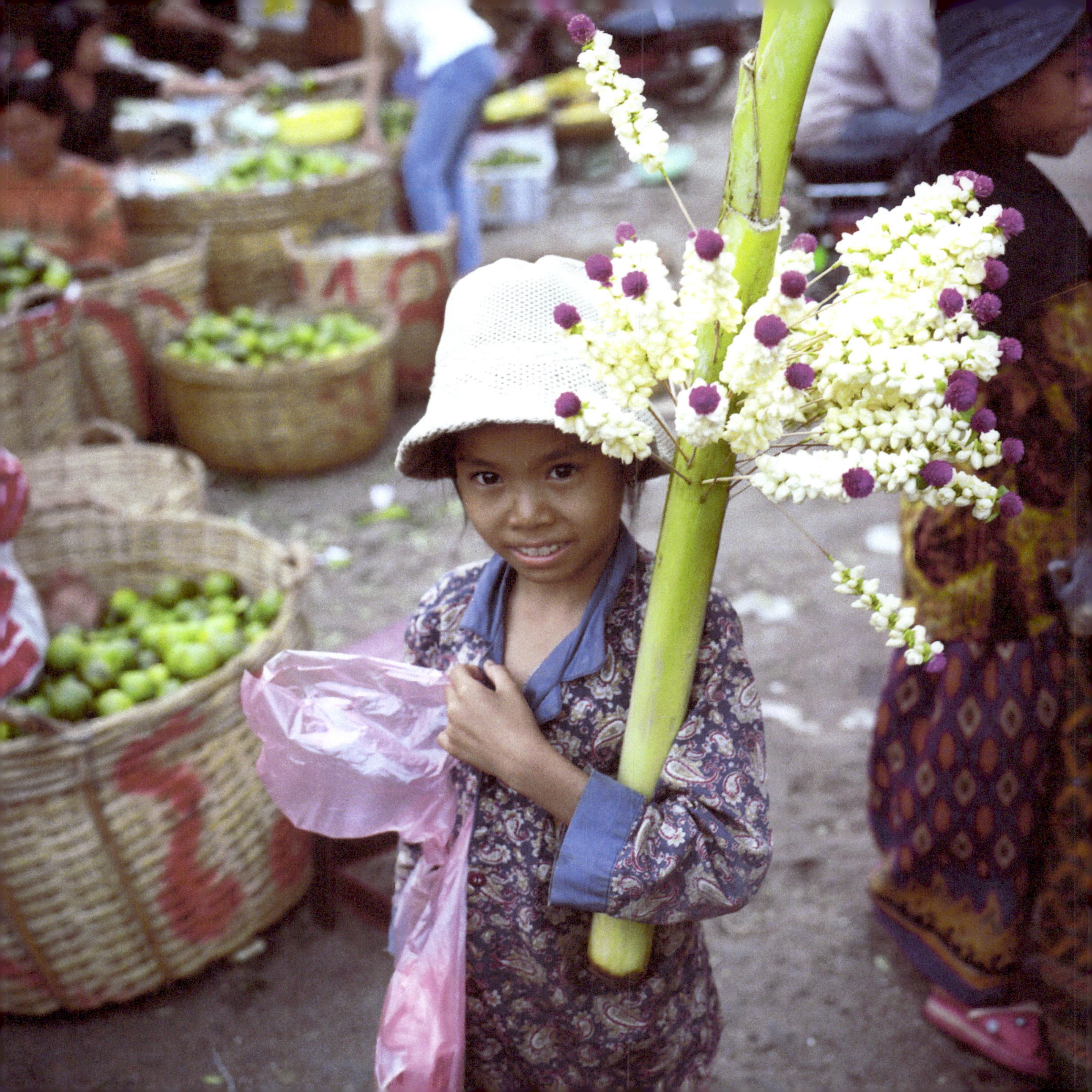

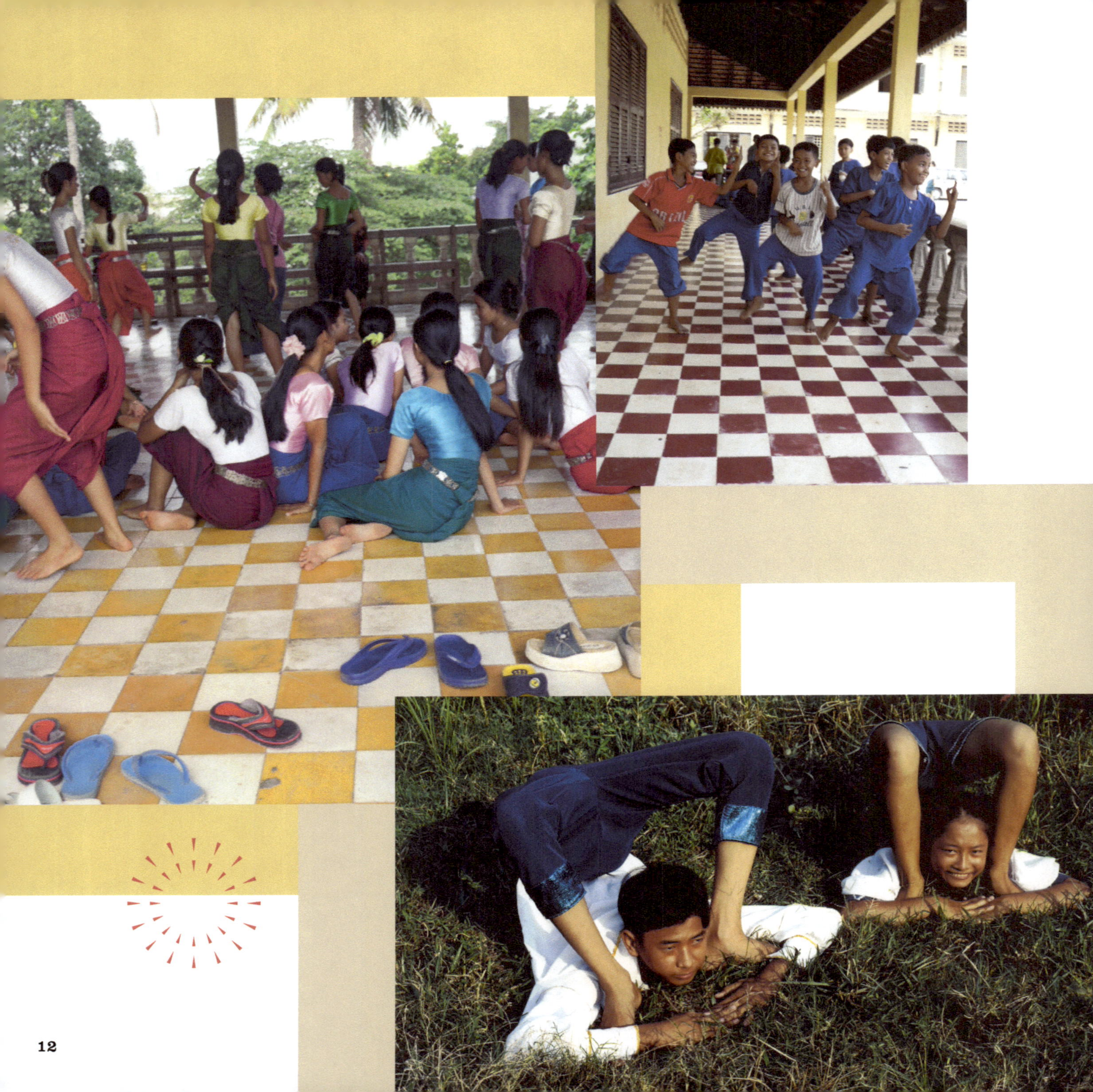

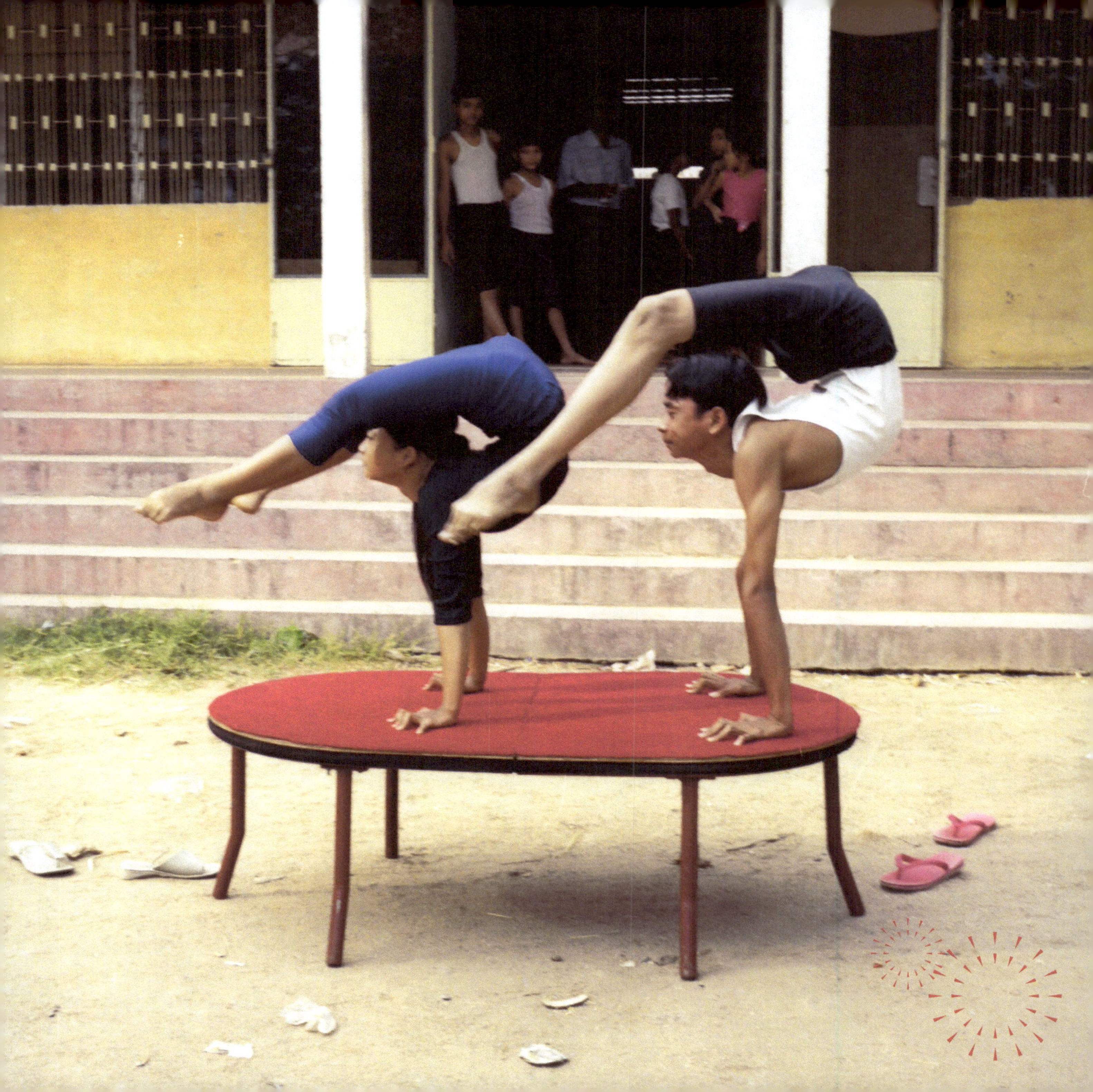

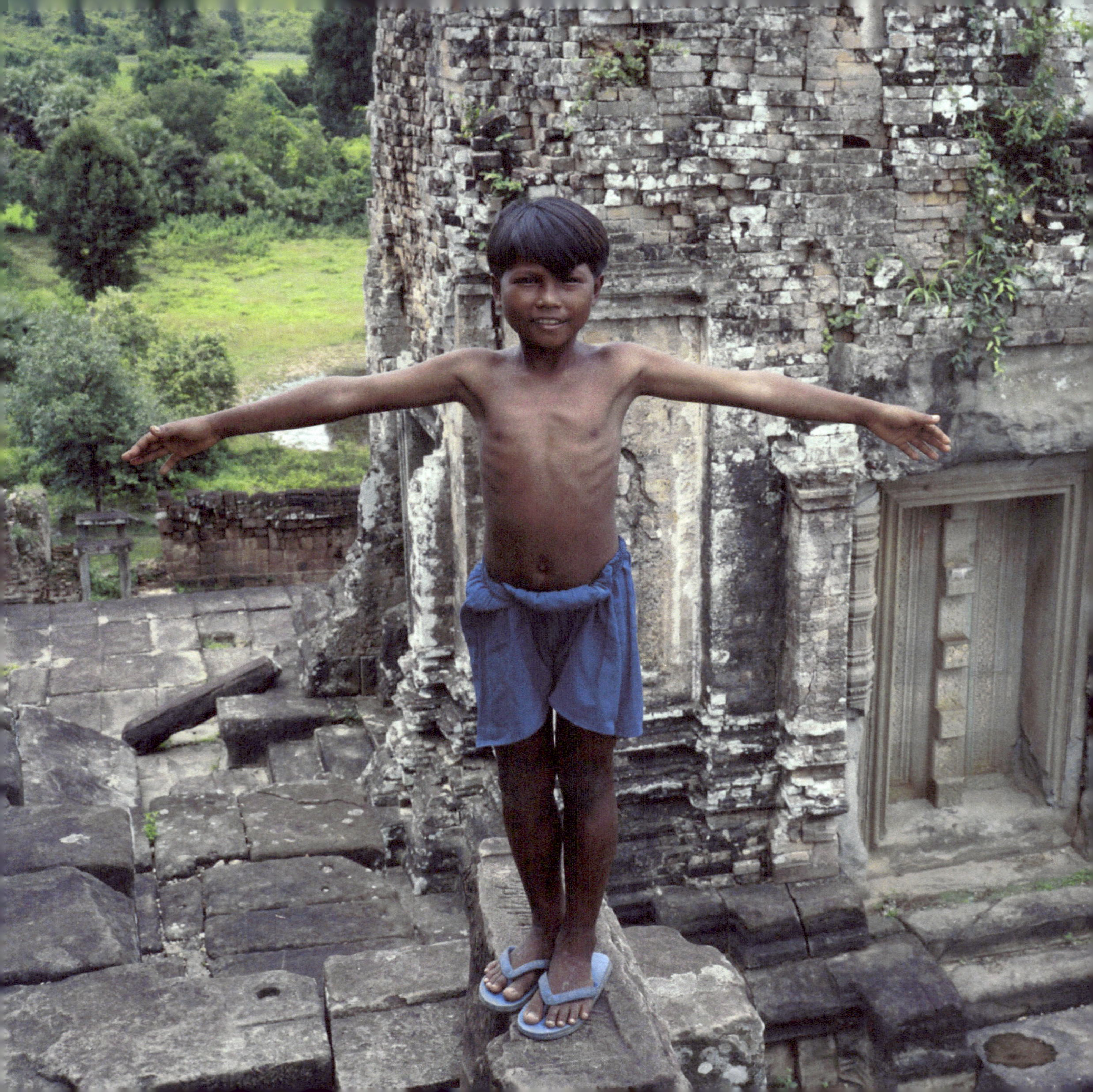

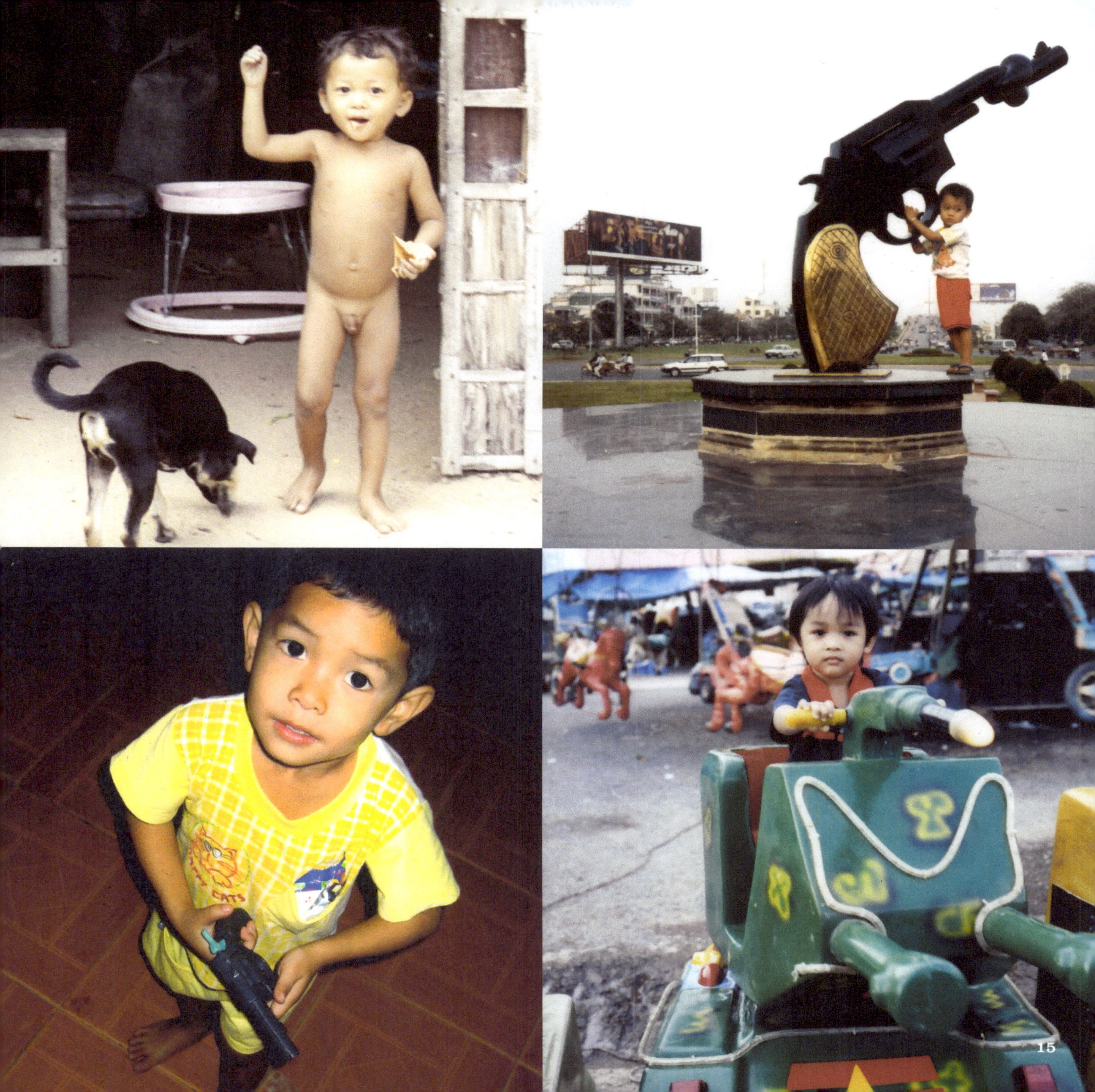

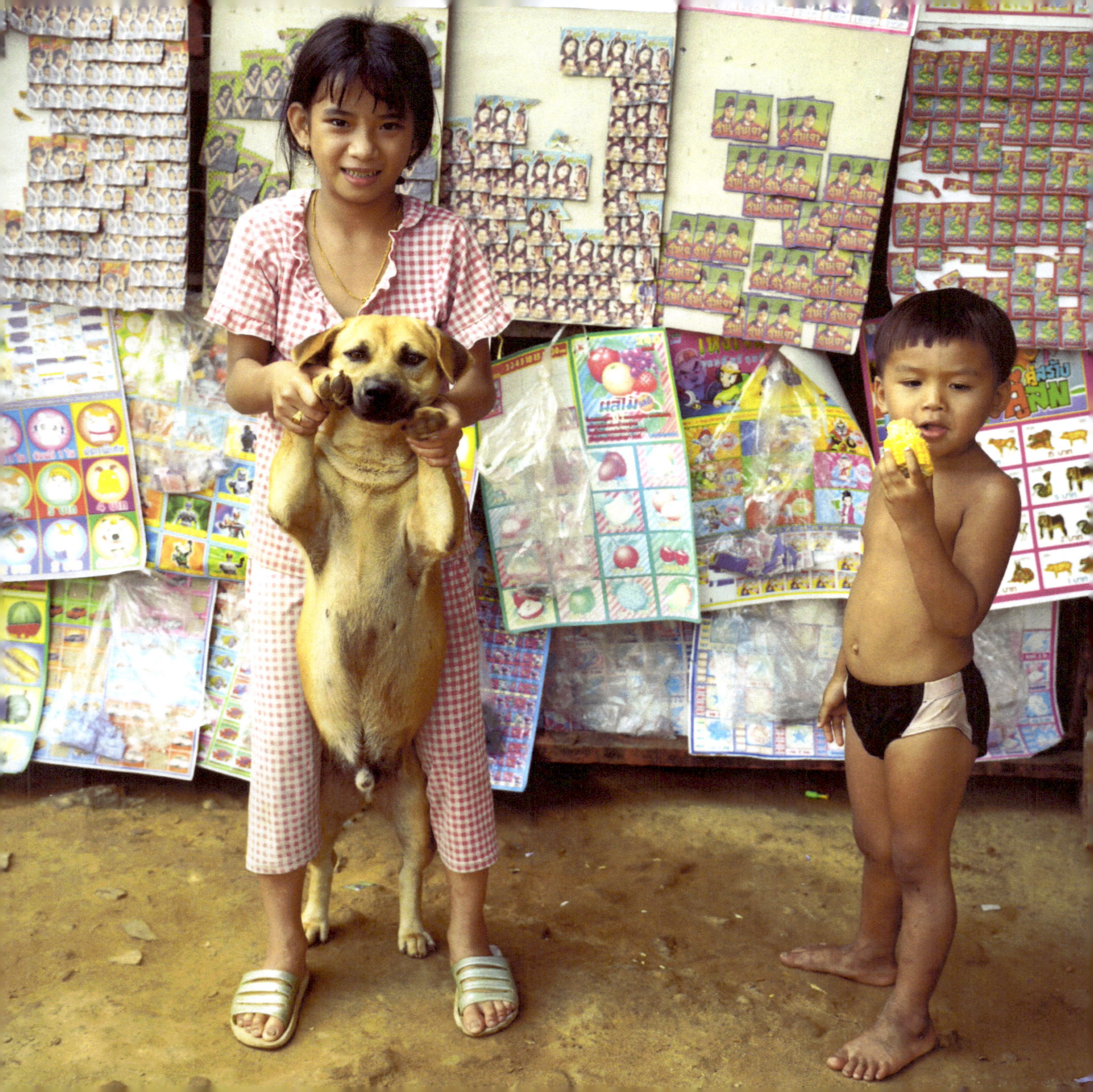

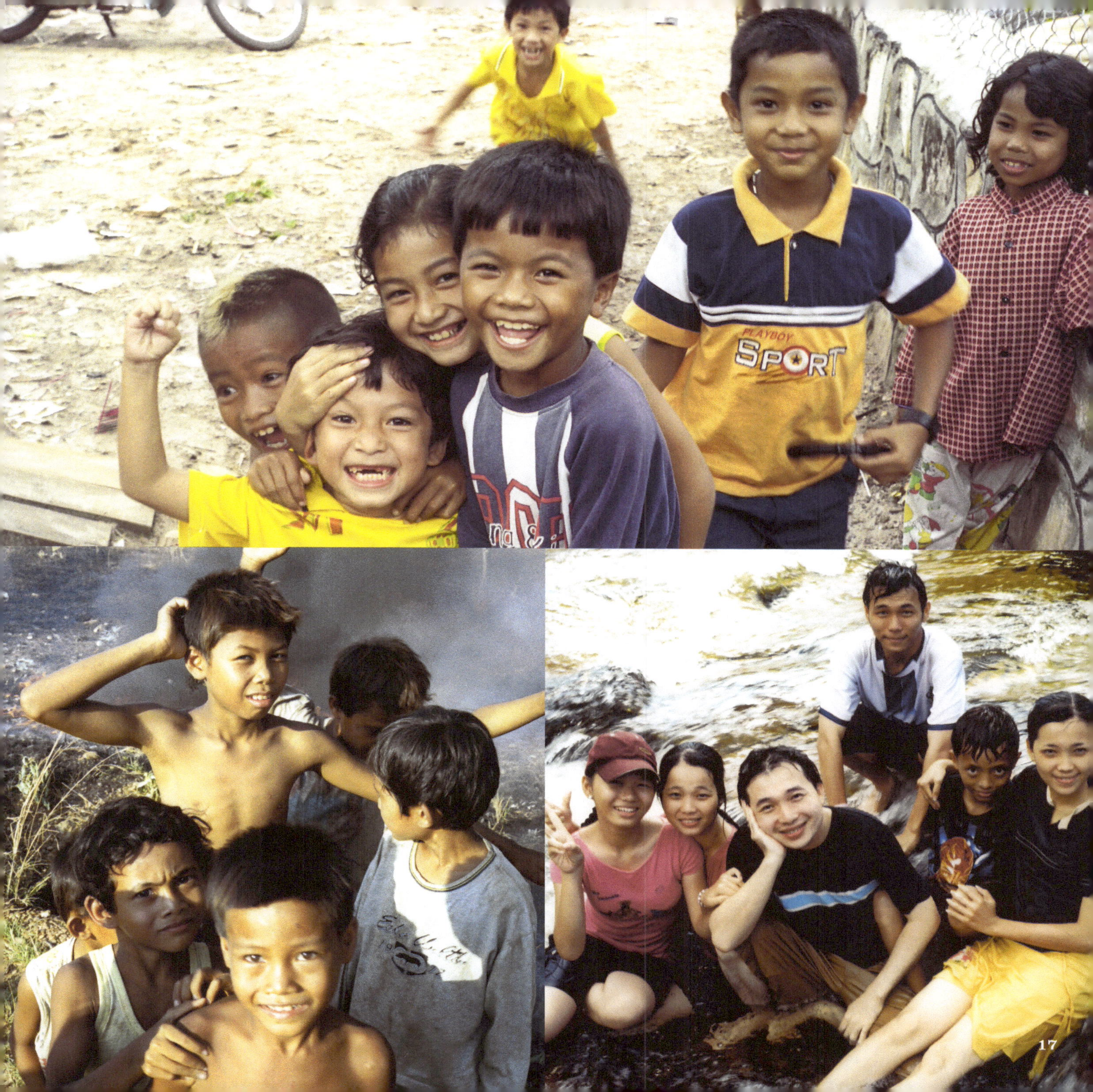
PLAYBOY
SPORT

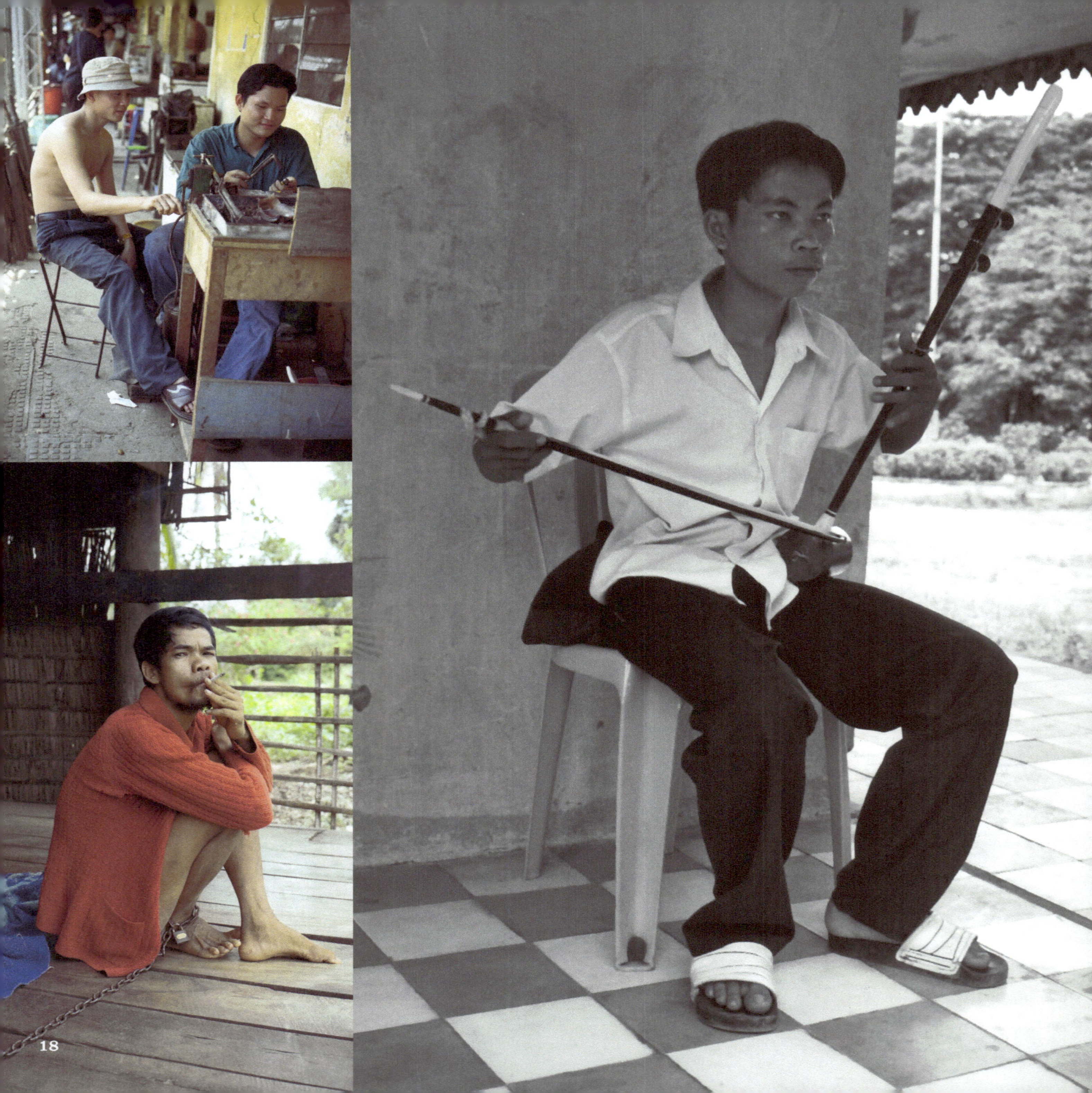

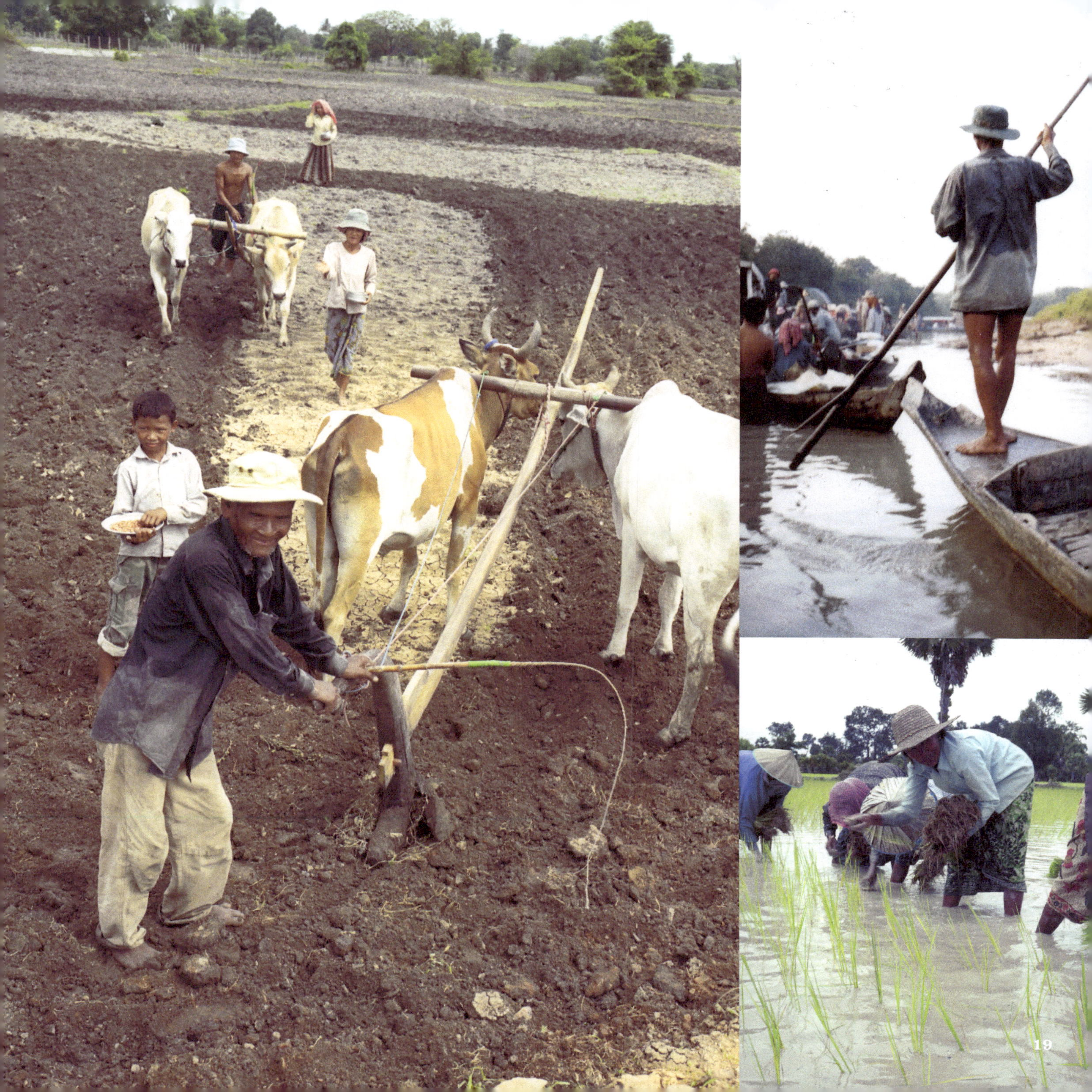

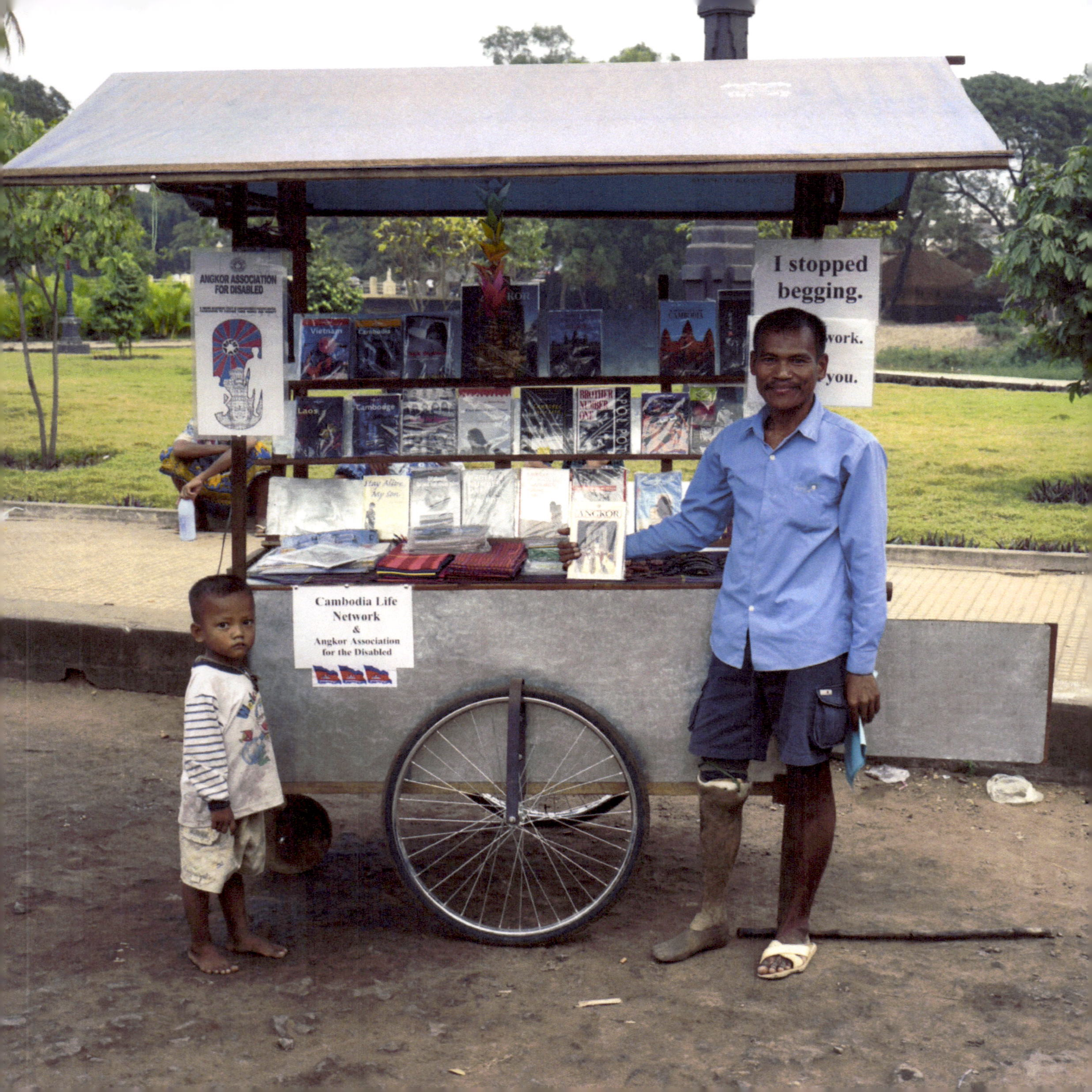
ANGKOR ASSOCIATION FOR DISABLED
I stopped begging.
work.
you.
Vietnam
Cambodia
Laos
Cambodge
BROTHER NUMBER ONE
POL POT
Stay Alive, My Son
ANGKOR
Cambodia Life Network & Angkor Association for the Disabled

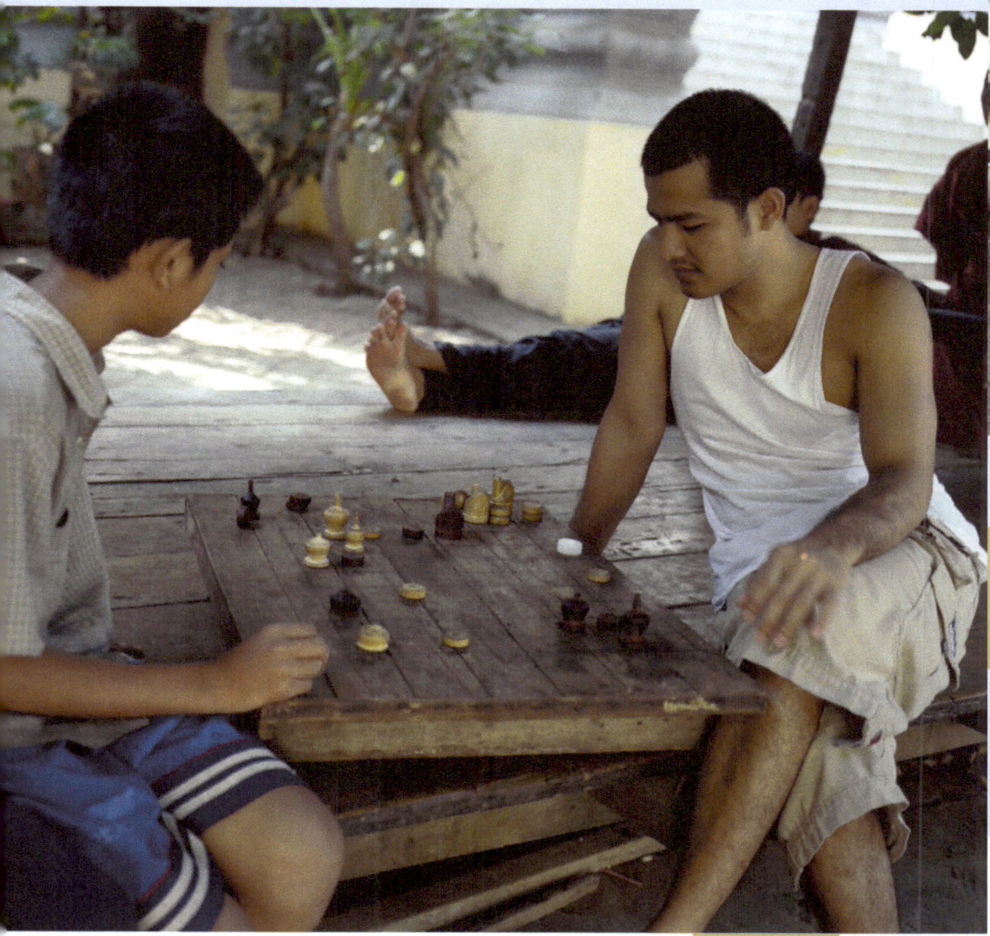

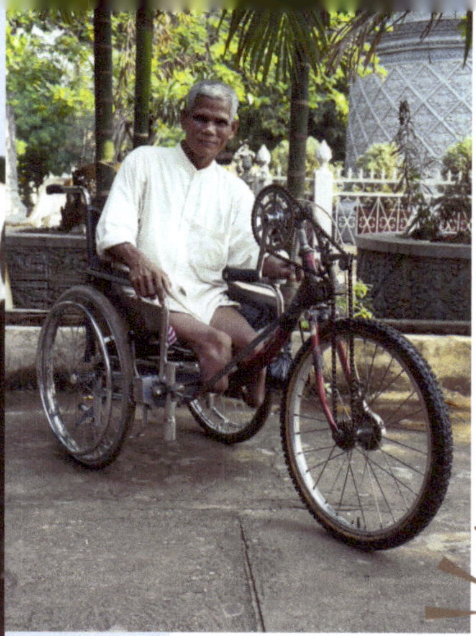

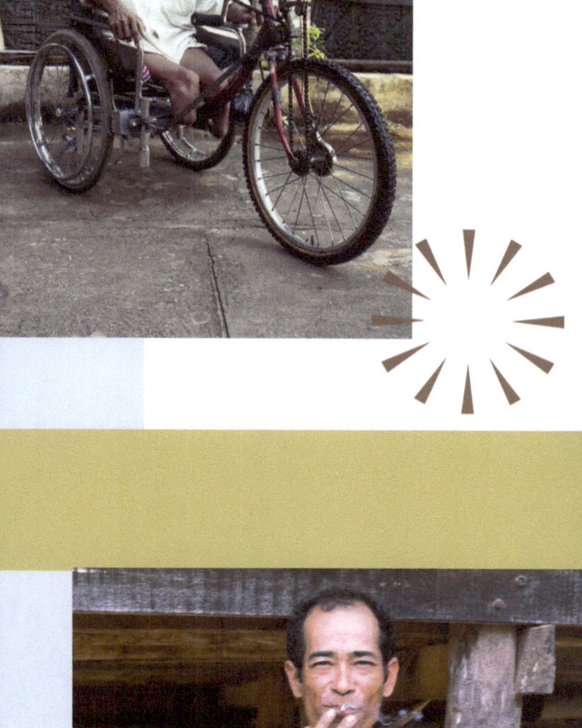

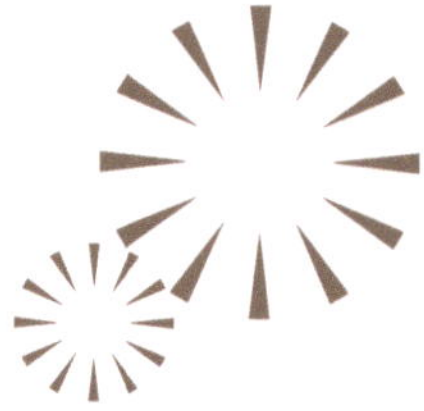

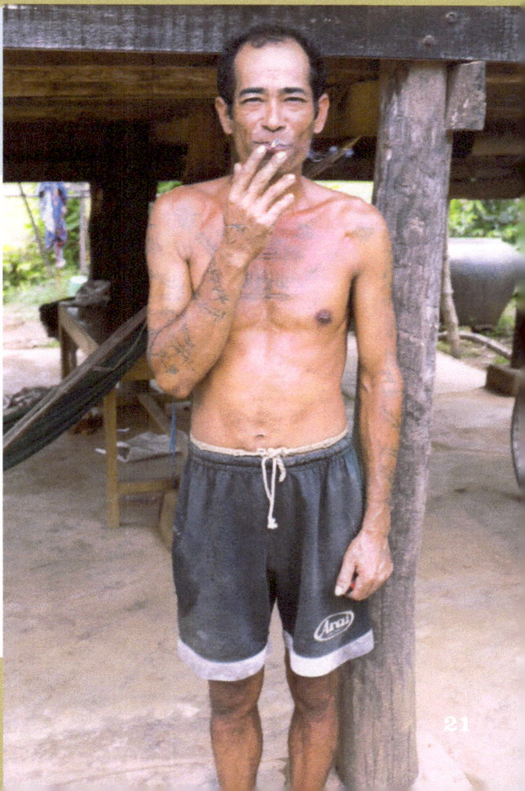

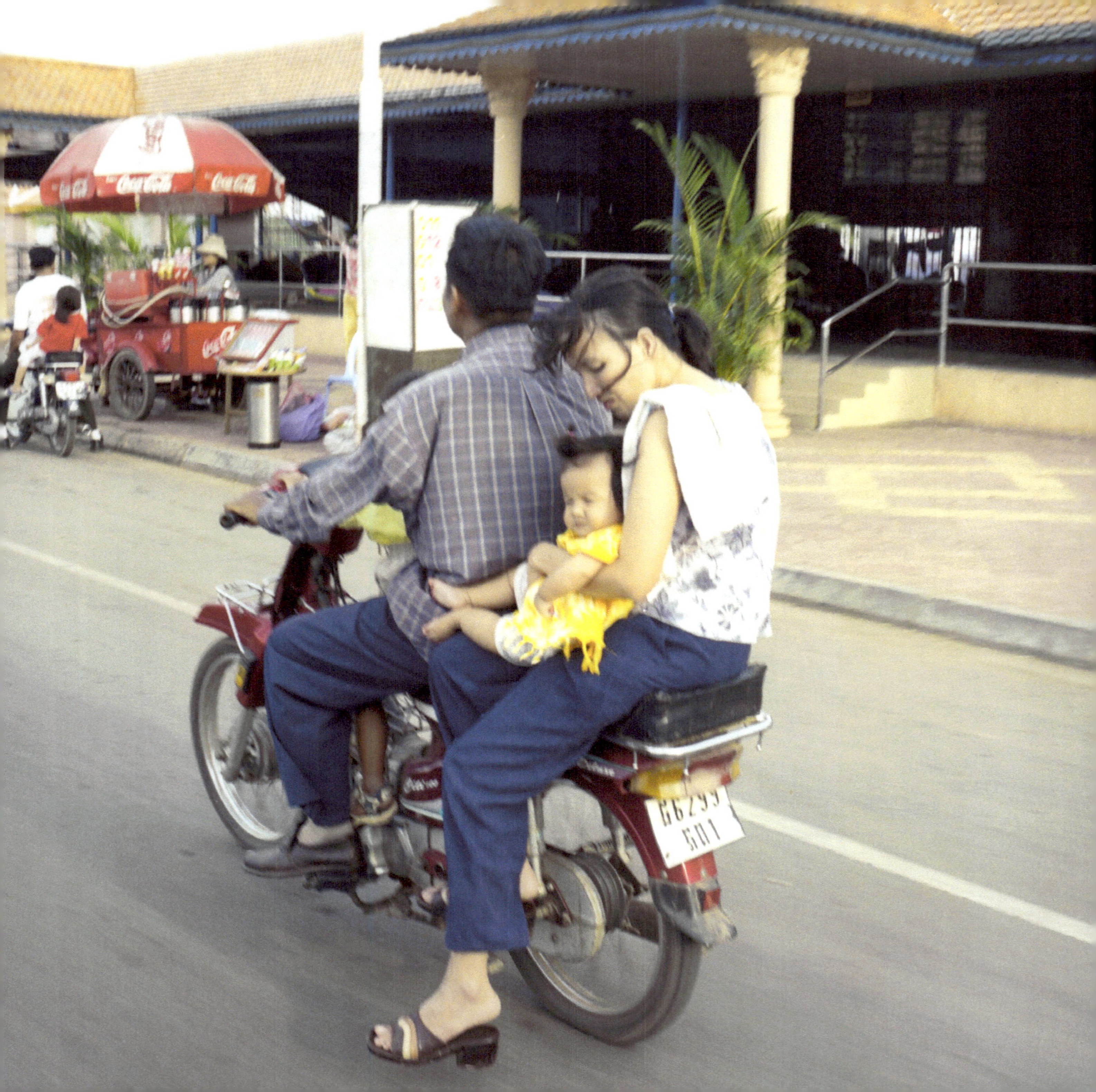
Coca-Cola
Coca-Cola

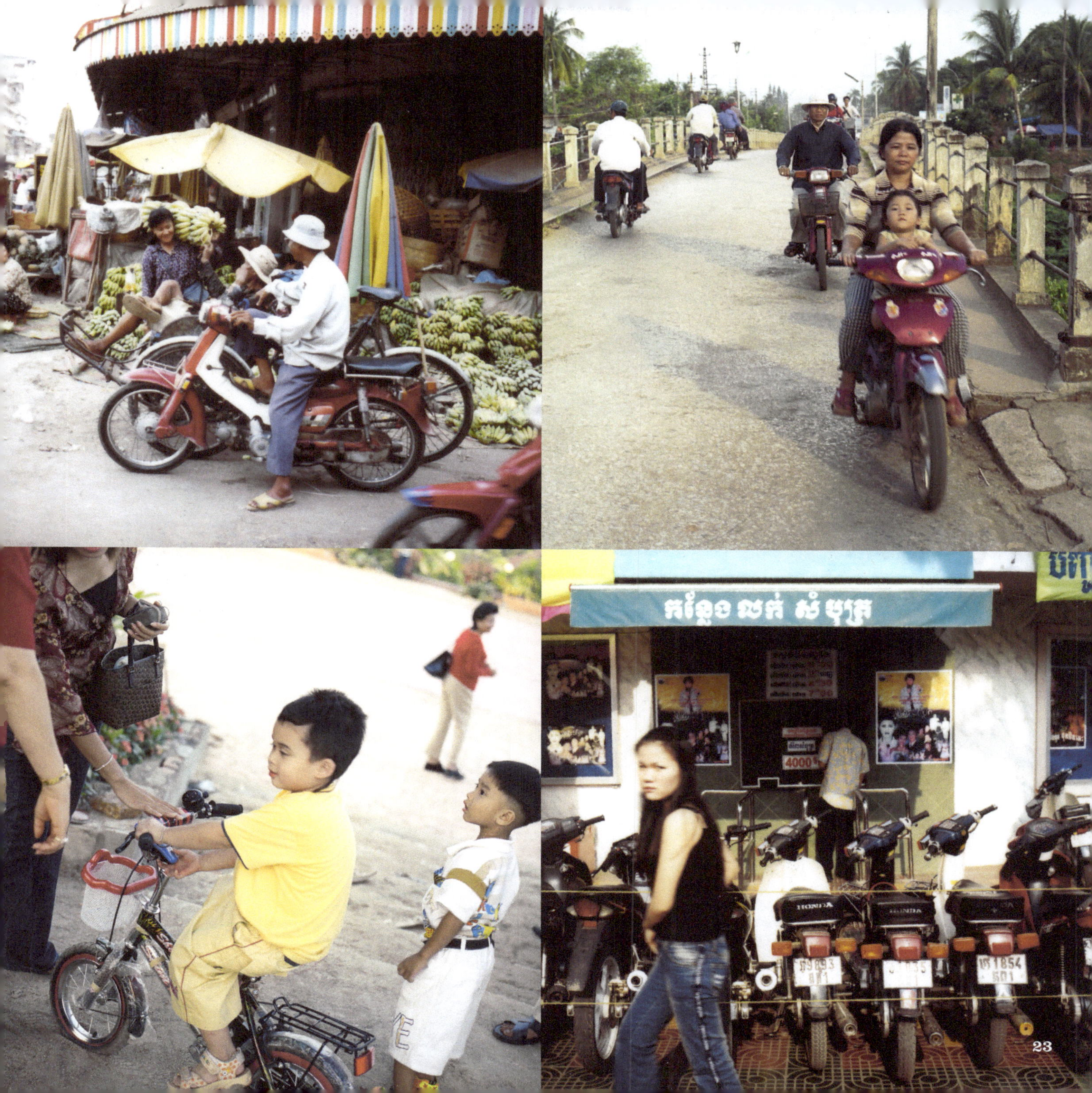
កន្លែង លក់ សំបុត្រ
4000
HONDA

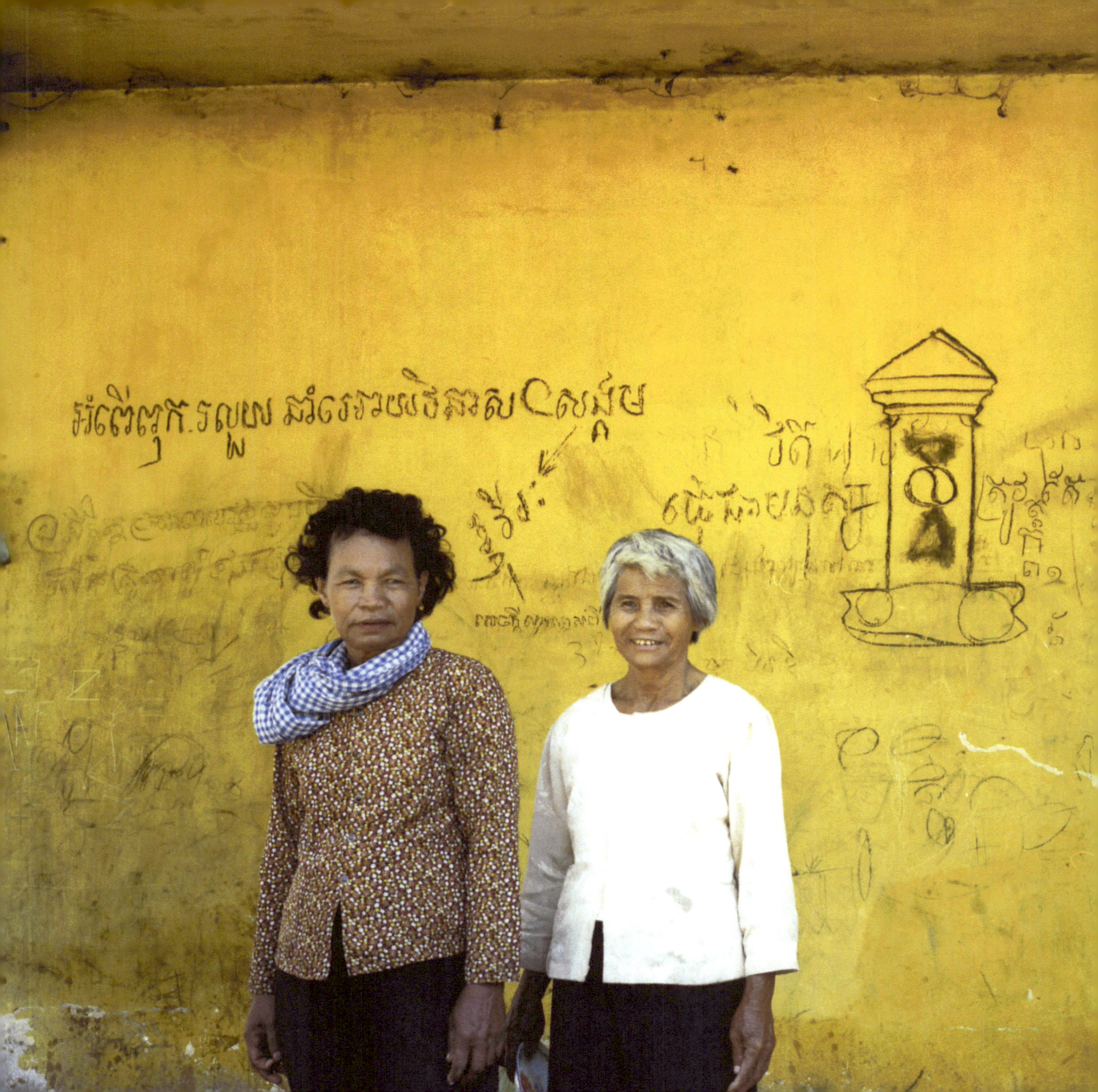

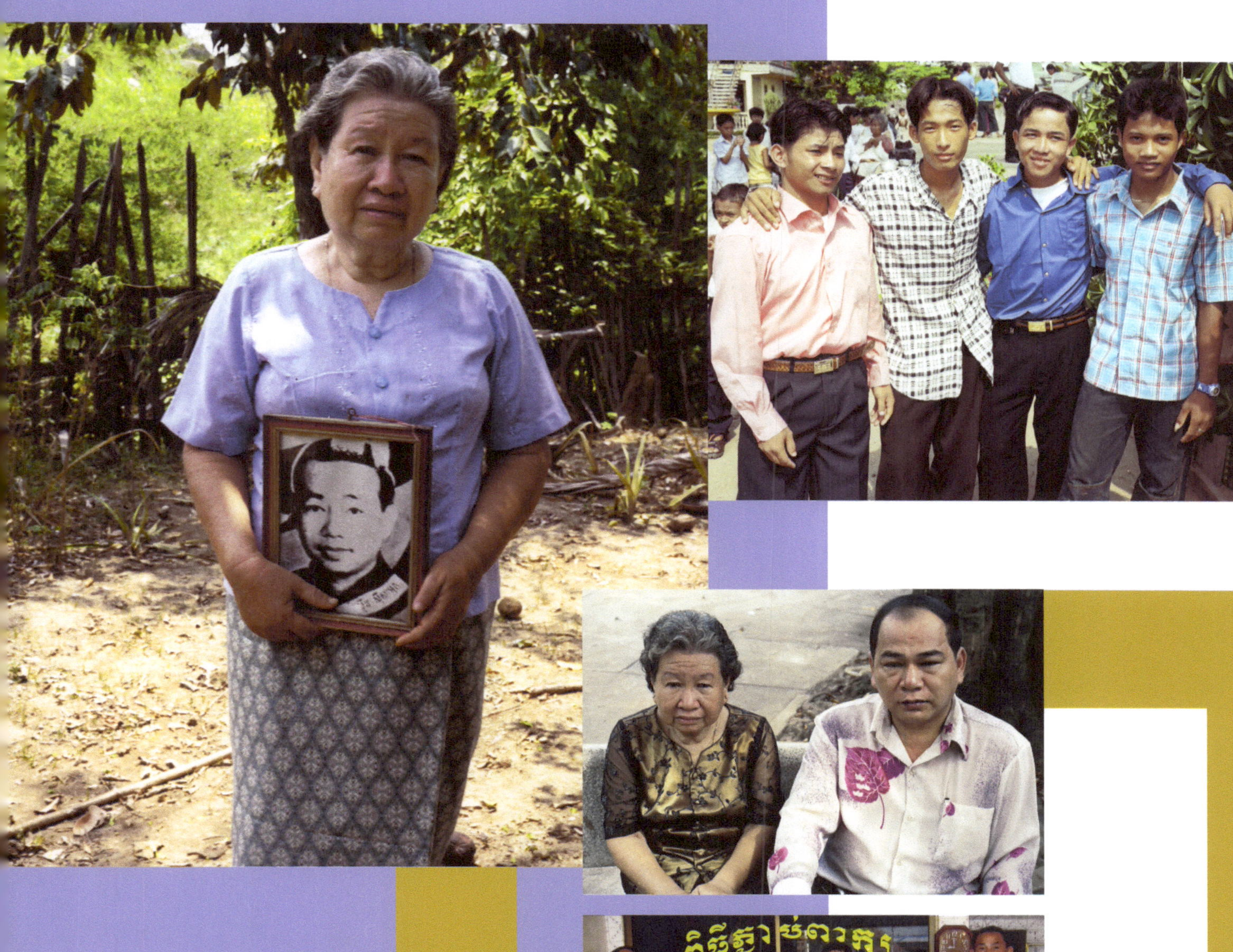

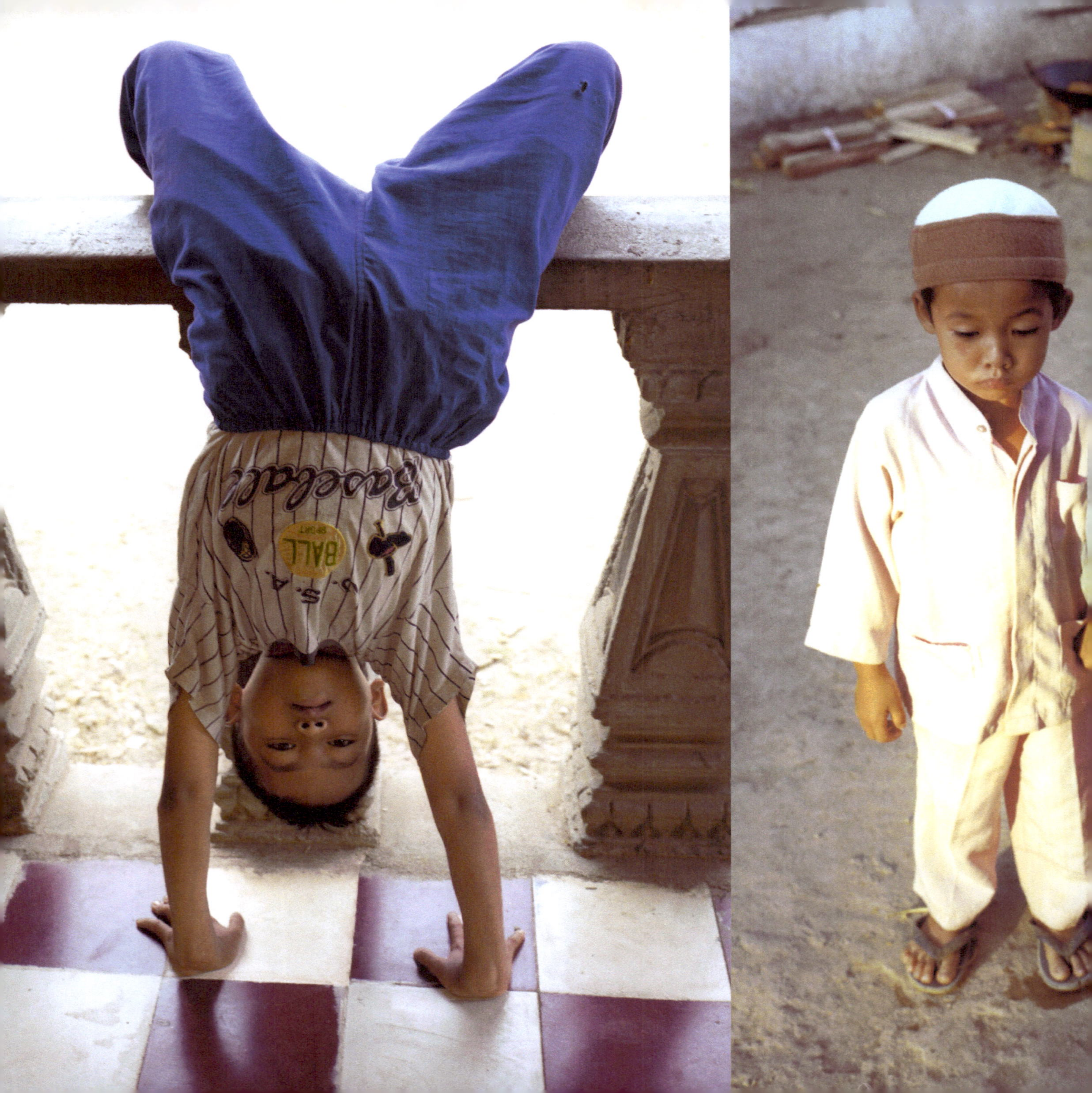
Baseball
BALL

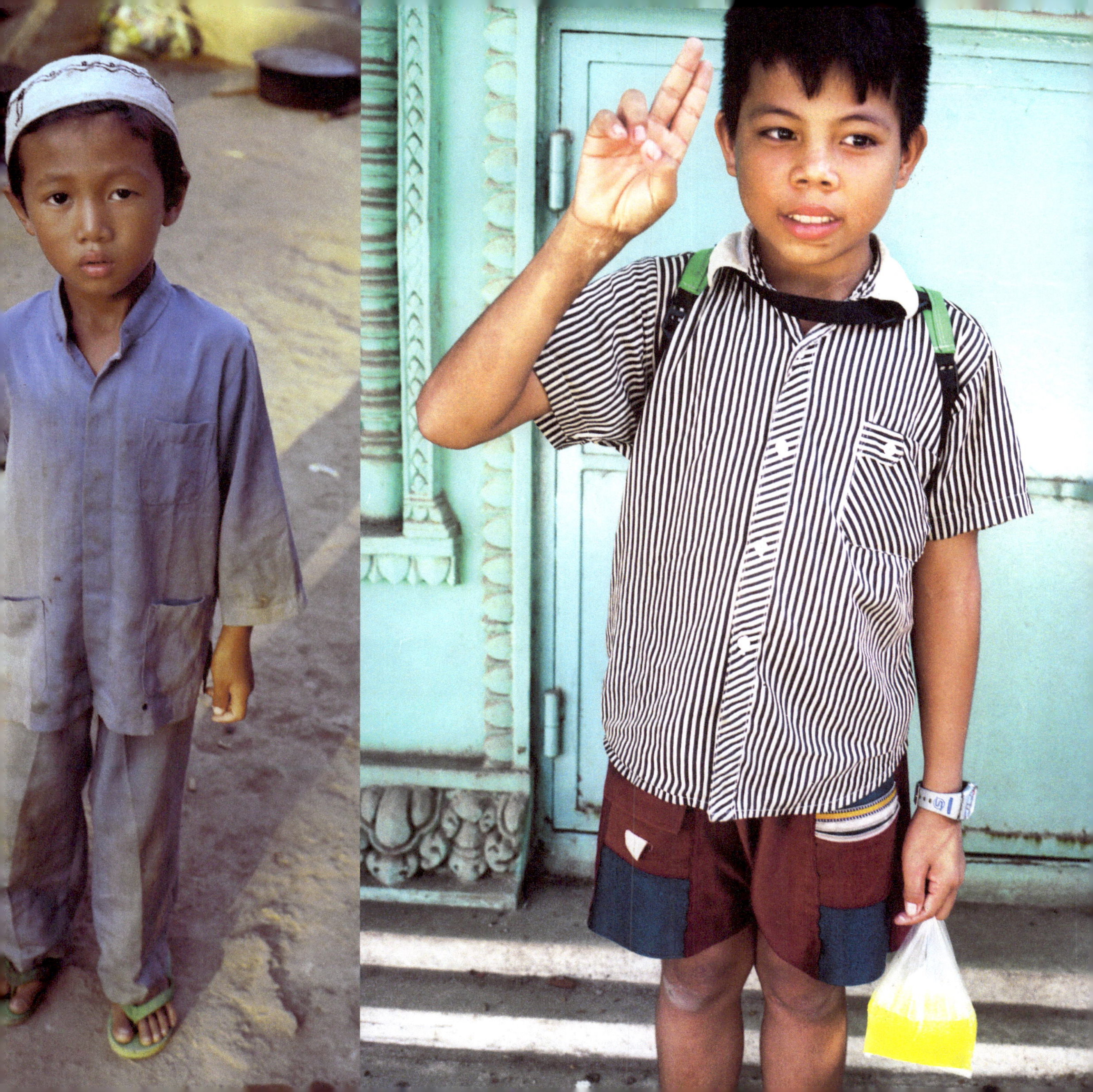

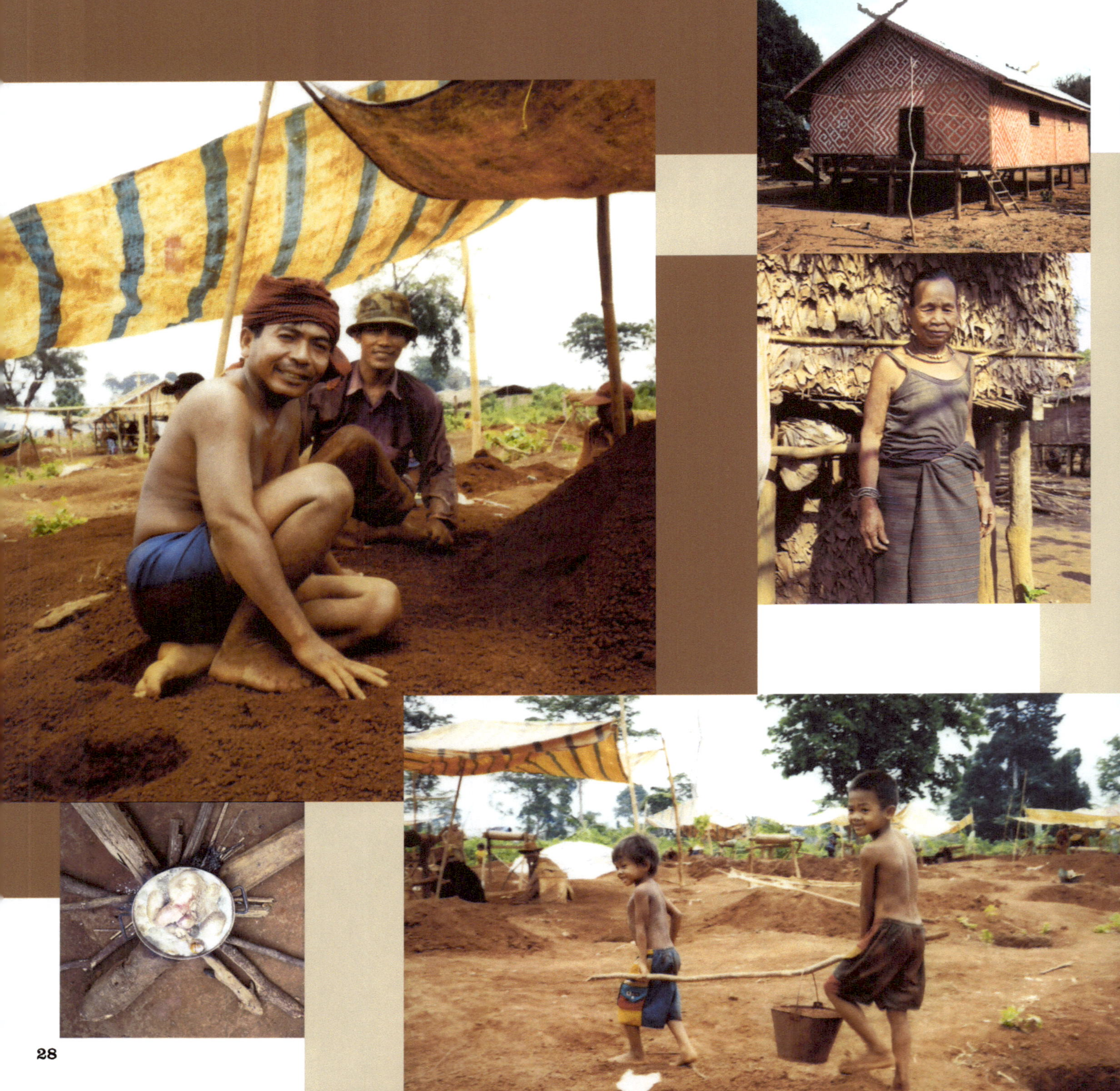

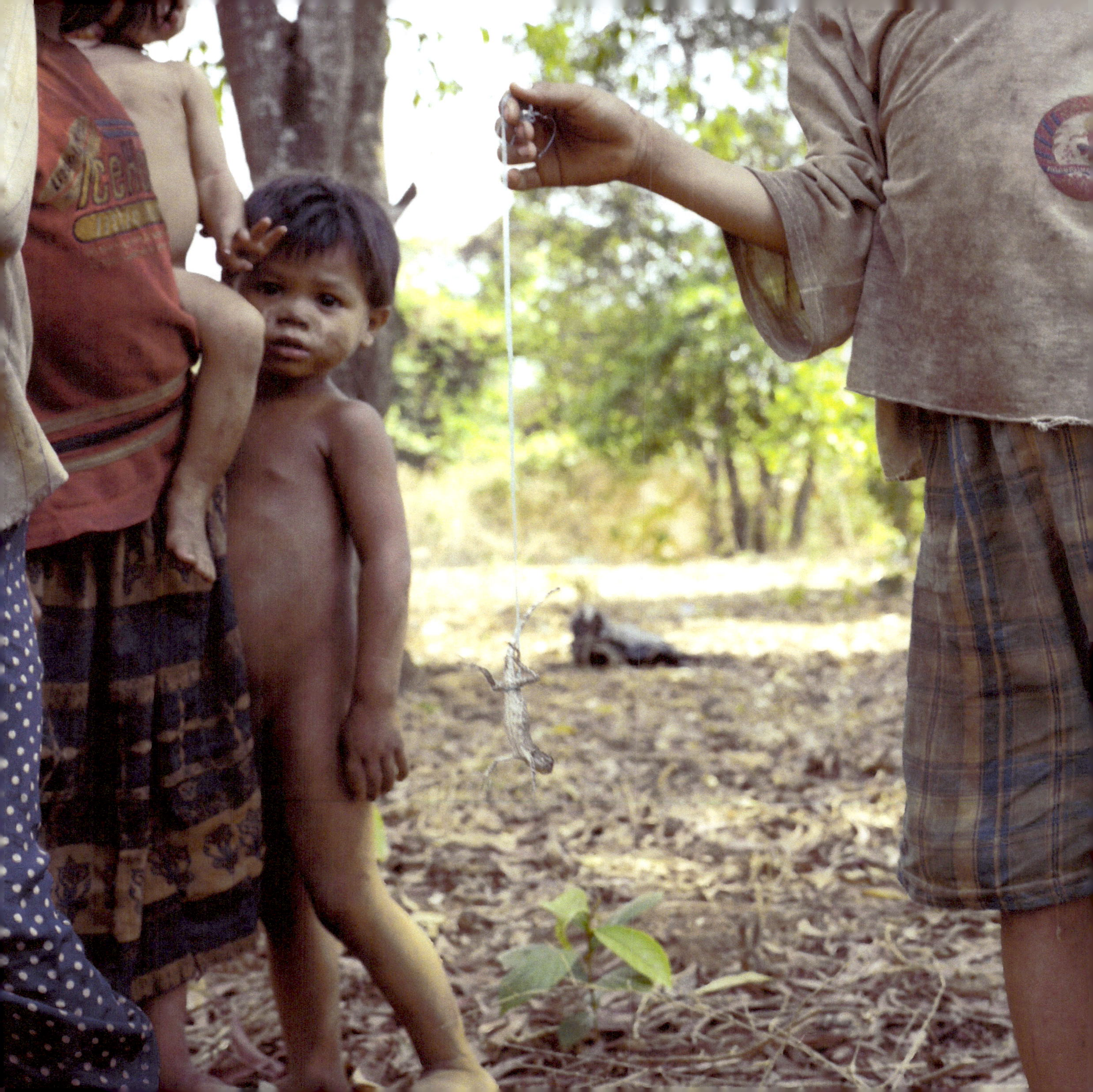

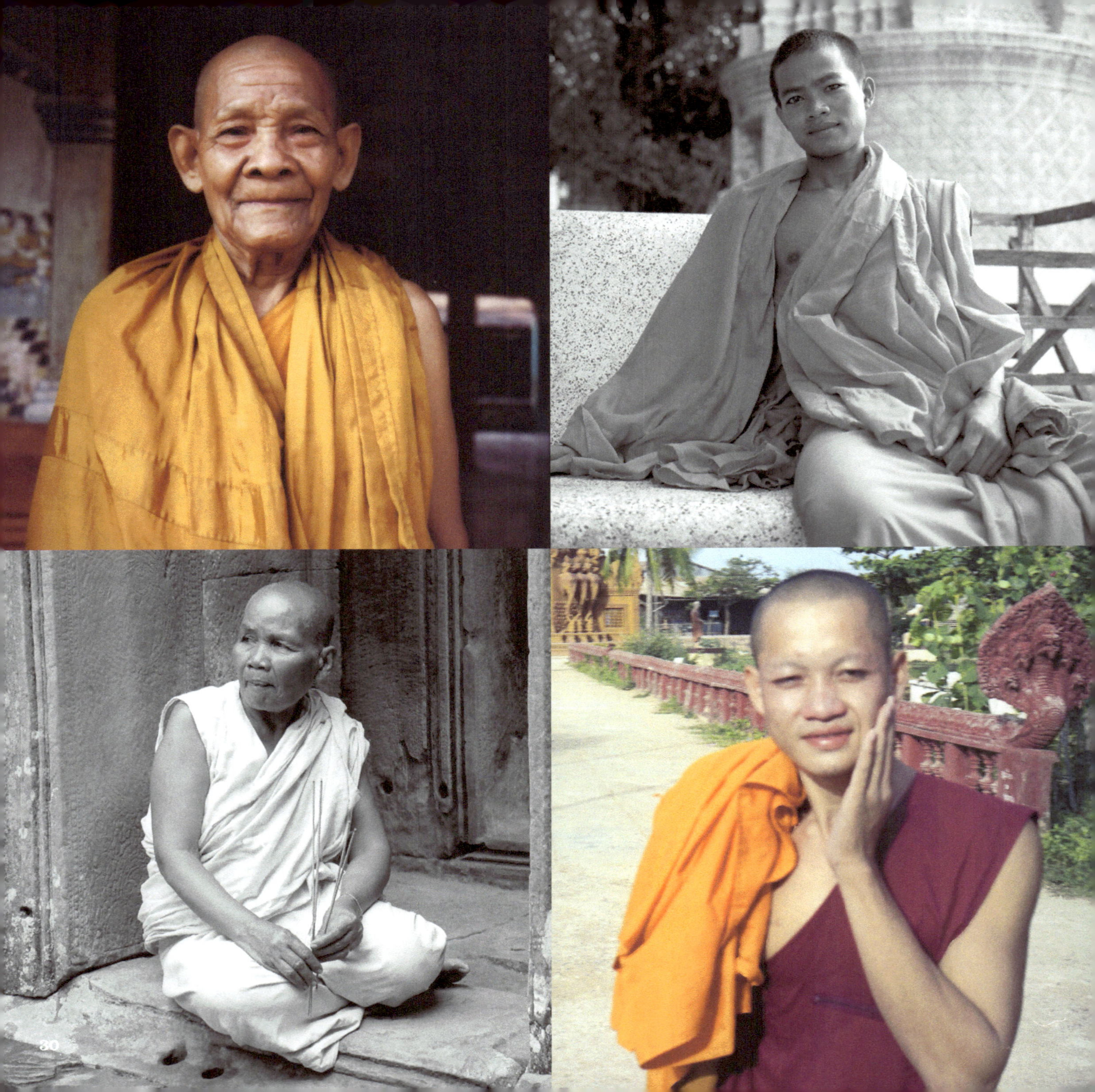

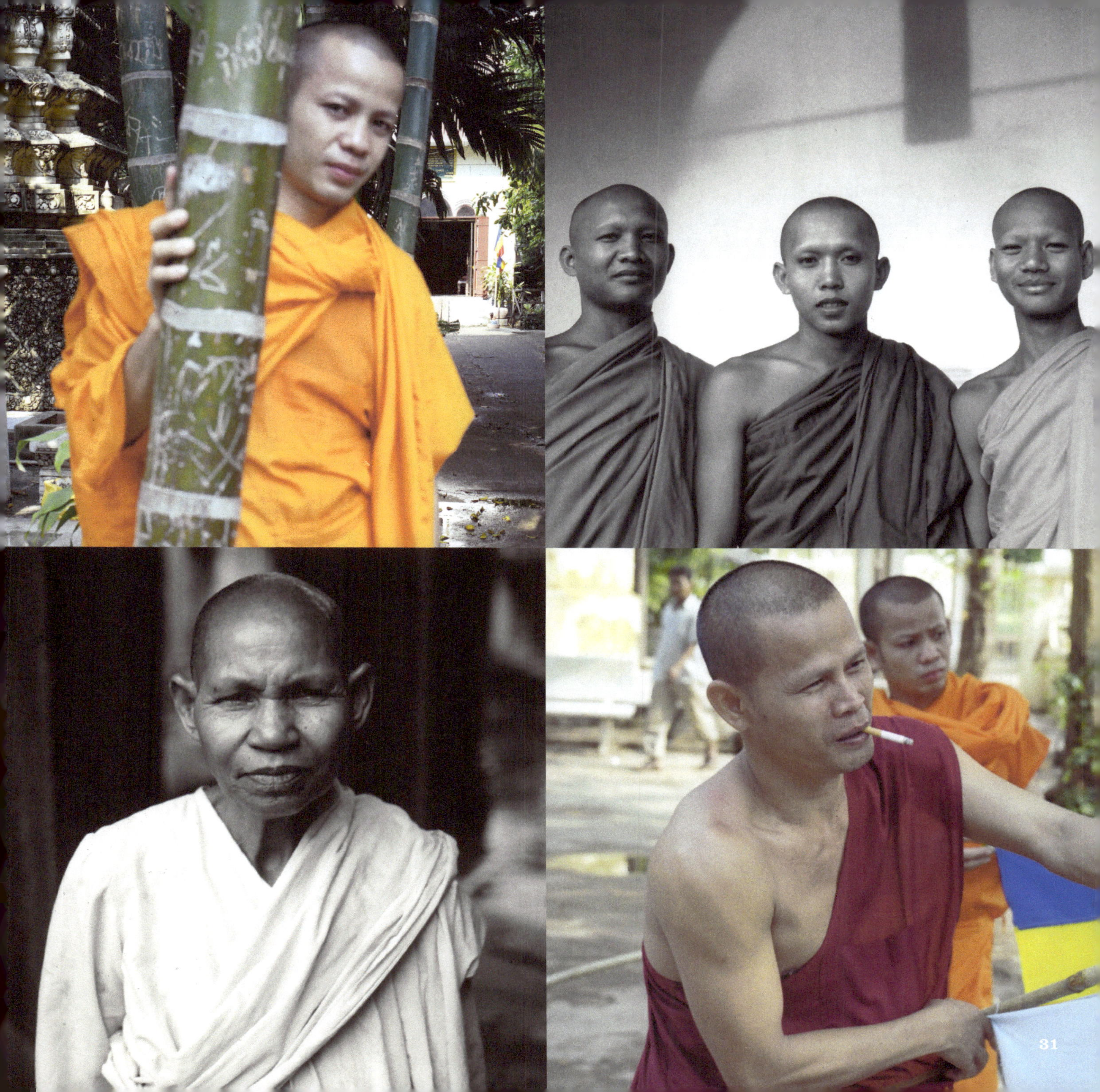

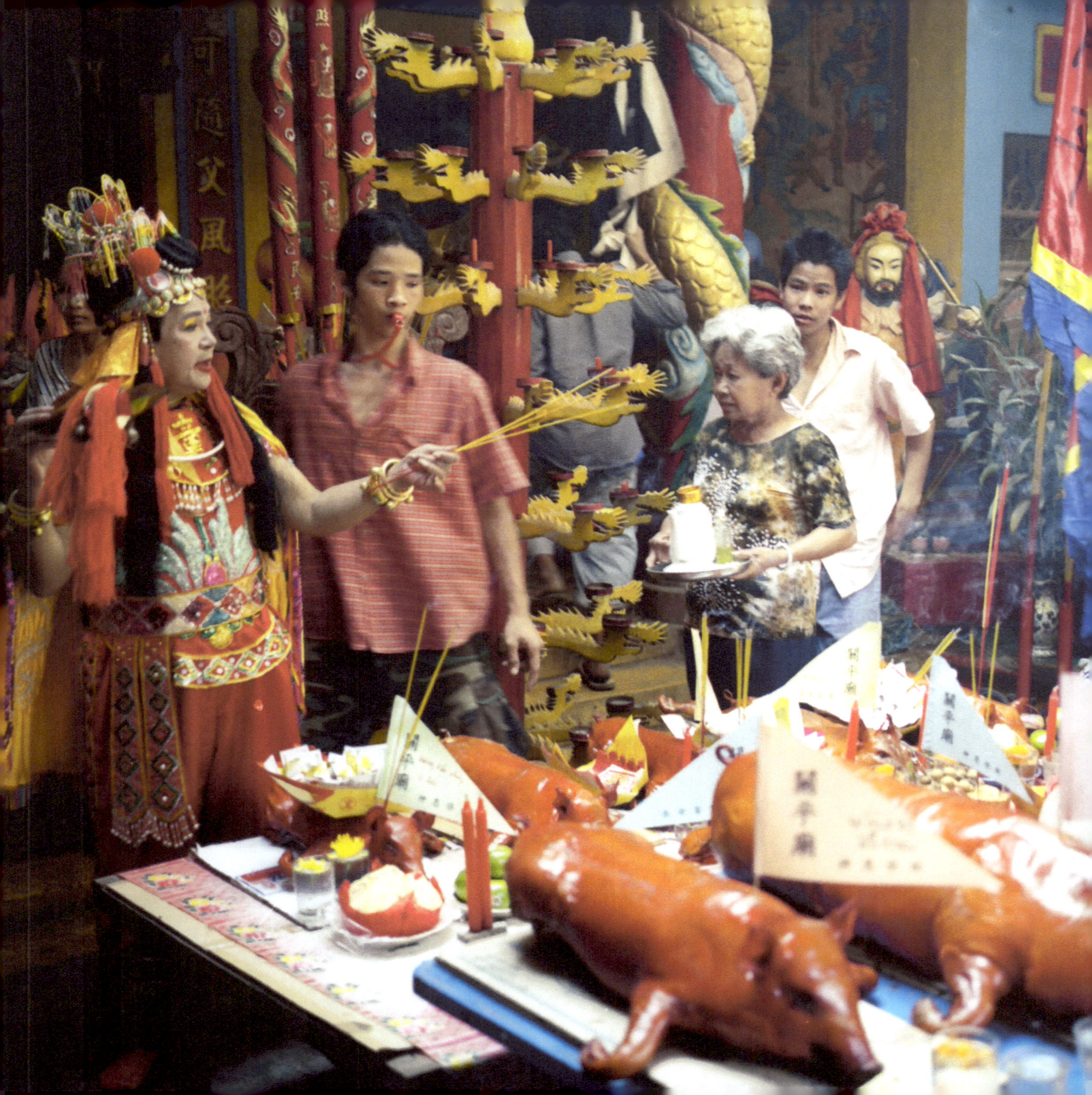

CELEBRATIONS,

holidays, ceremonies and night life are fantastic in your country! The way you entertain with your traditional music, dance and spiritual rituals are a wonder to see and be a part of. Water Festival, Chinese New Year and Khmer New Year are awesome spectacles. Even your beer gardens booming with Karaoke–though it is a little westernized–are great fun! Your traditional engagement parties, weddings and funerals are also special to witness.

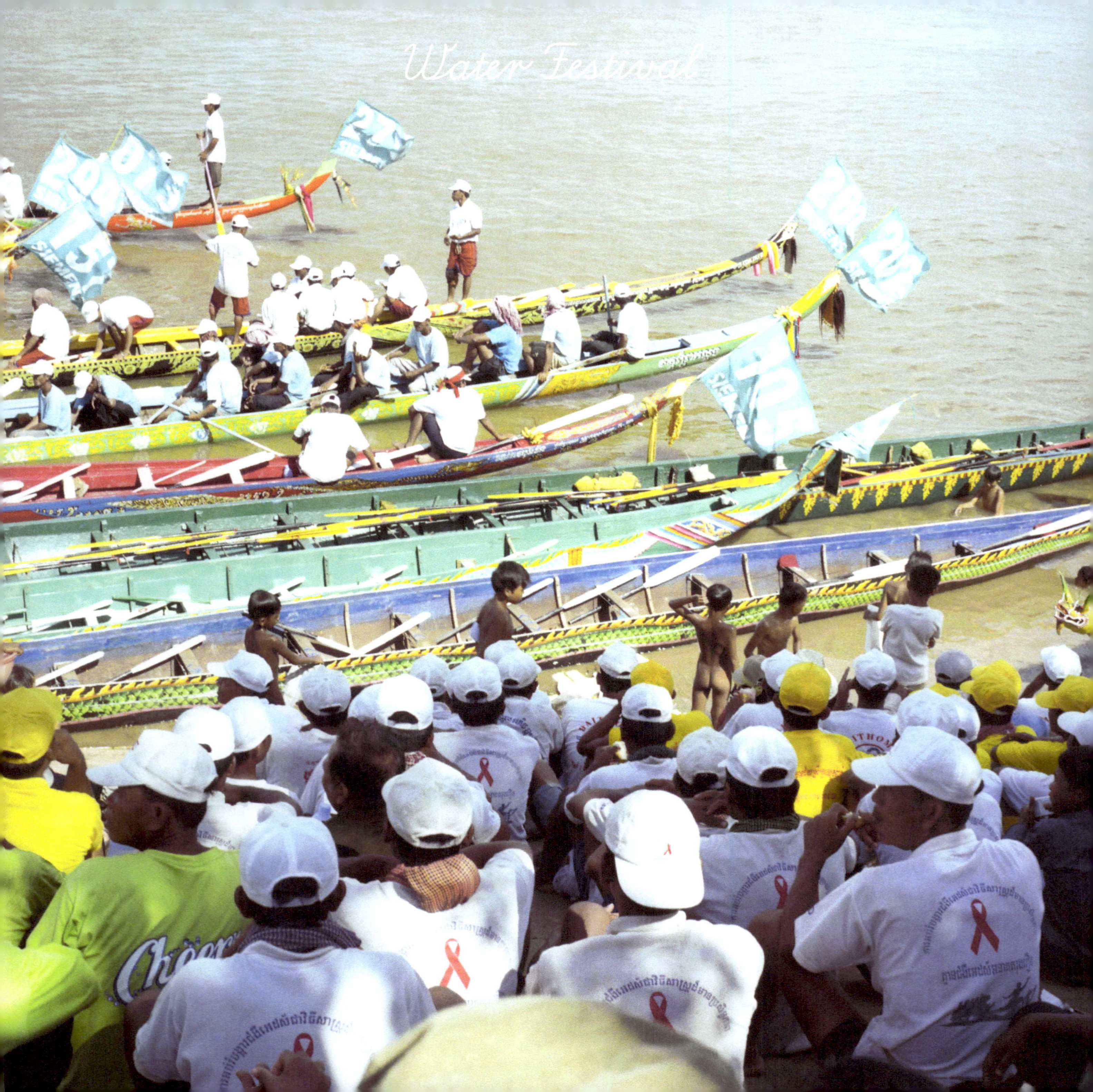

Water Festival

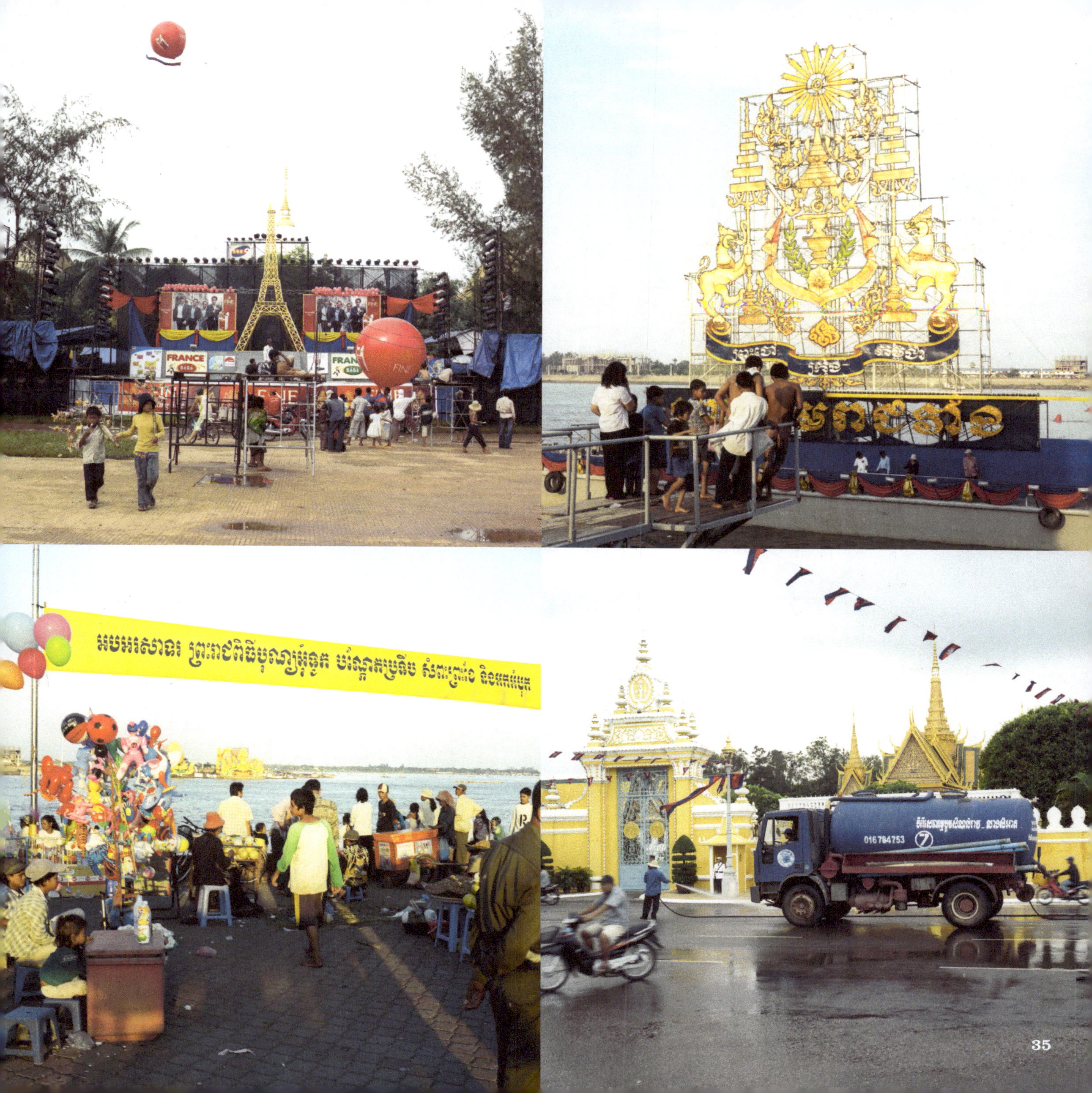
FRANCE
អបអរសាទរ ព្រះរាជពិធីបុណ្យអុំទូក បណ្តែតប្រទីប សំពះព្រះខែ និងអកអំបុក
016784753

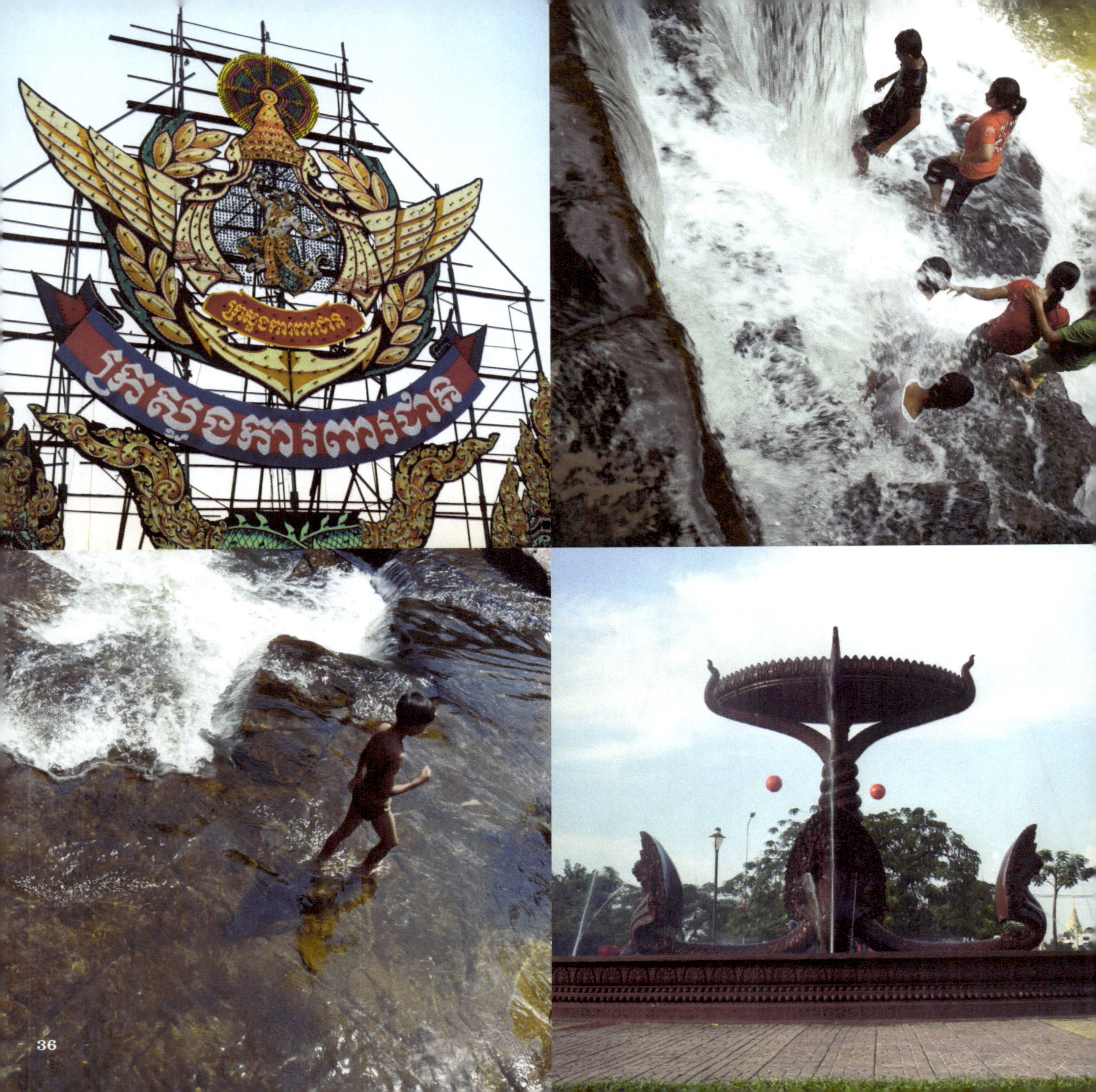
ក្រសួងការពារជាតិ

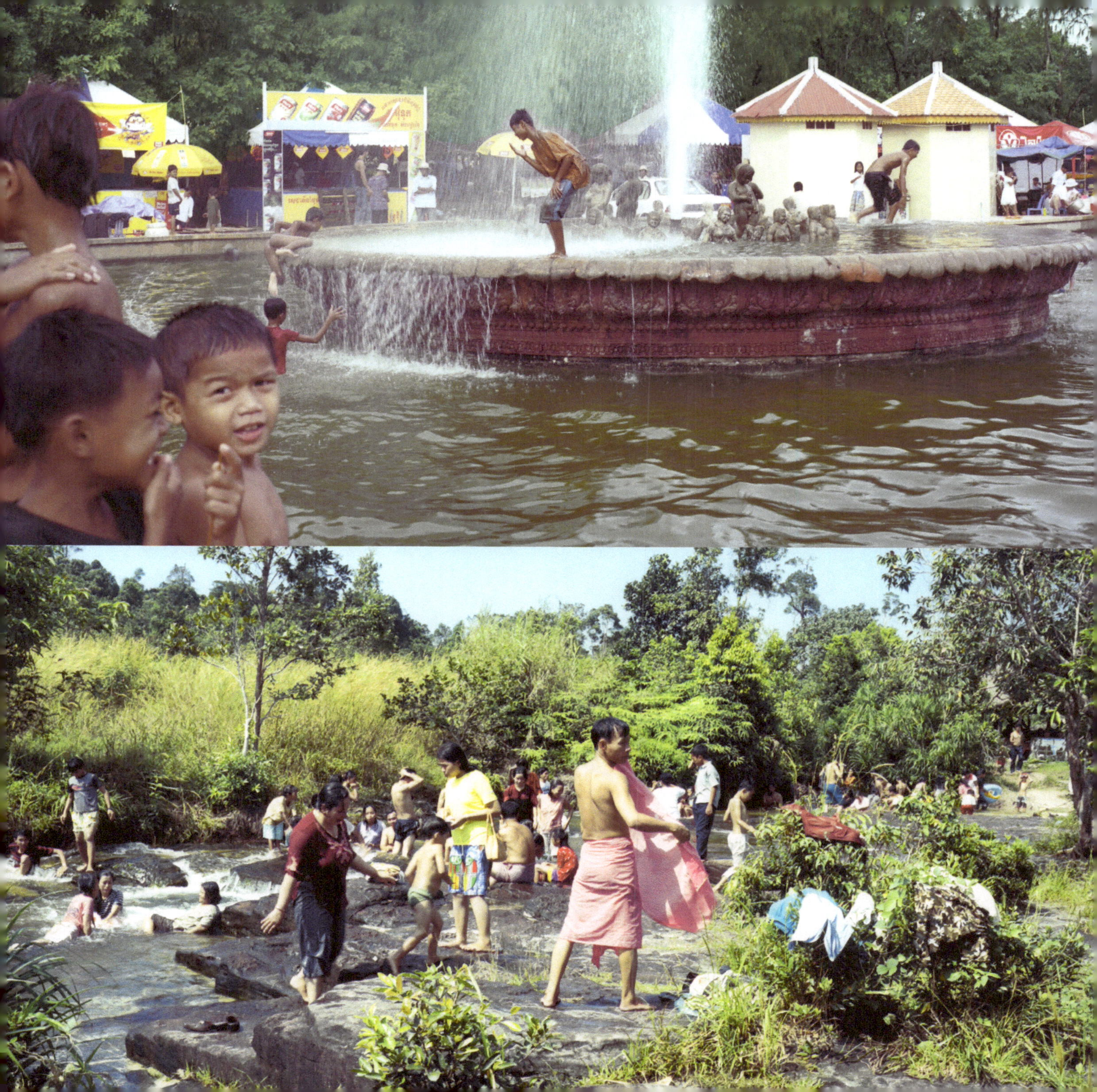

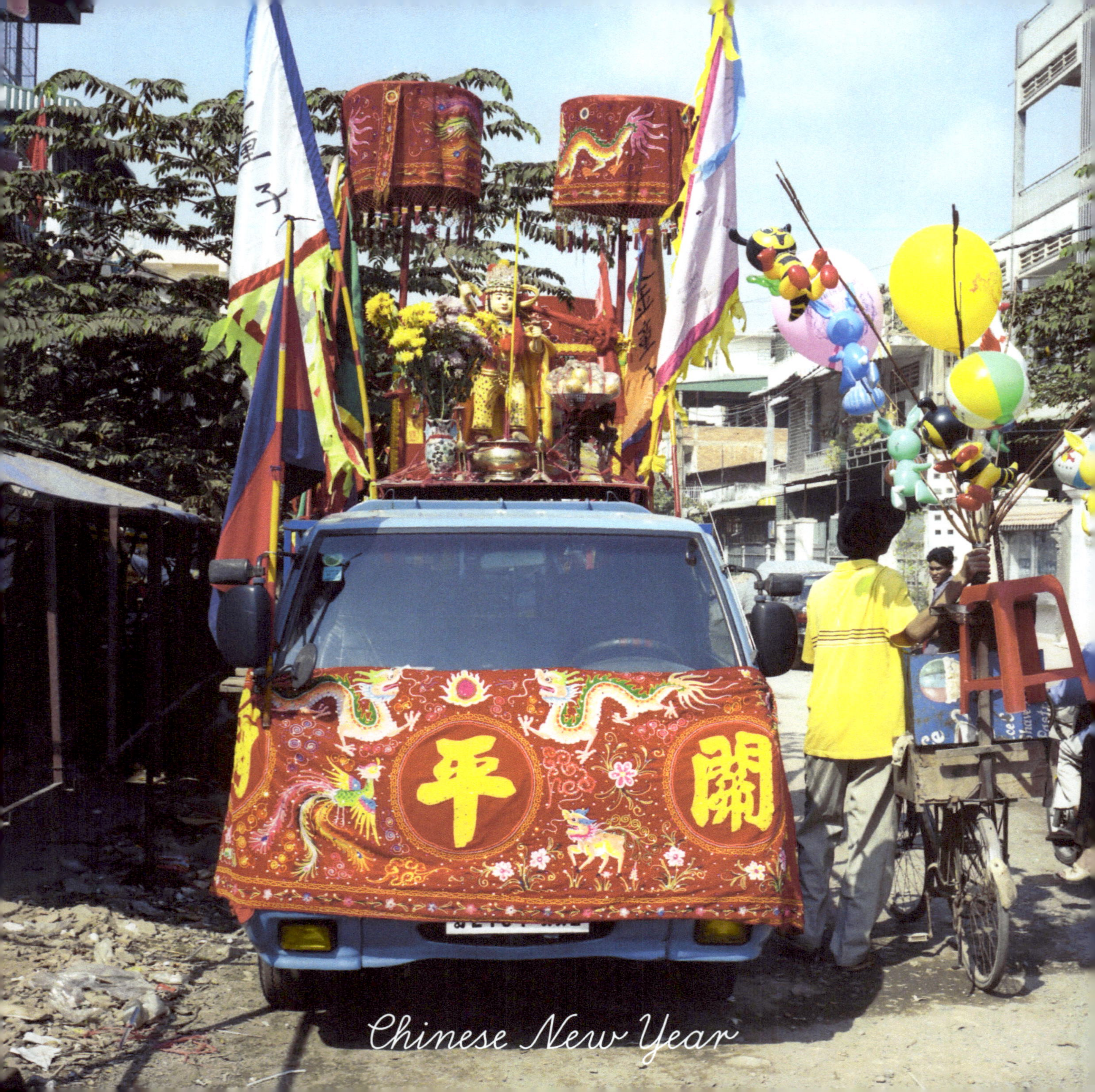

Chinese New Year

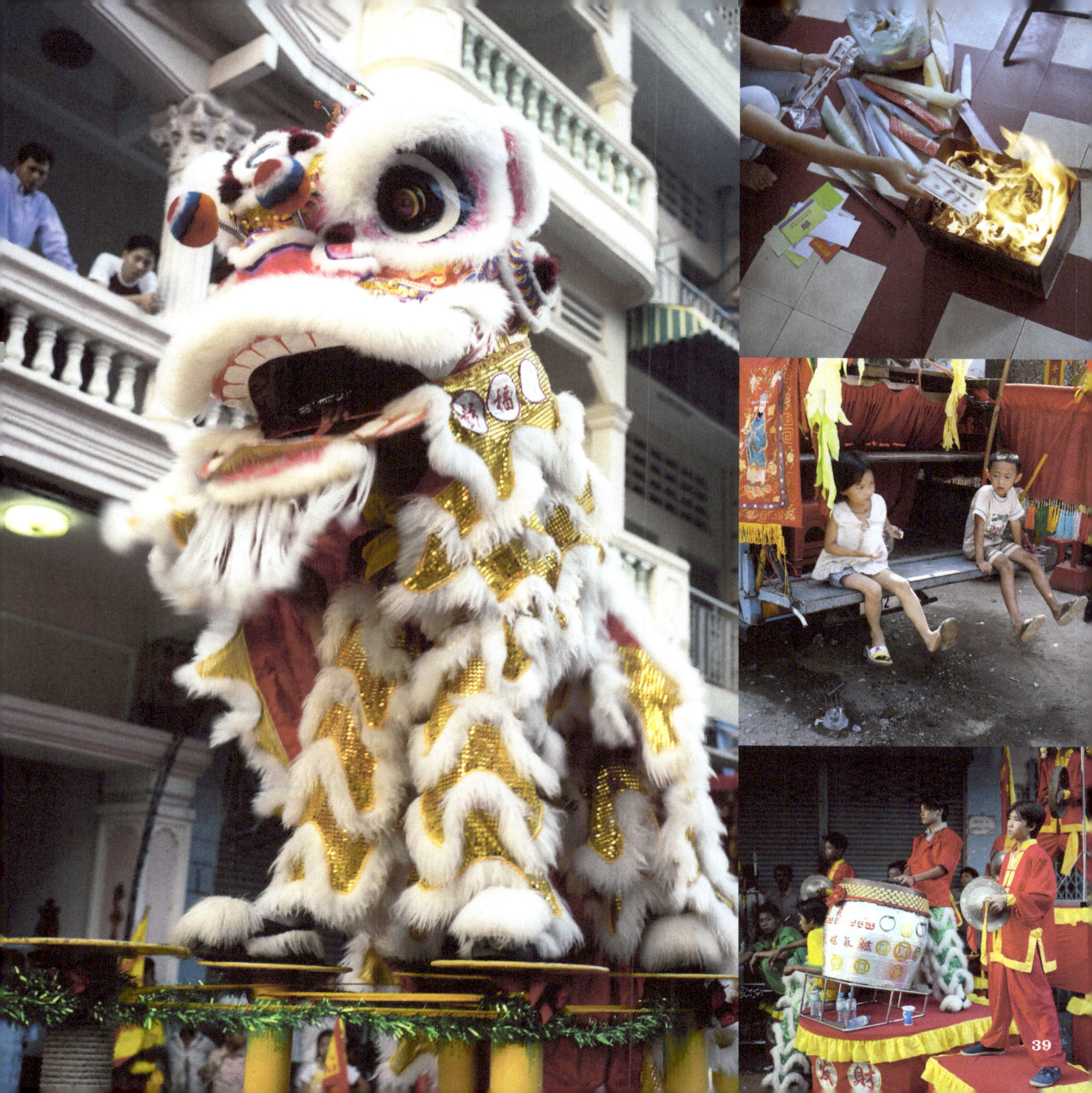
福

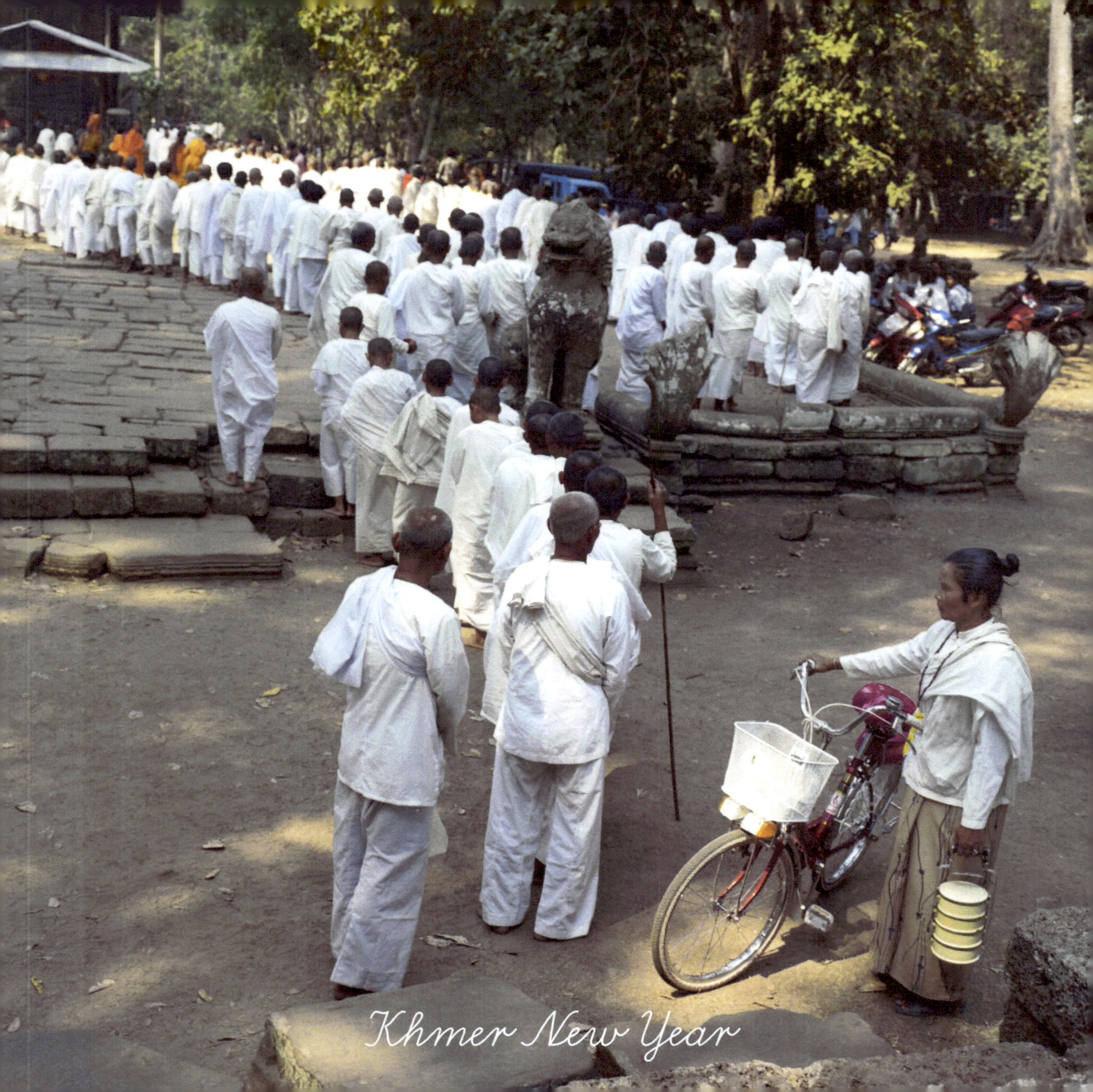

Khmer New Year

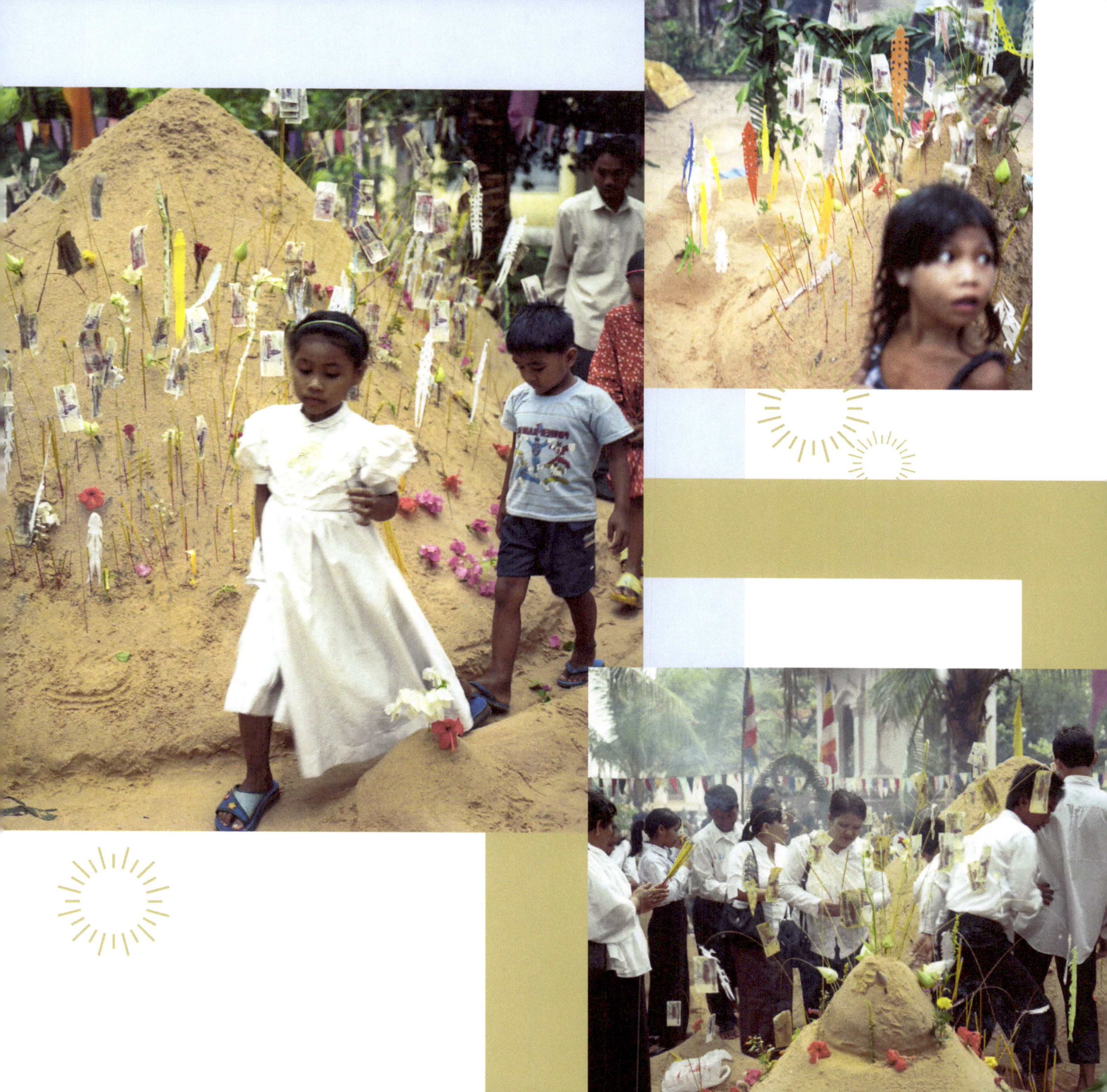

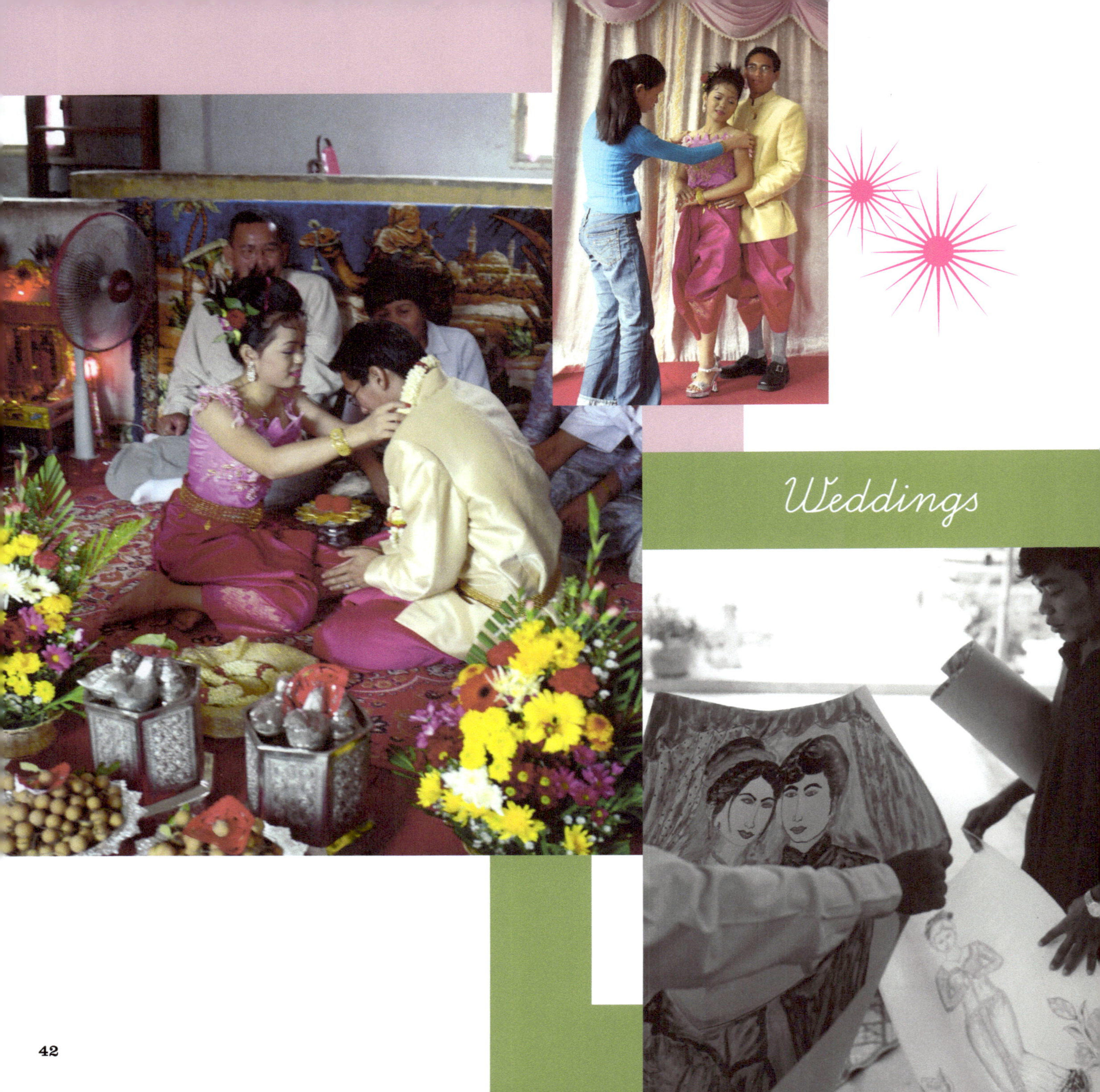

Weddings

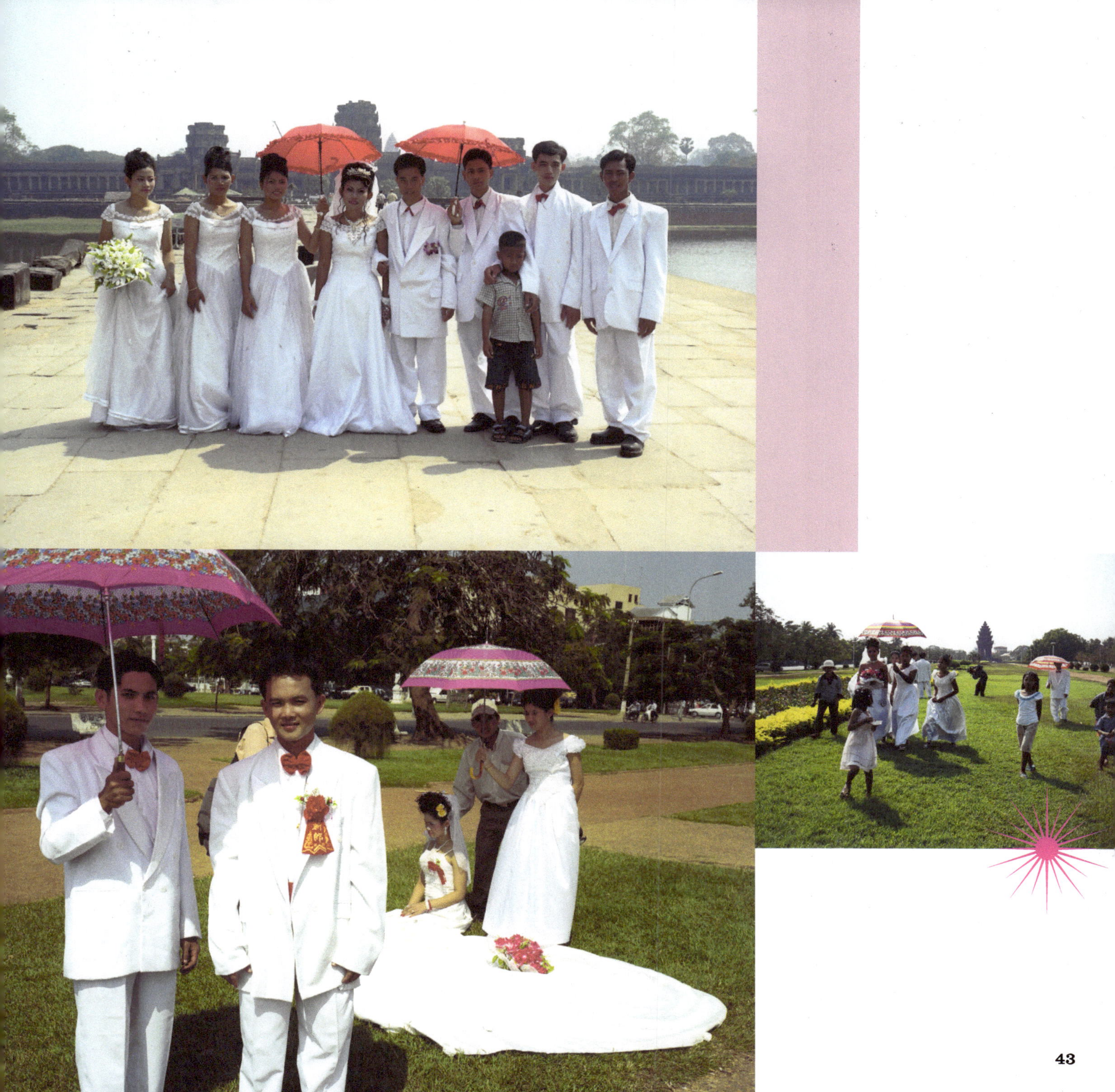

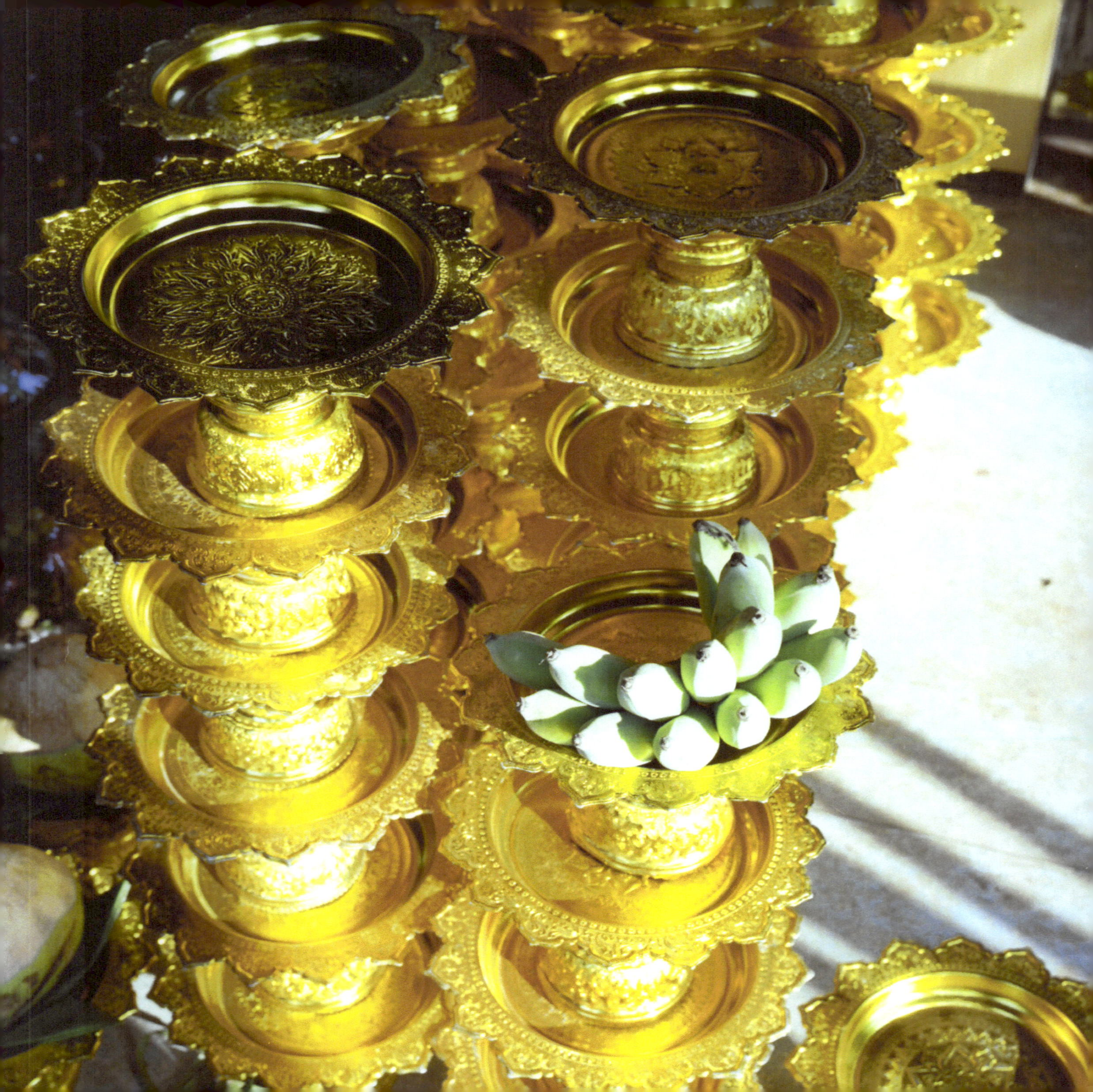

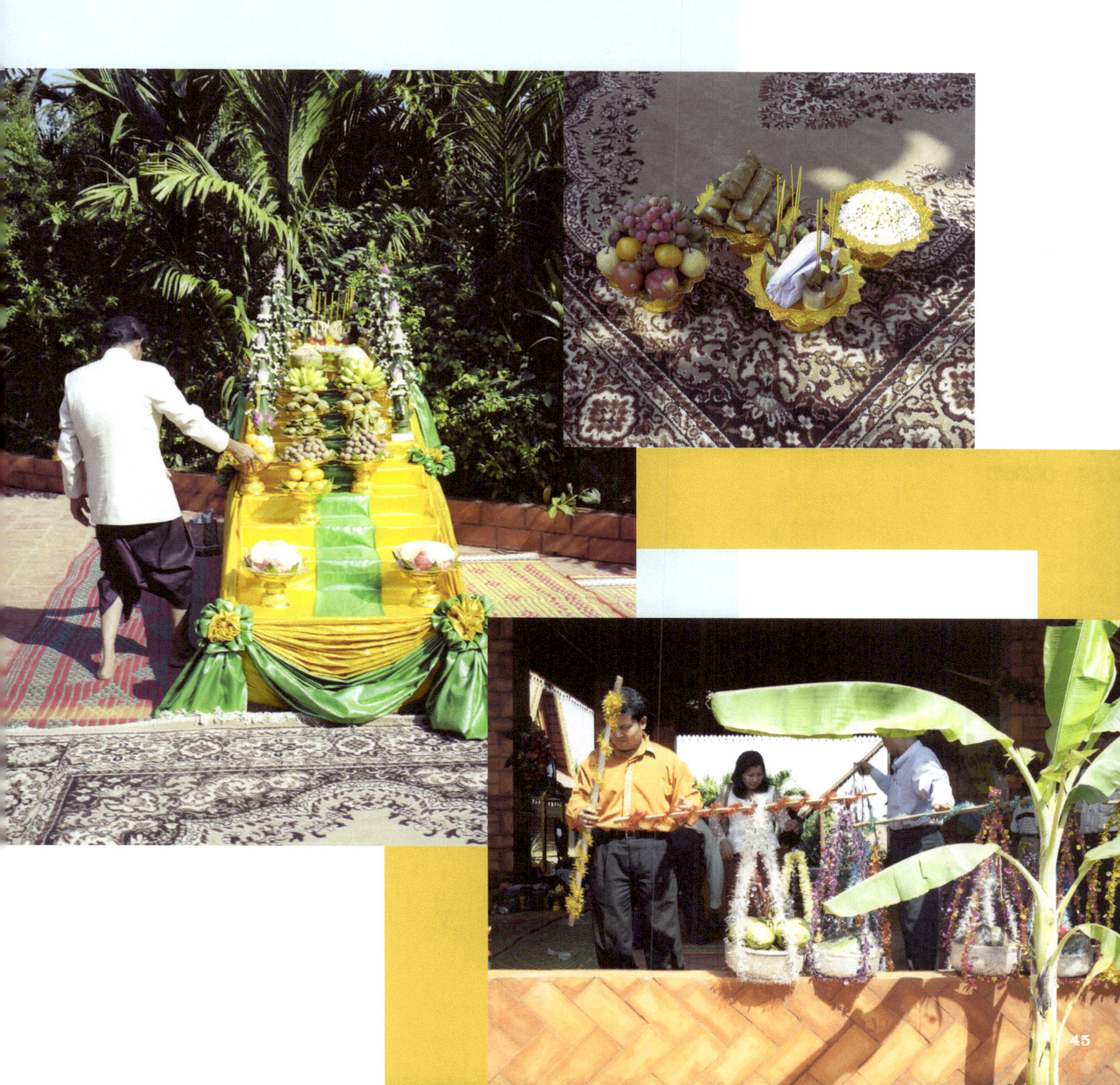

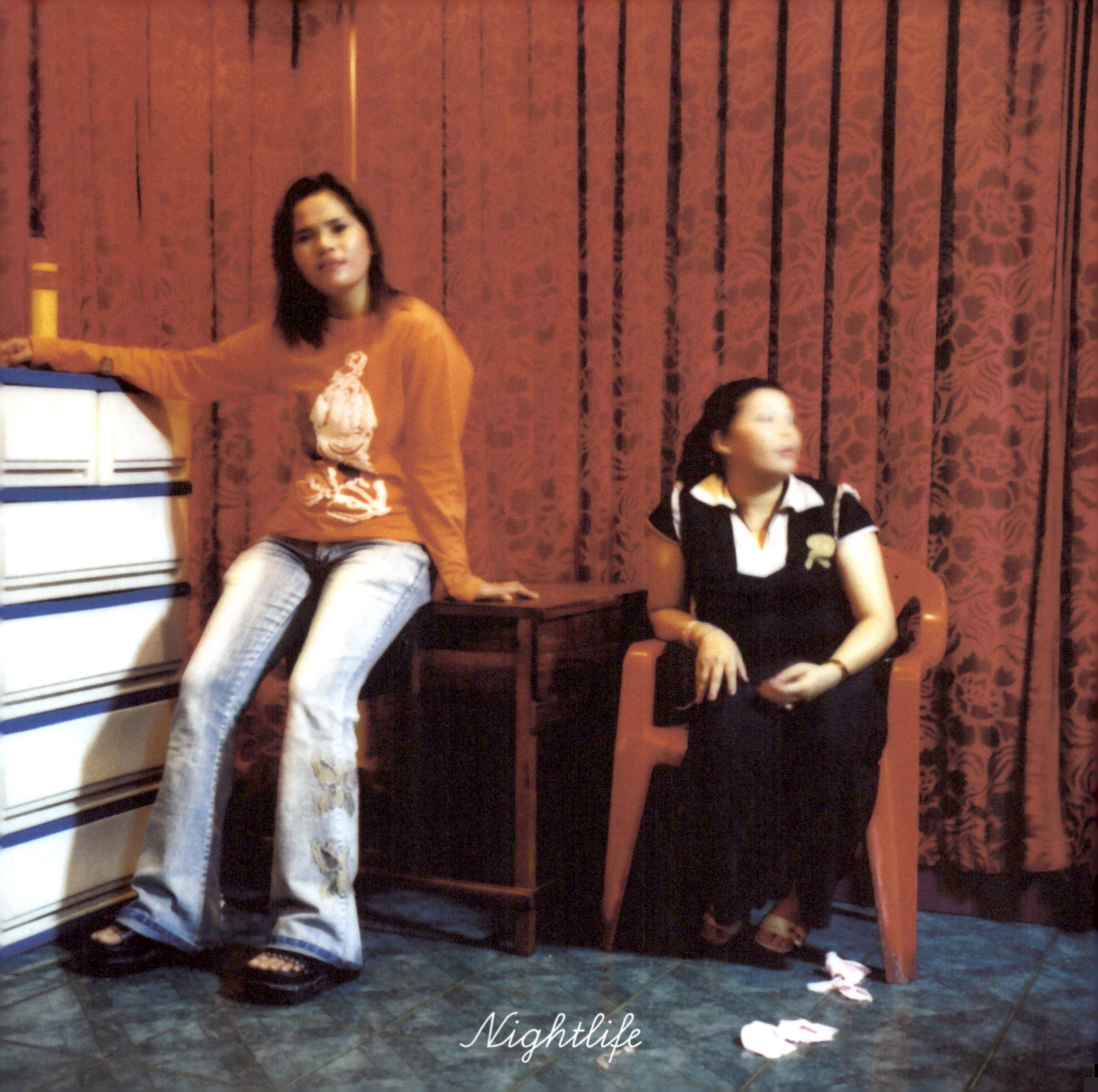

Nightlife

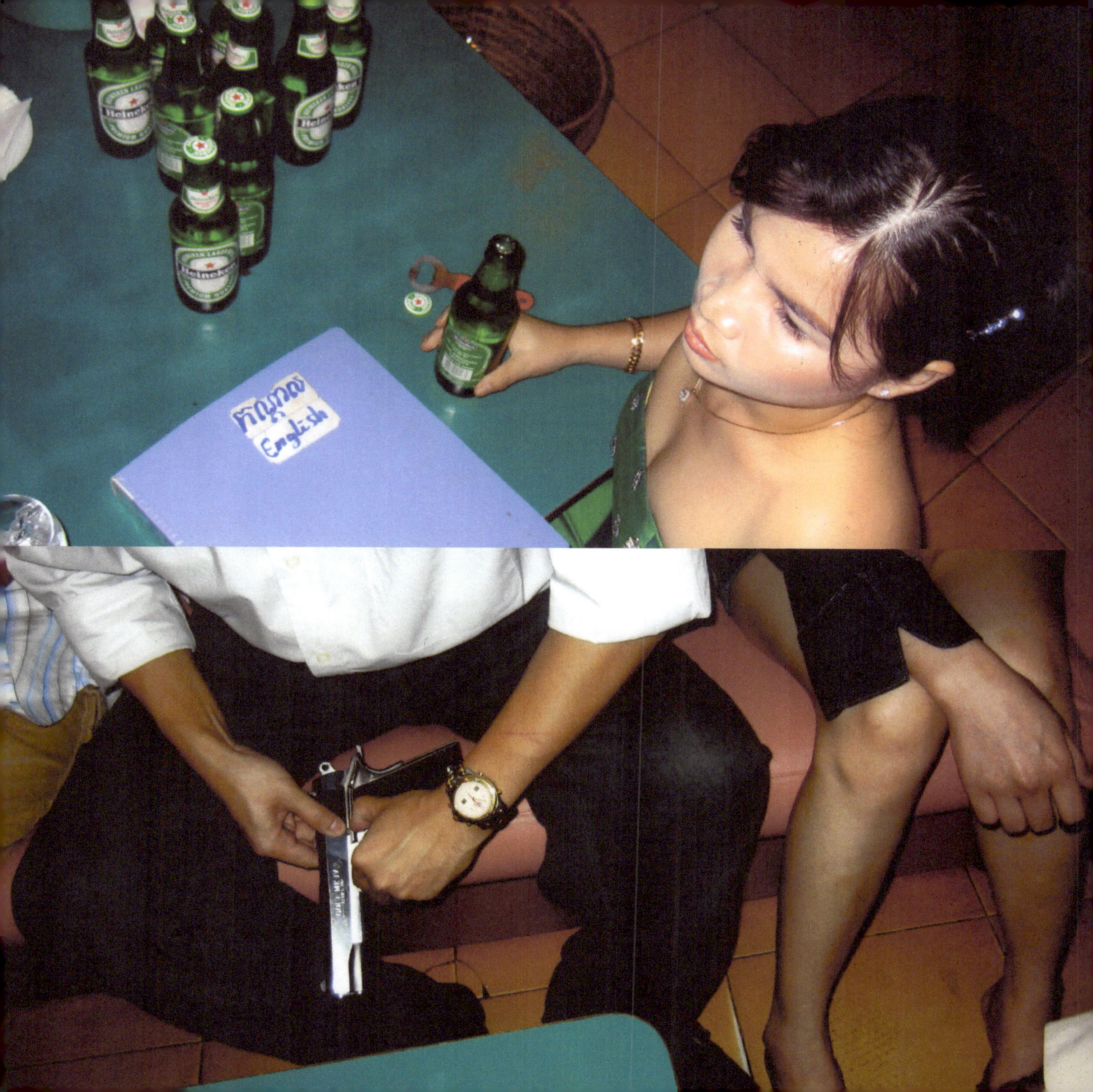
Heineken
English

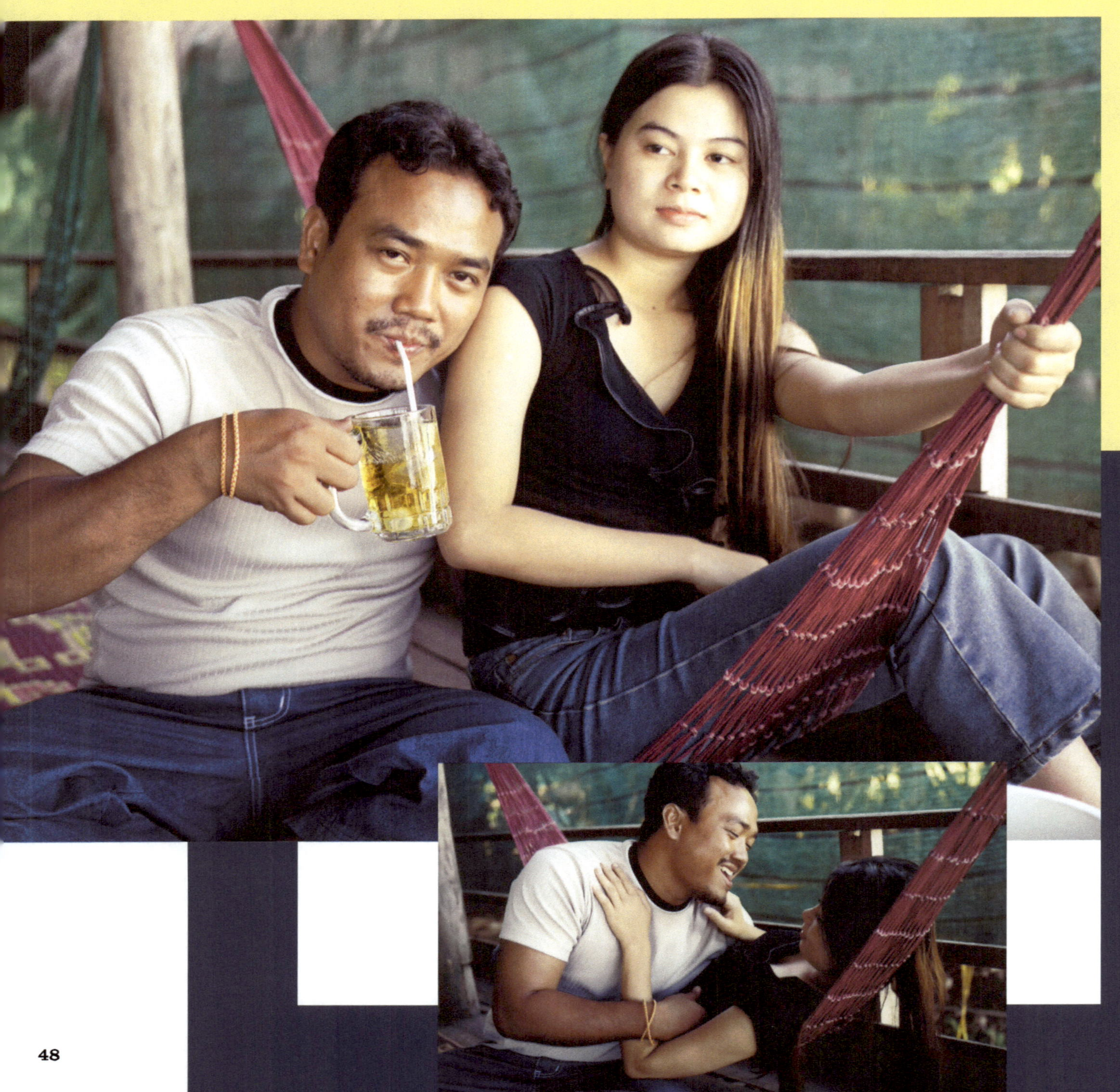

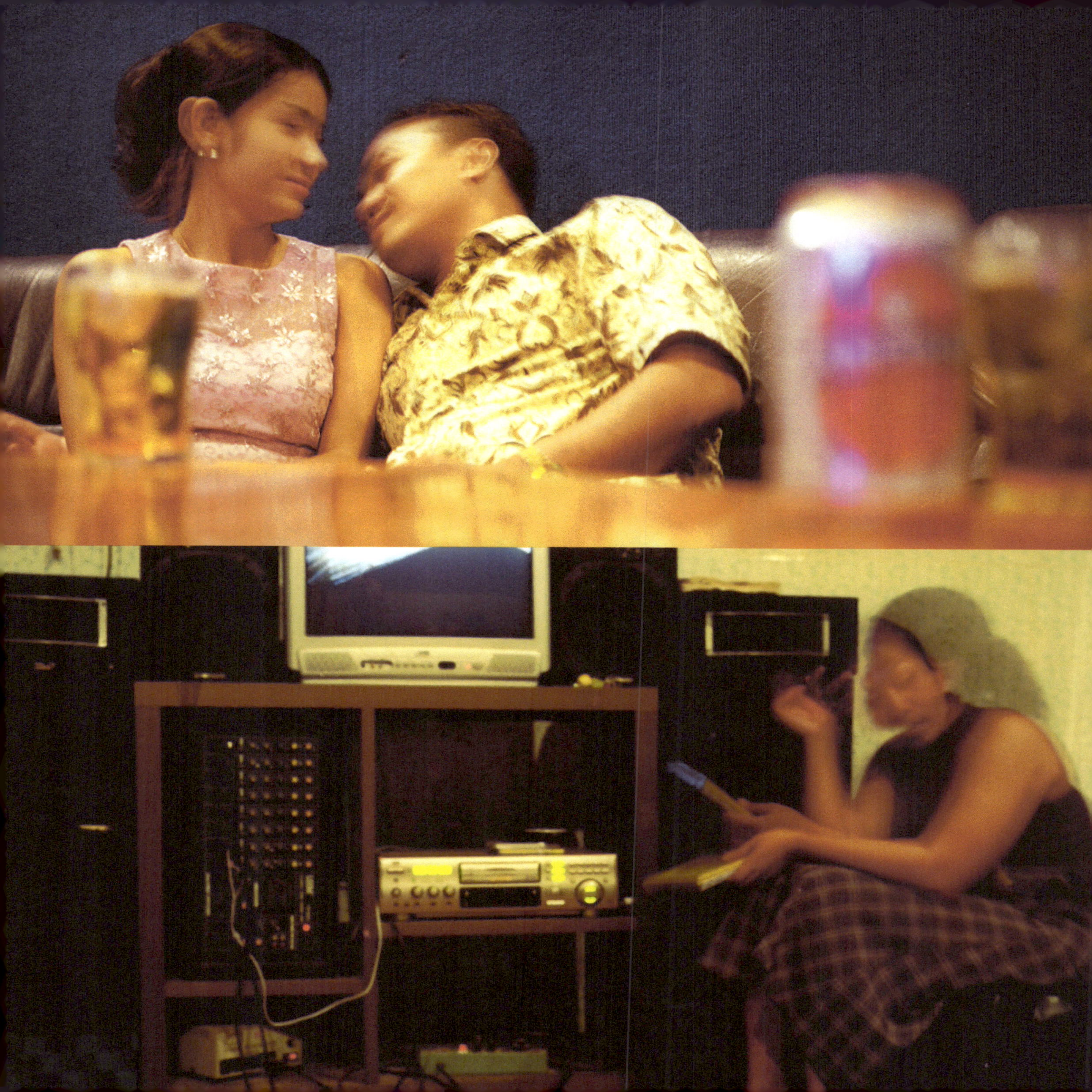

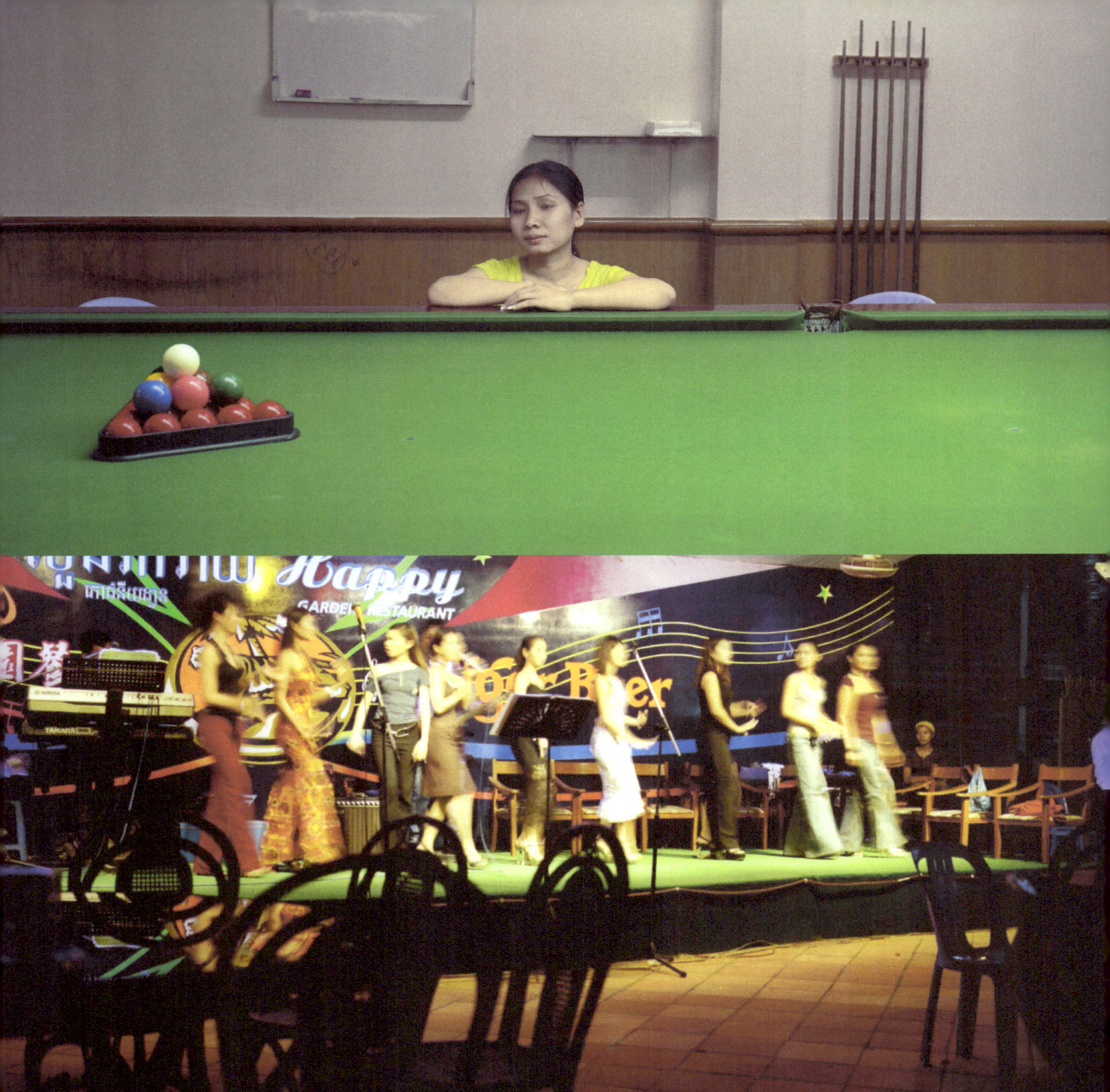
Happy
RESTAURANT
YAMAHA
YAMAHA

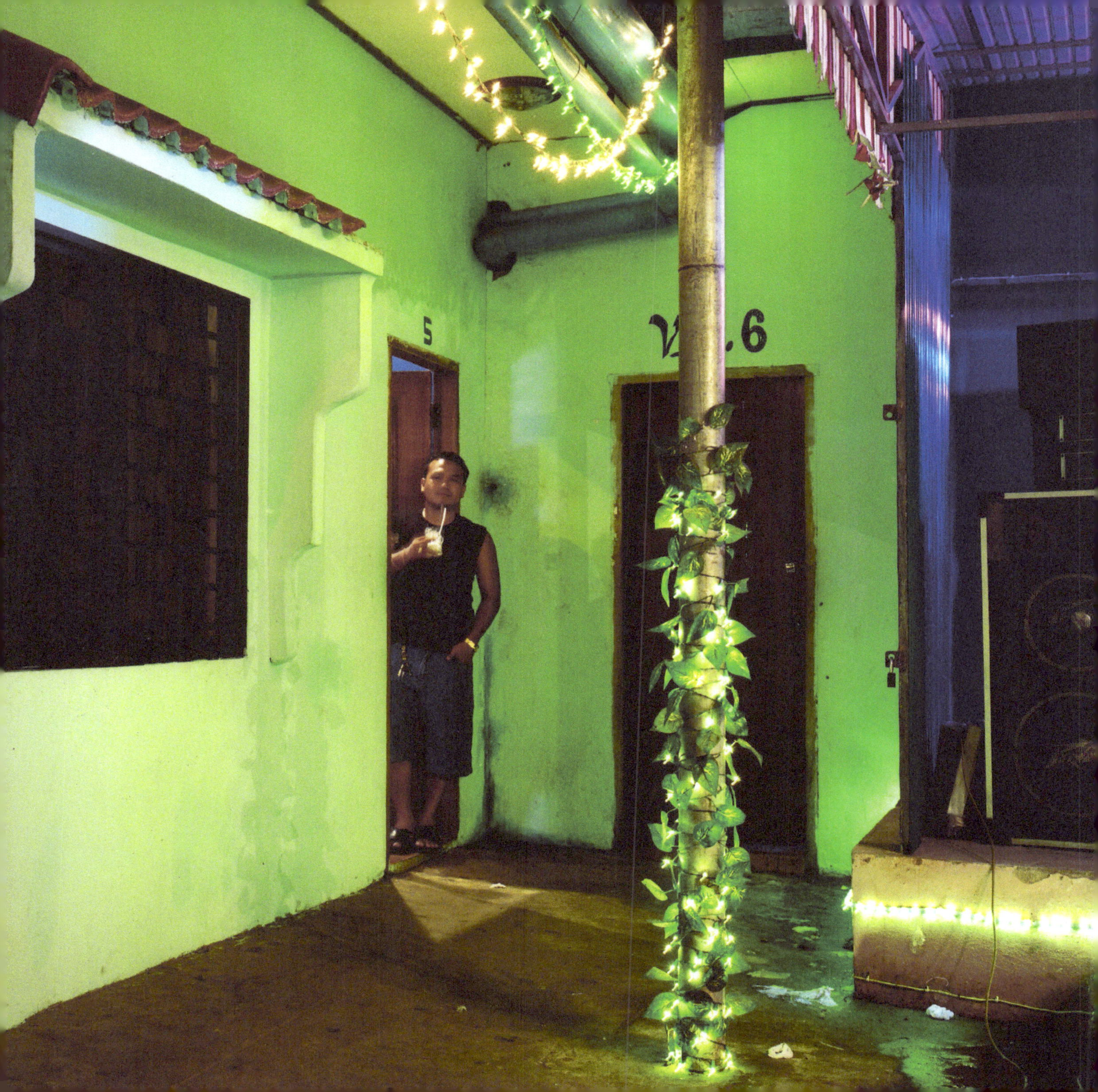
5
6

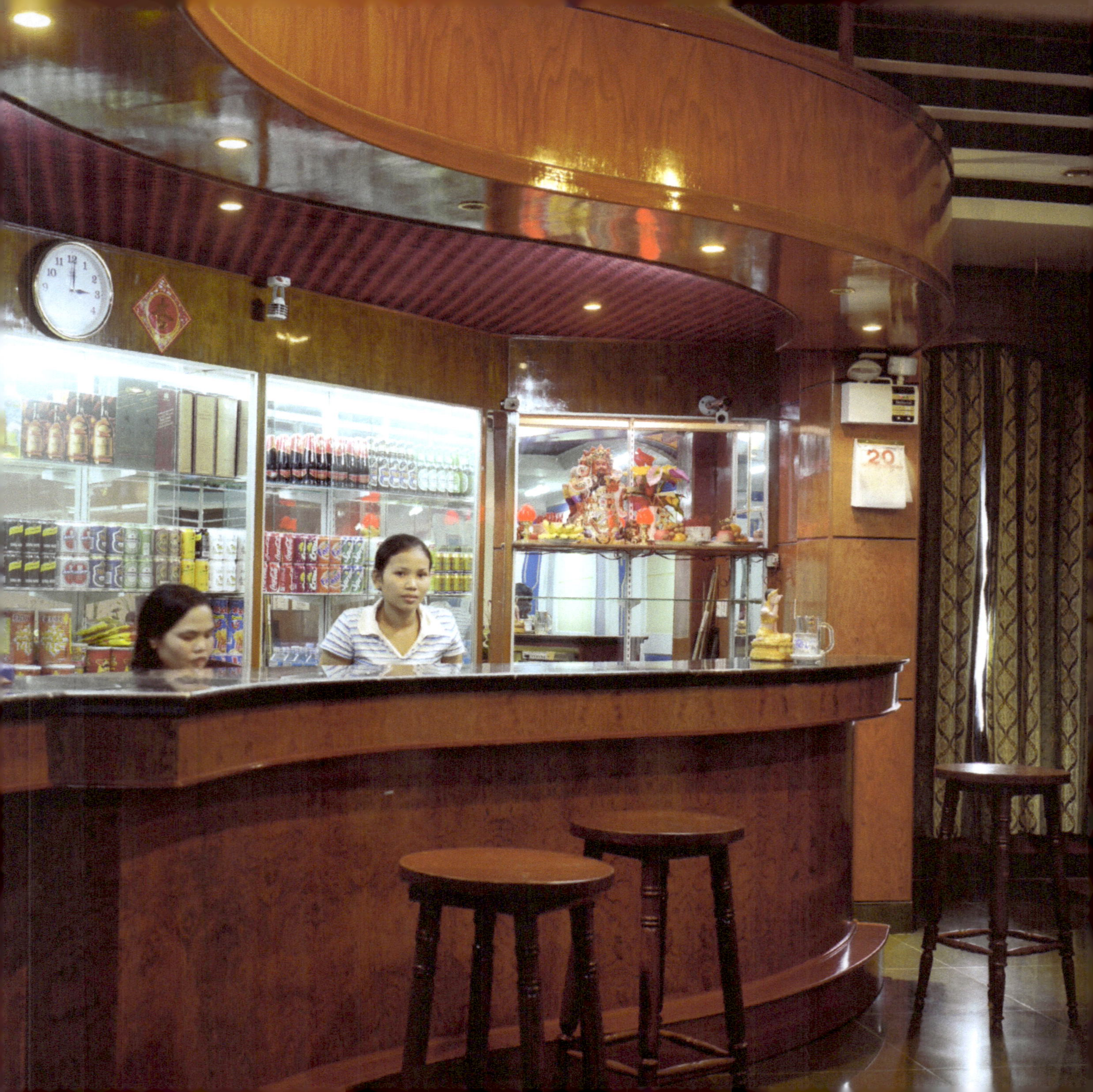

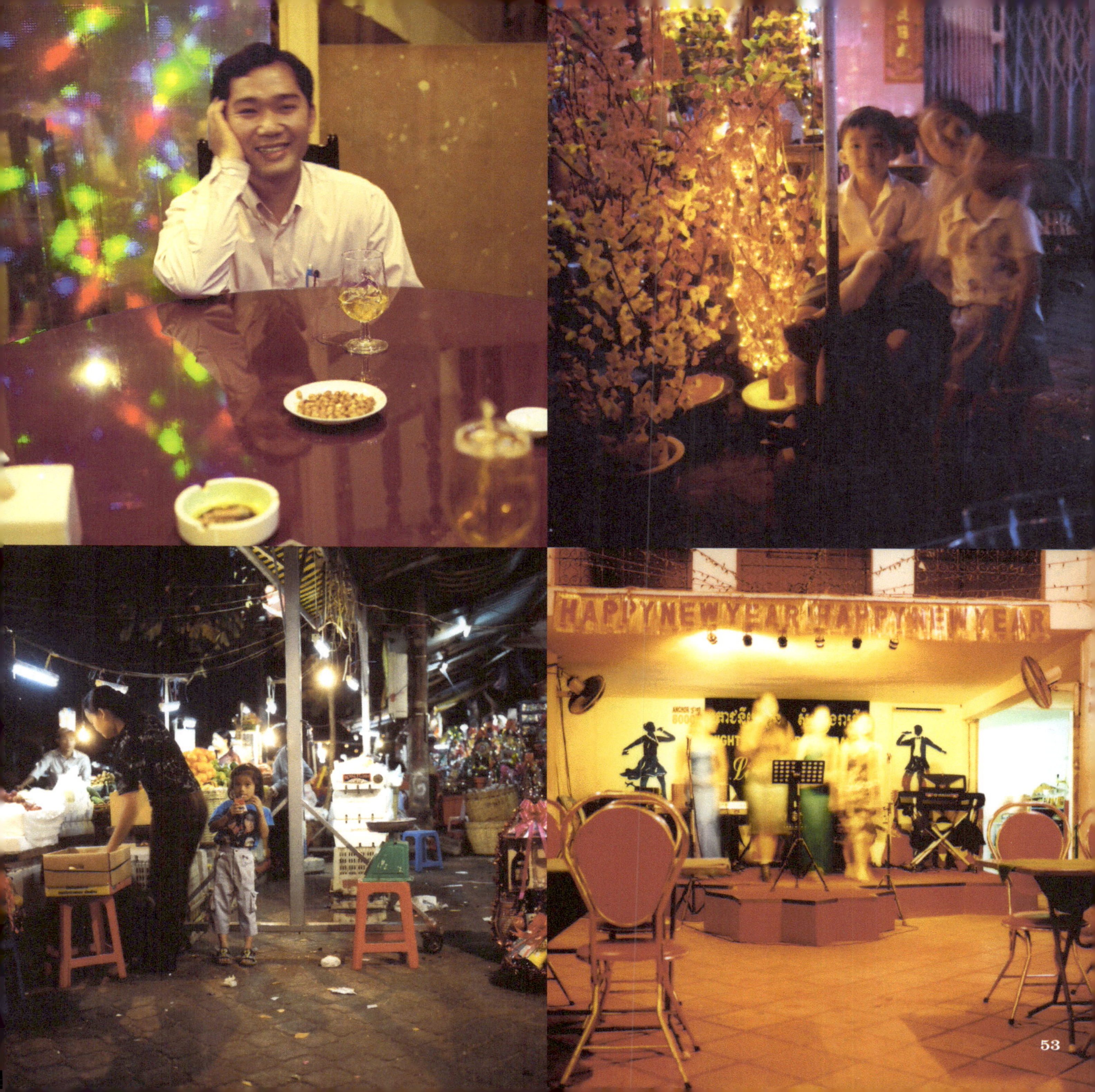
HAPPY NEW YEAR HAPPY NEW YEAR

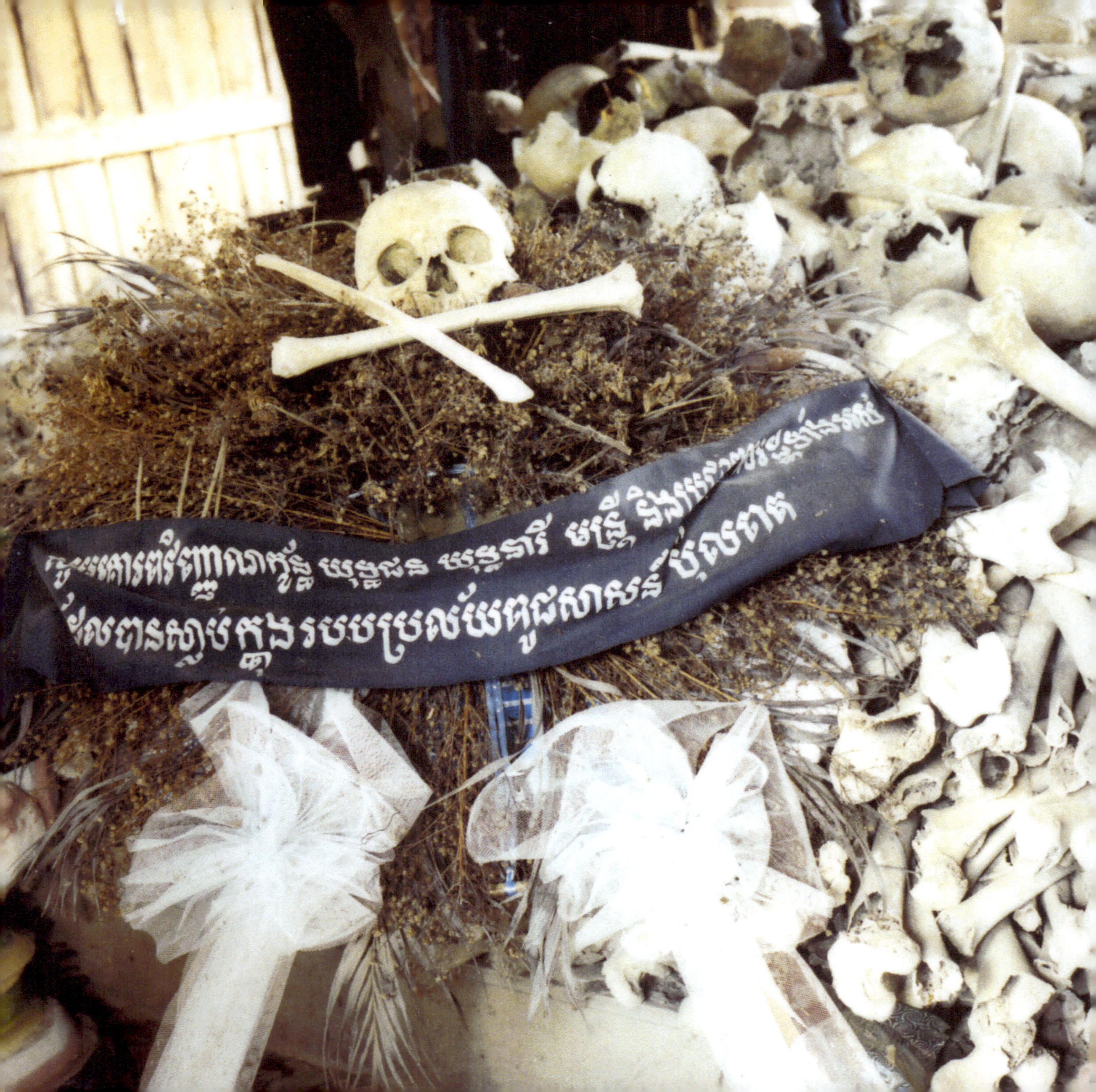
គោរពវិញ្ញាណក្ខន្ធ យុទ្ធជន យុទ្ធនារី មន្ត្រី និង
ដែលបានស្លាប់ក្នុងរបបប្រល័យពូជសាសន៍ ប៉ុលពត

REMEMBER

that the rest of us will not forget. Your country has suffered so much harm from social and political upheavals. The world needs to learn from the tragedy of the millions of innocent people who died during the Khmer Rouge from 1975 to 1979. They need to hear the stories of the many honorable people whose lives were cut short. These accounts of struggles for survival can only be disclosed by Cambodians. When I hear them told, I am overwhelmed. I can't possibly imagine what it must have been like for your people.

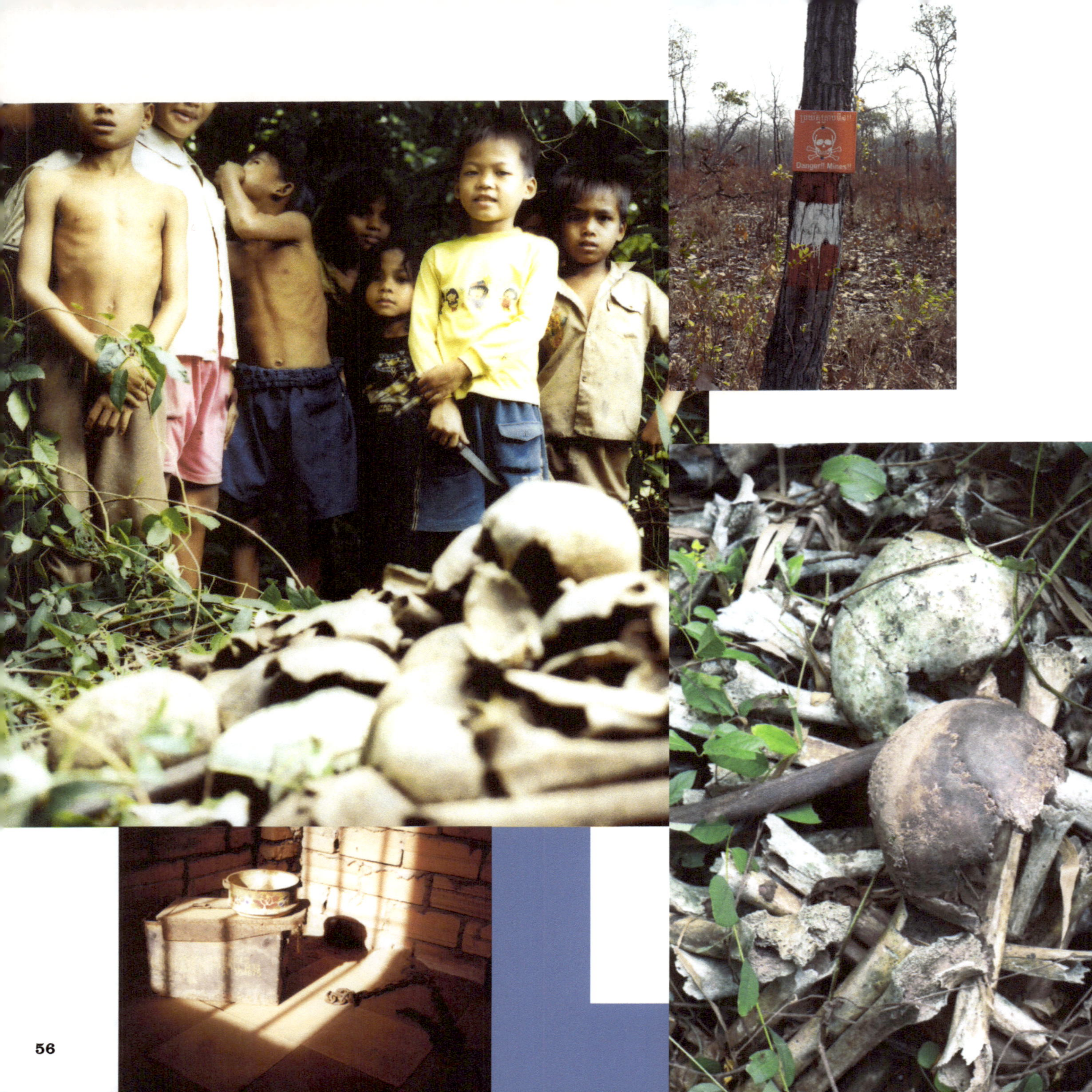
Danger!! Mines!!

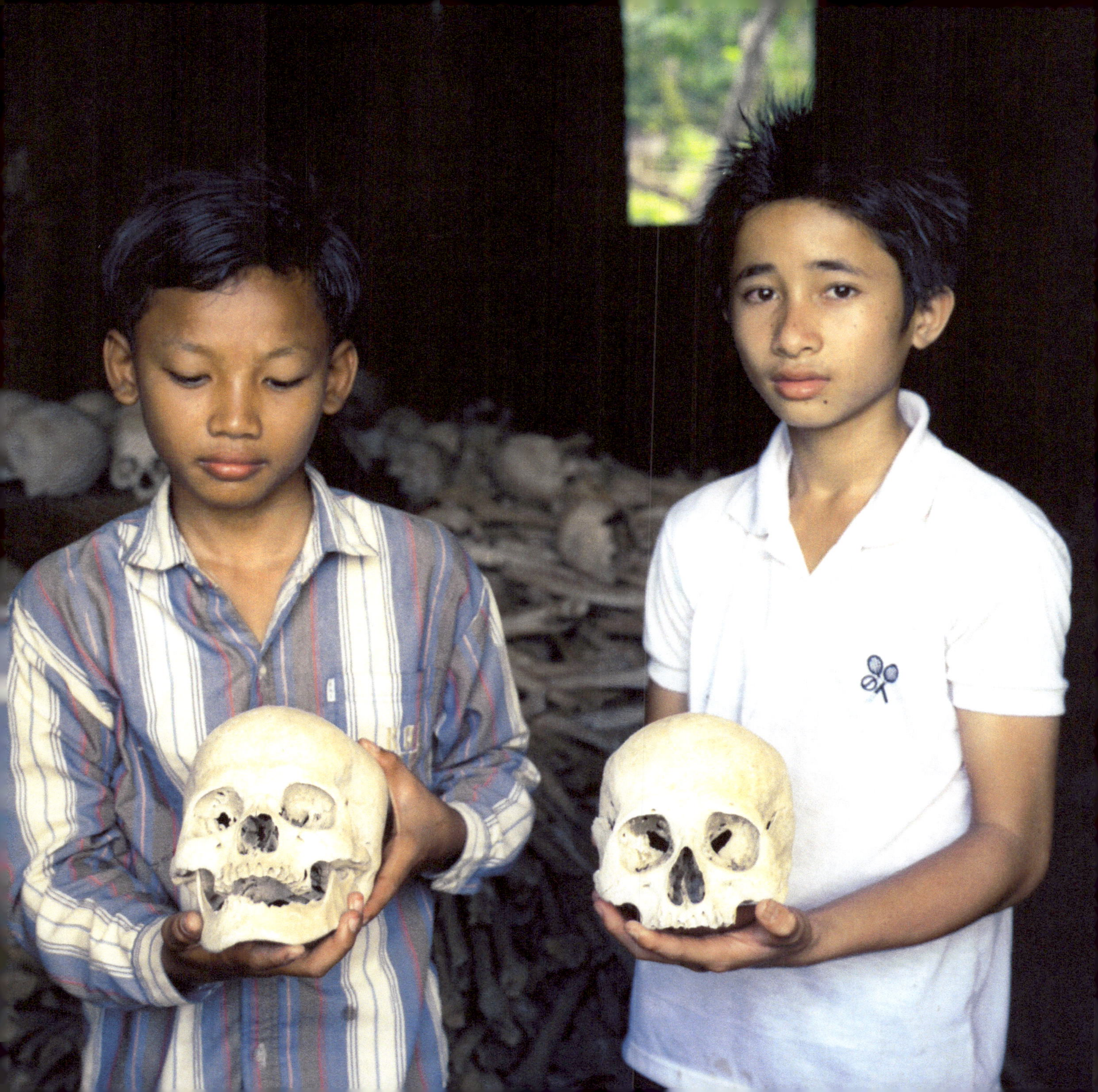

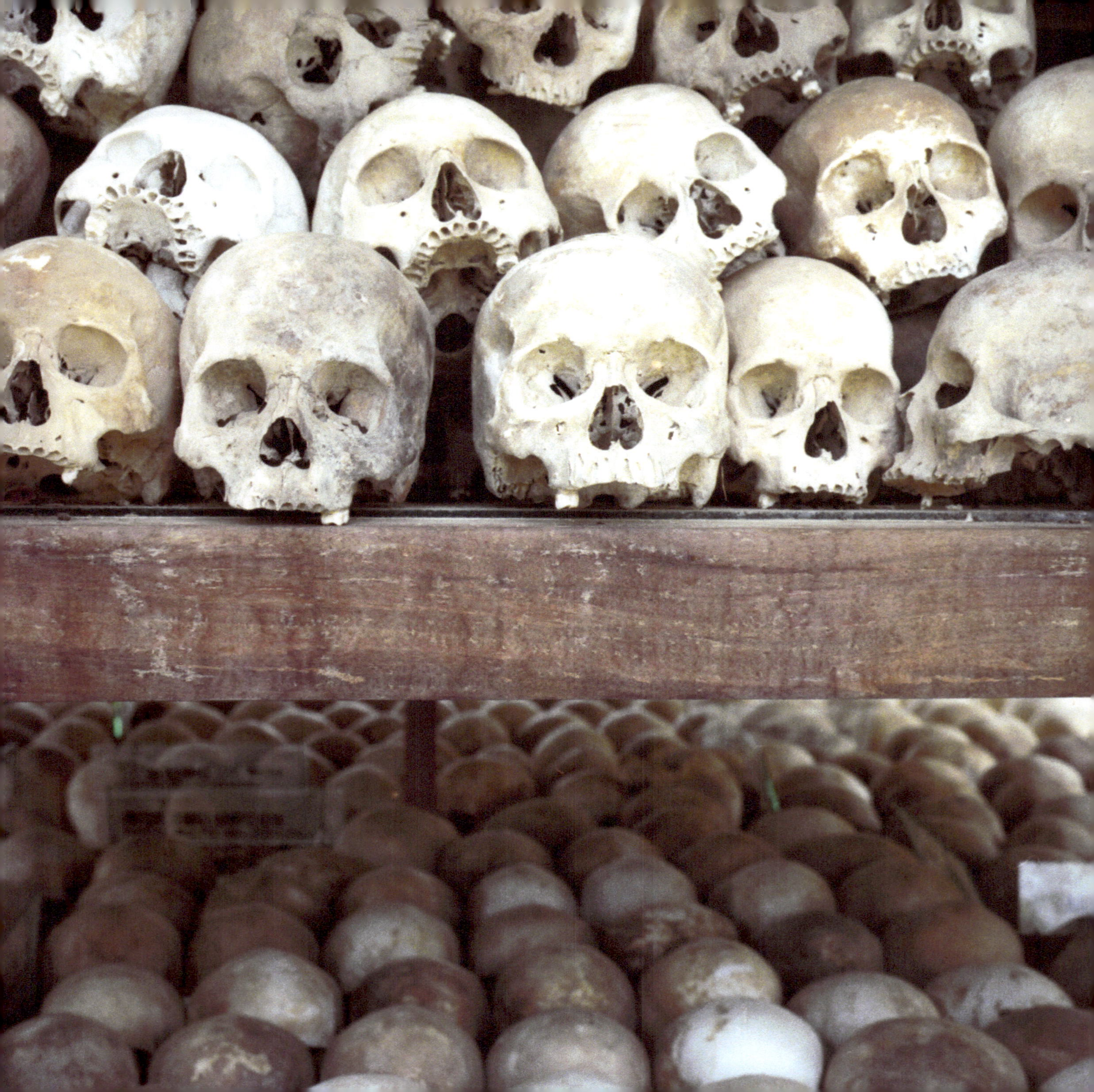

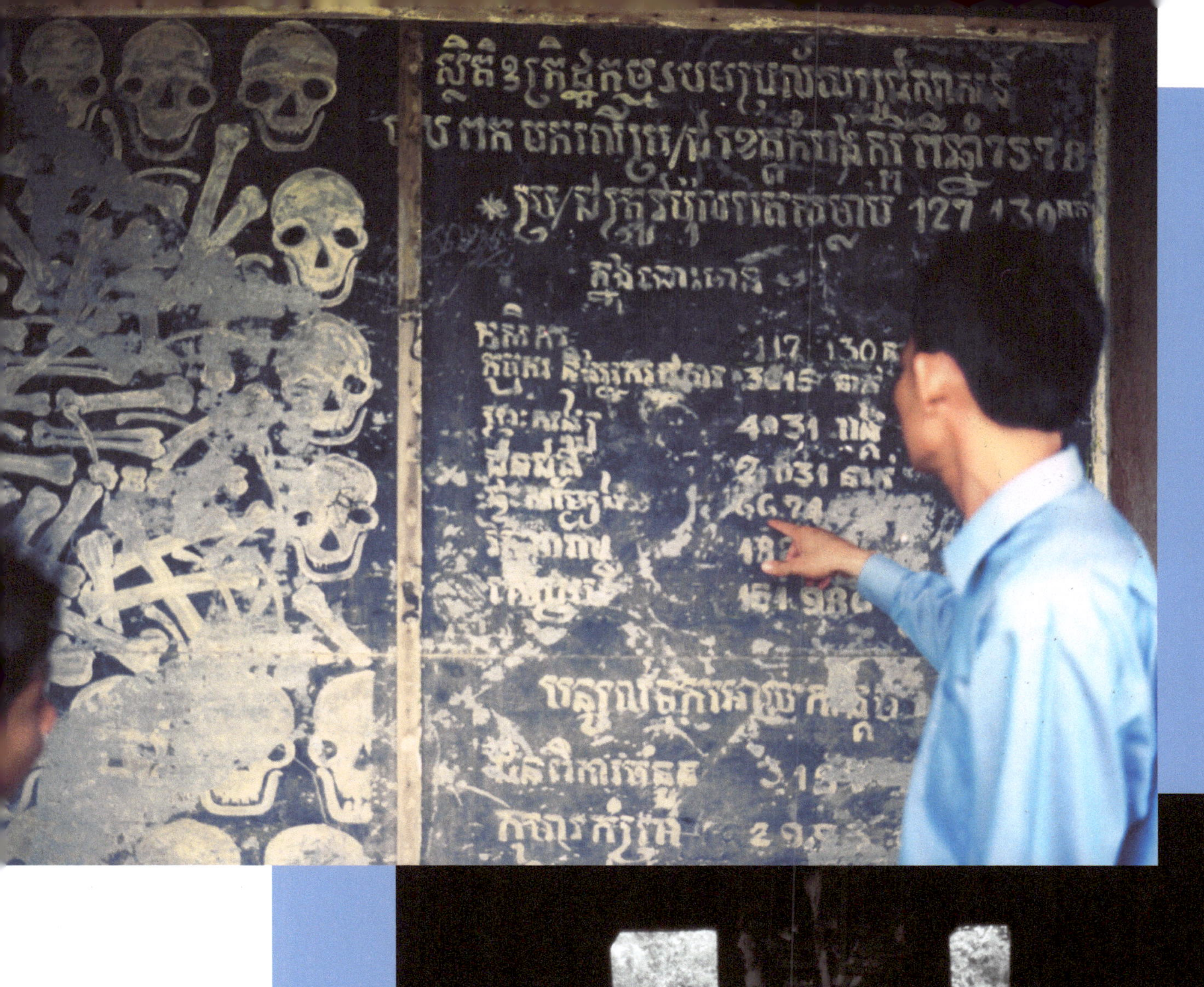

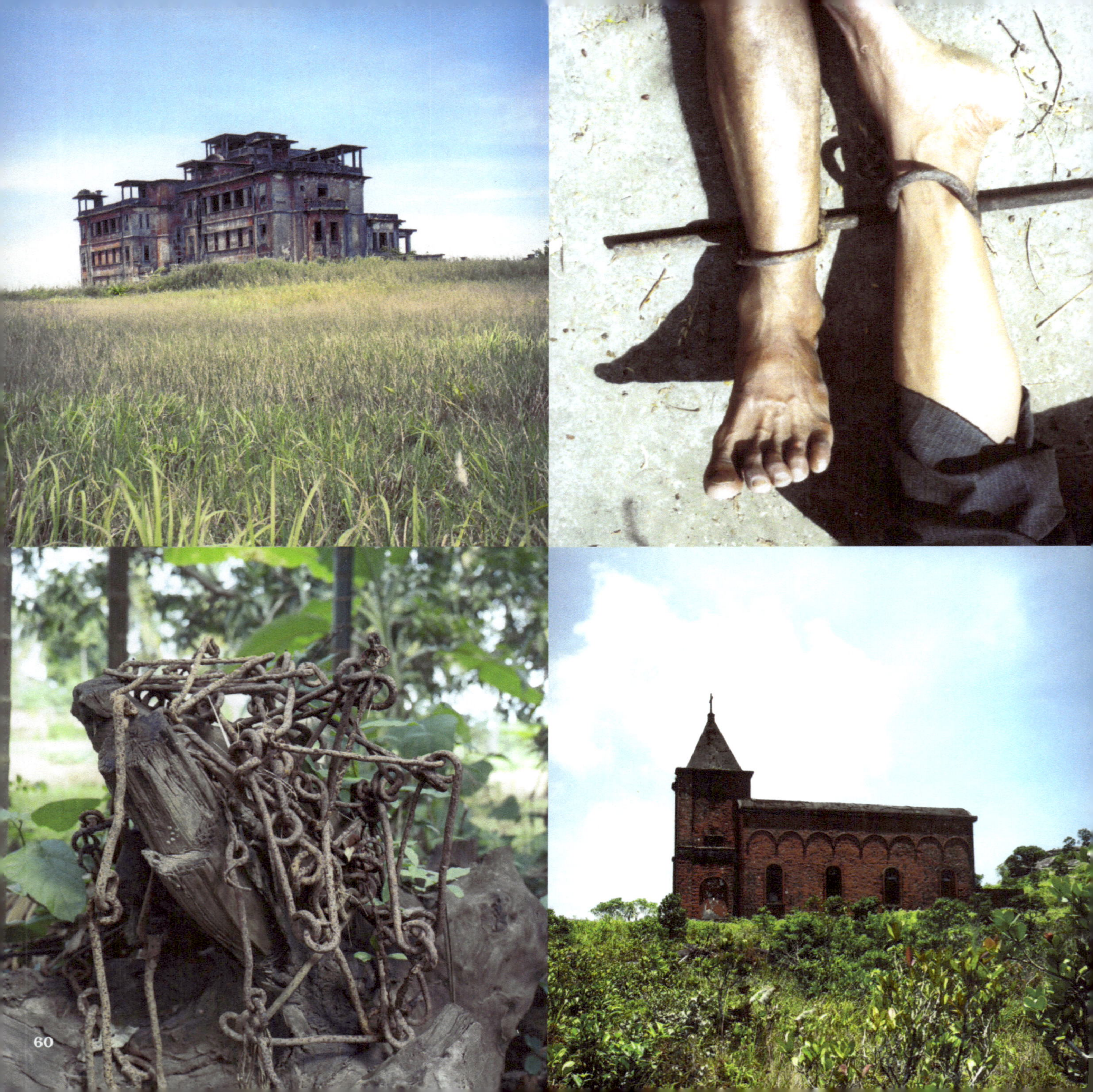

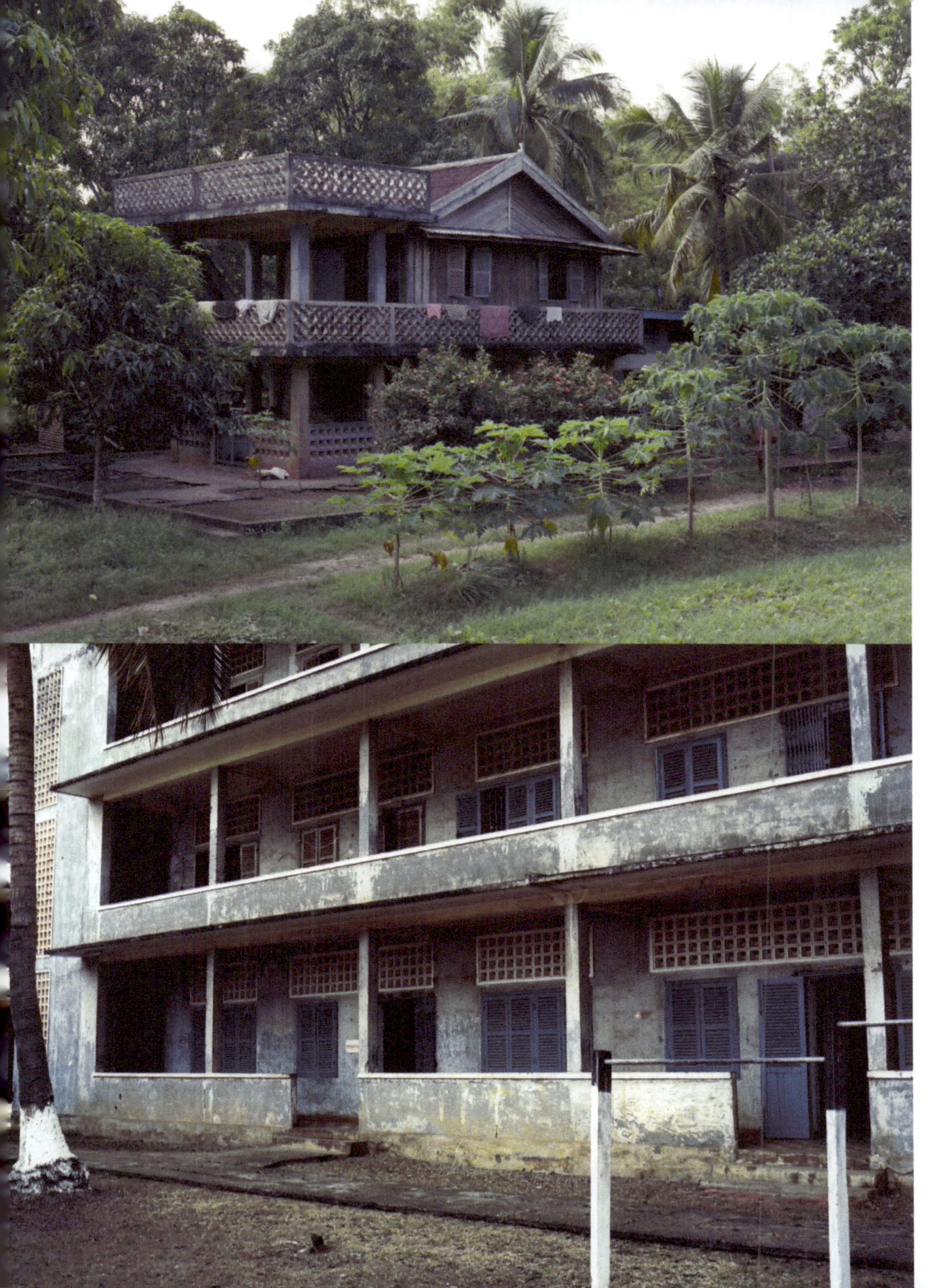

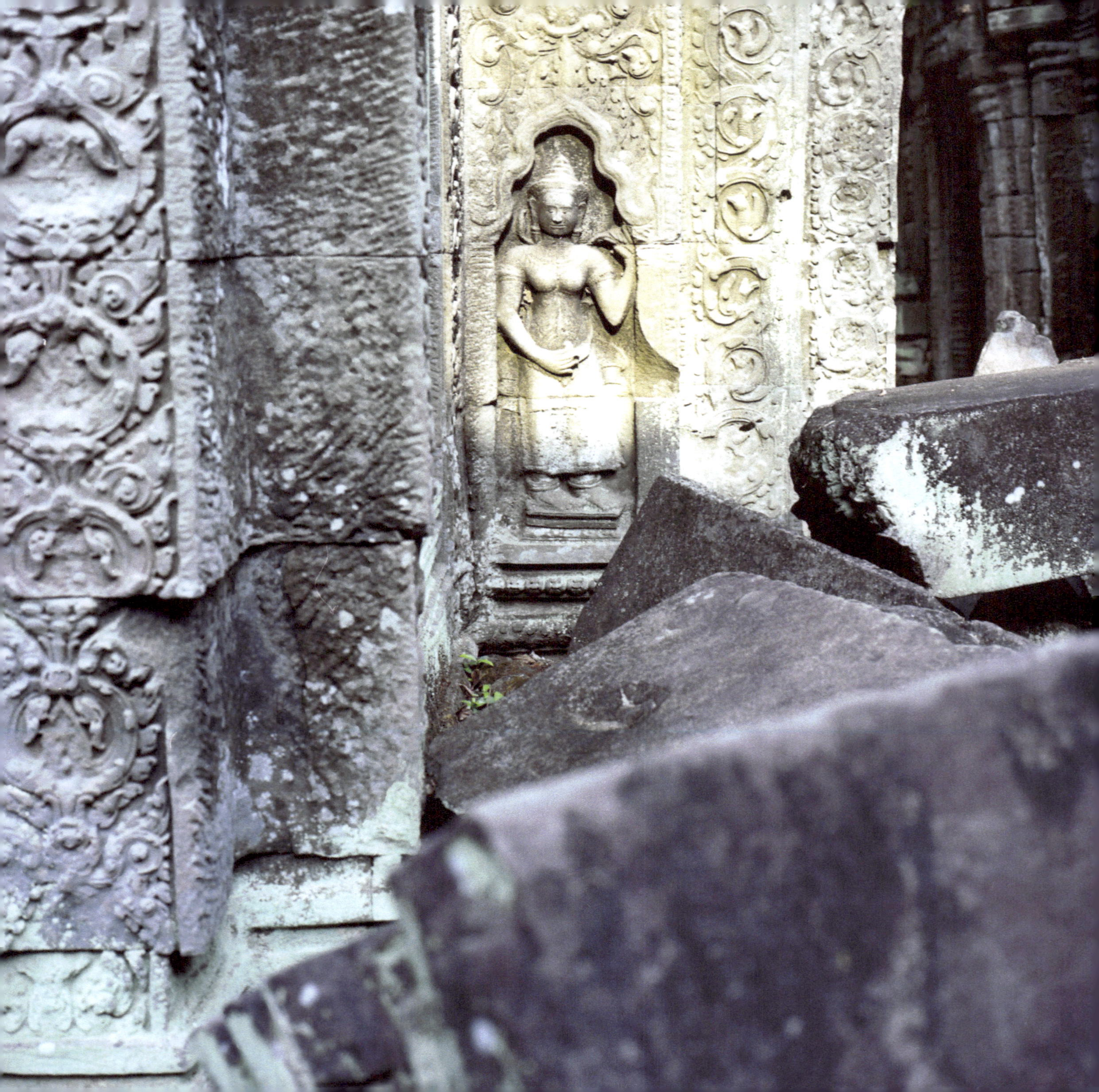

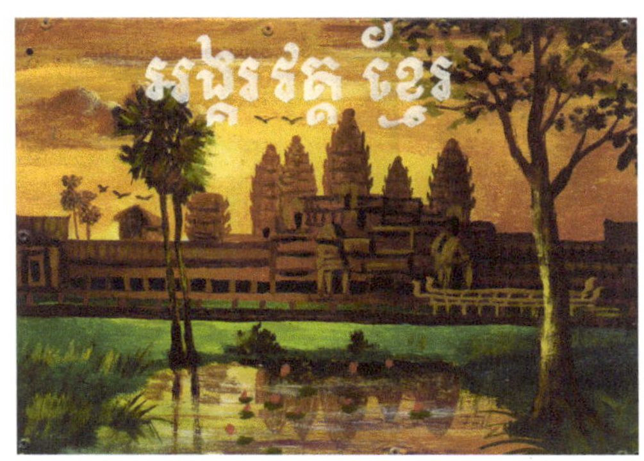

Dear Cambodia,

ANGKOR

is the ancient capital of the Khmer empire with its celebrated temples and palaces. One of the biggest sets of religious ruins, and one of the world's greatest treasures is amazing to see. But please... don't lose your cultural heritage by letting people take artifacts and architectural elements away from your archaeological sites. I beg you to slow attempts to cash in on the country's rise in tourism. You can upset the ground where Angkor Wat sits which could lead to parts of it sinking and eventually falling down. Take a look at what you and the world would miss...

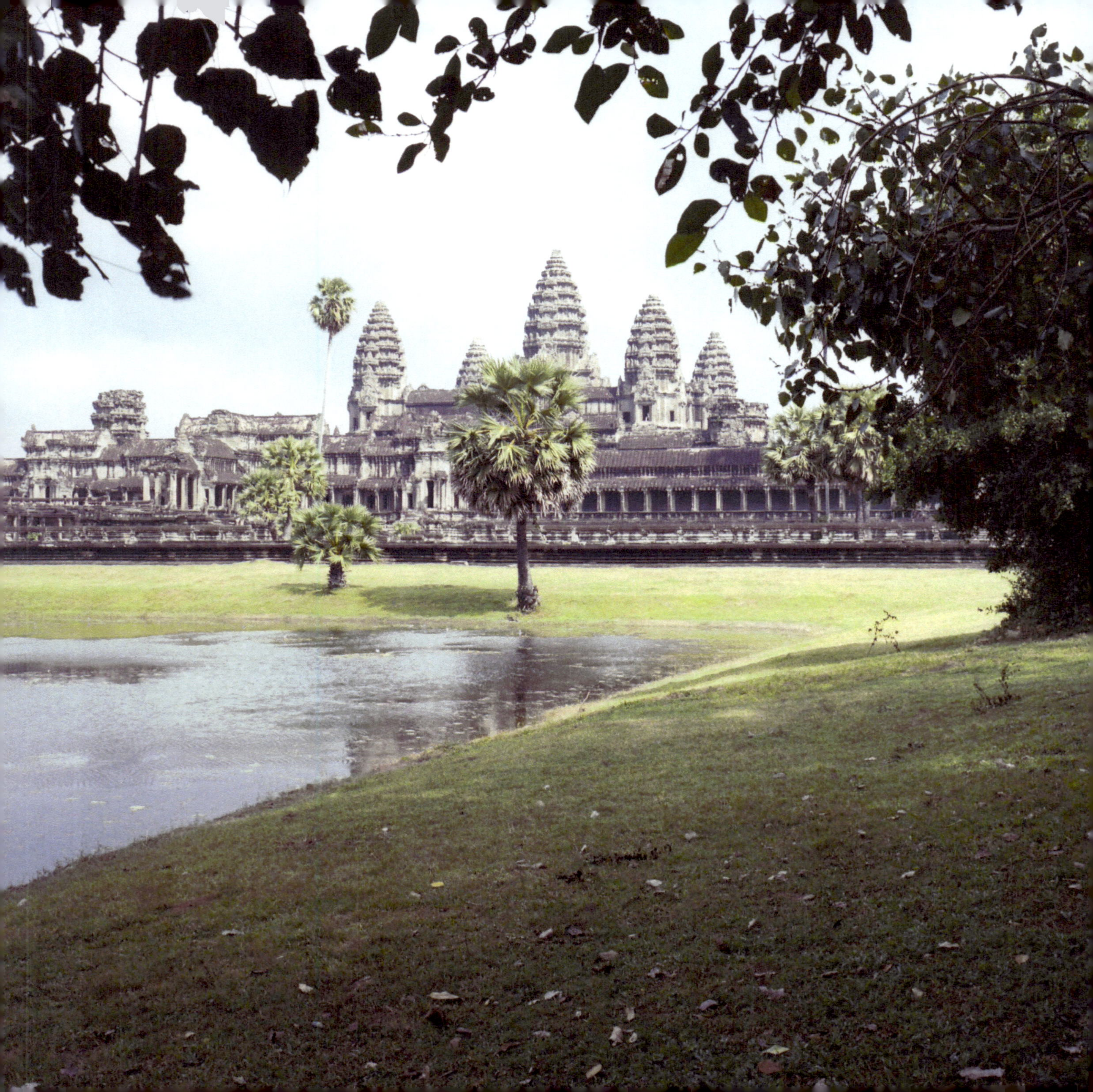

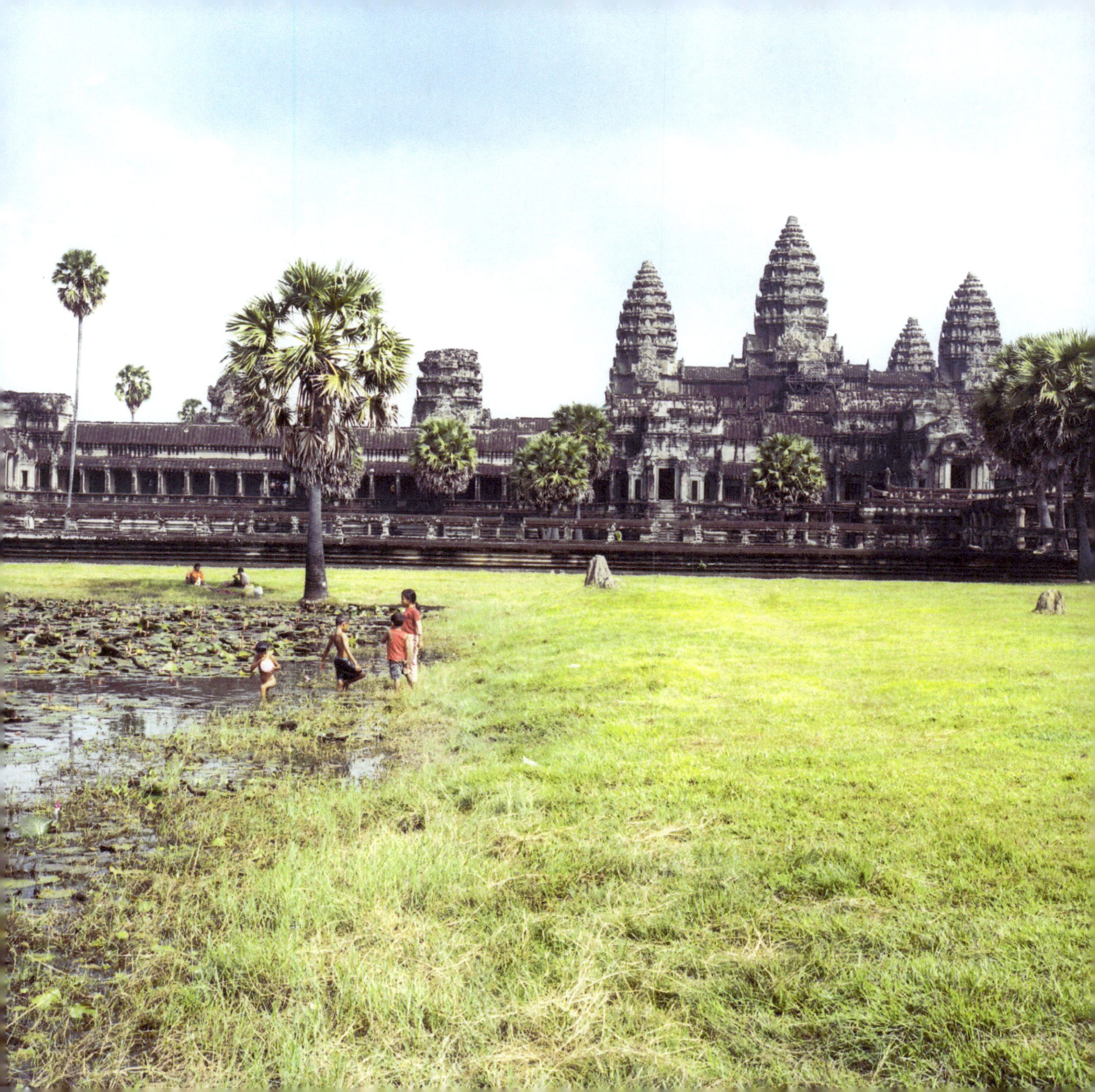

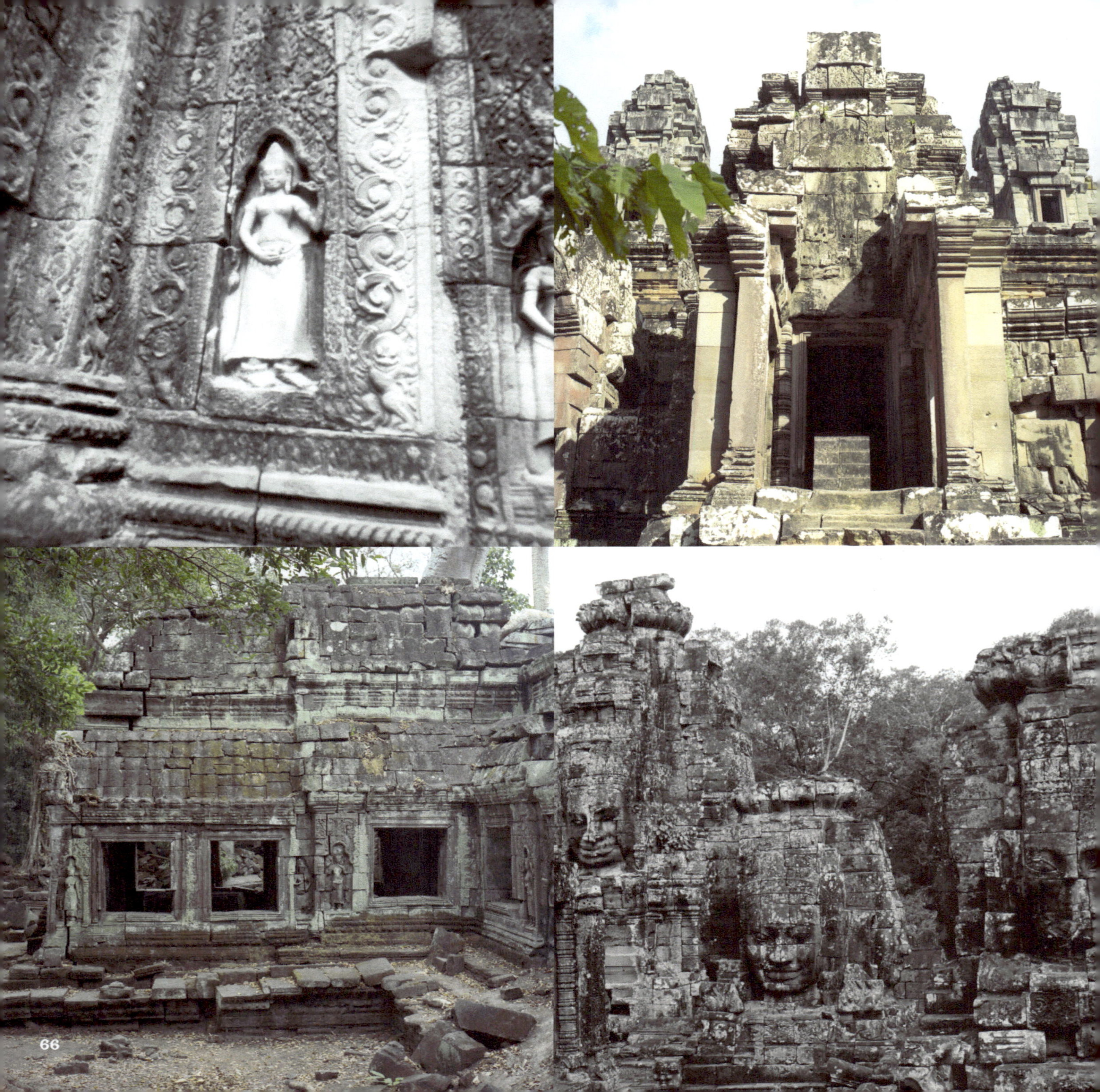

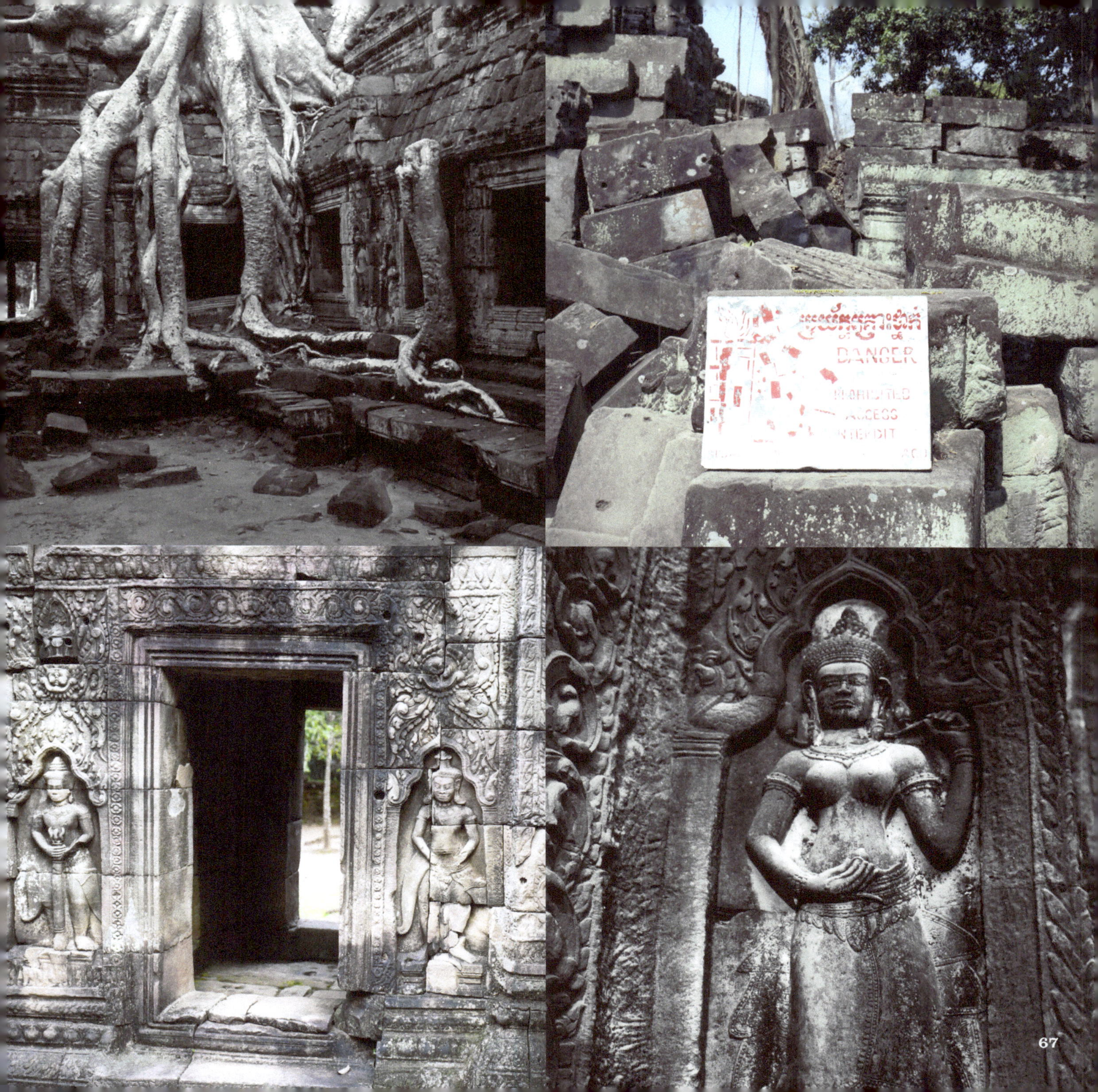
DANGER

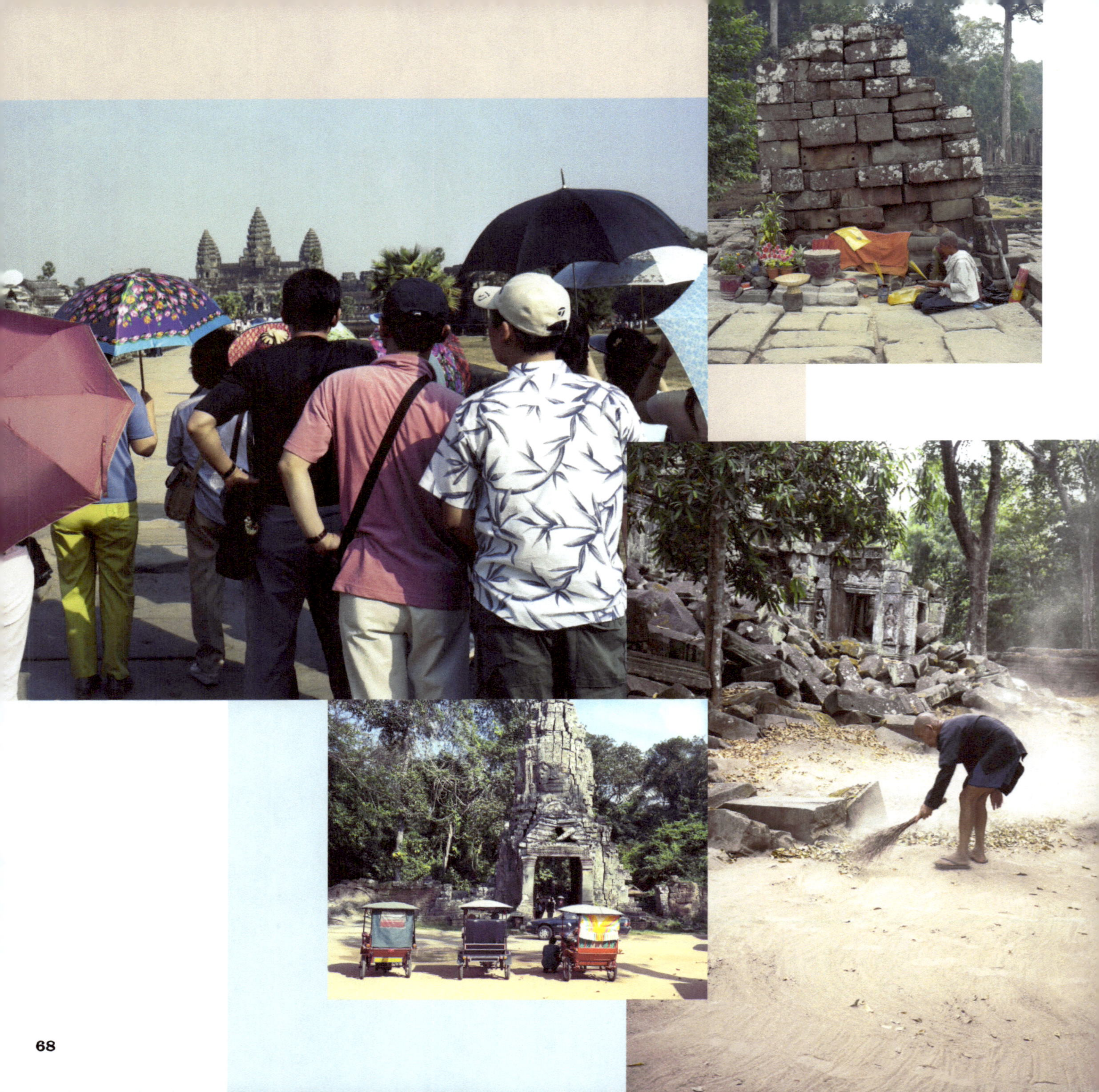

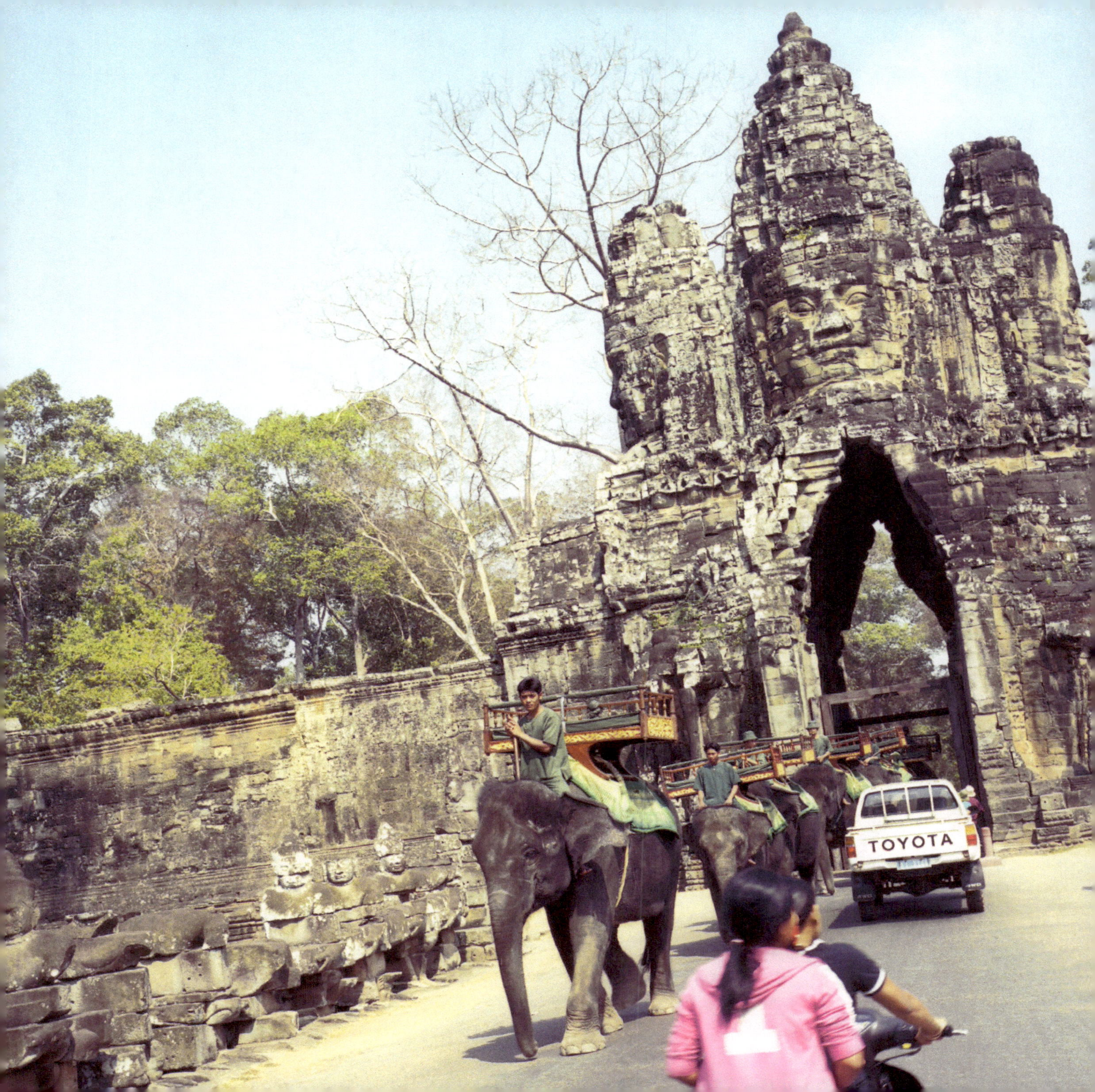
TOYOTA

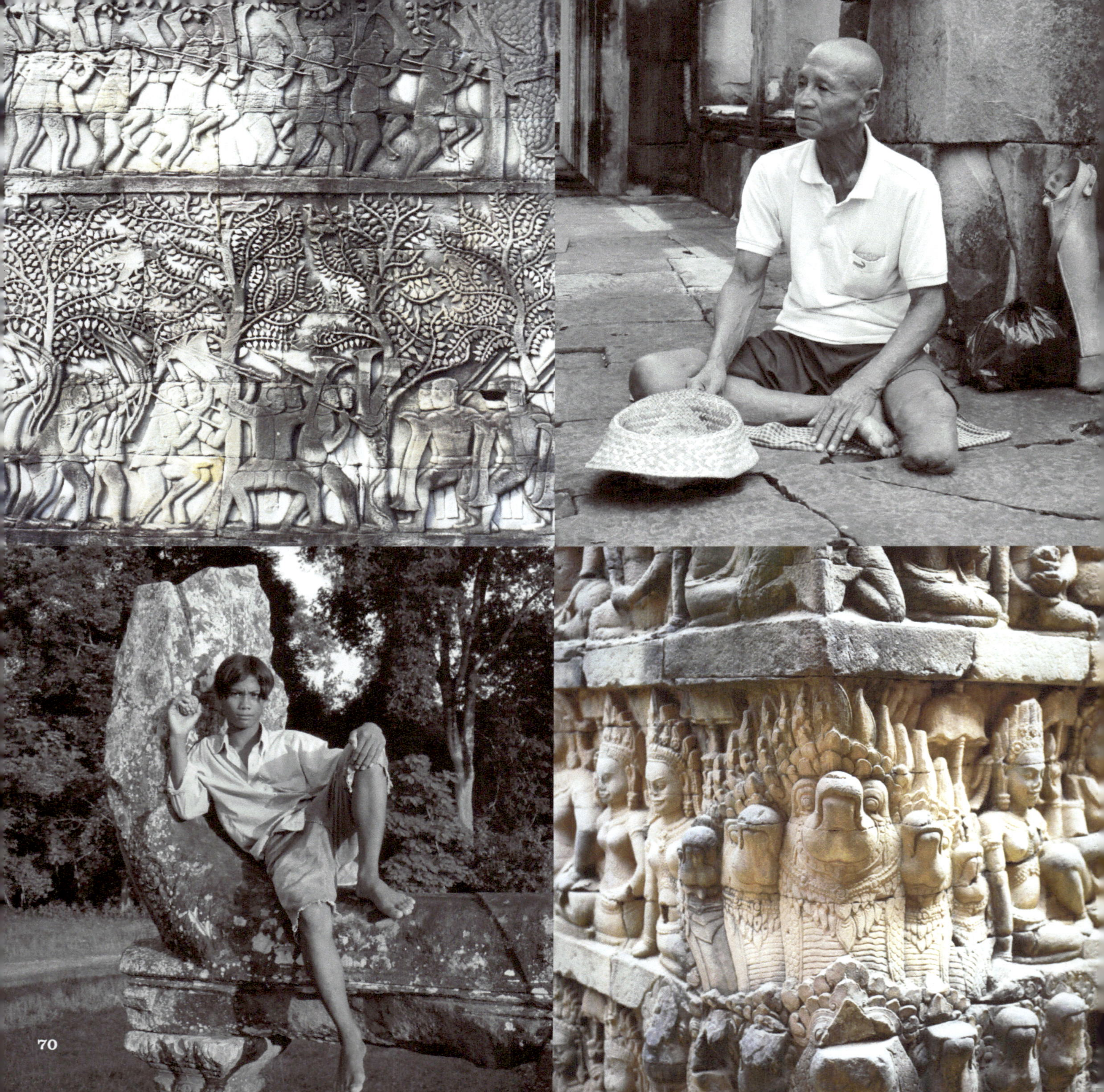

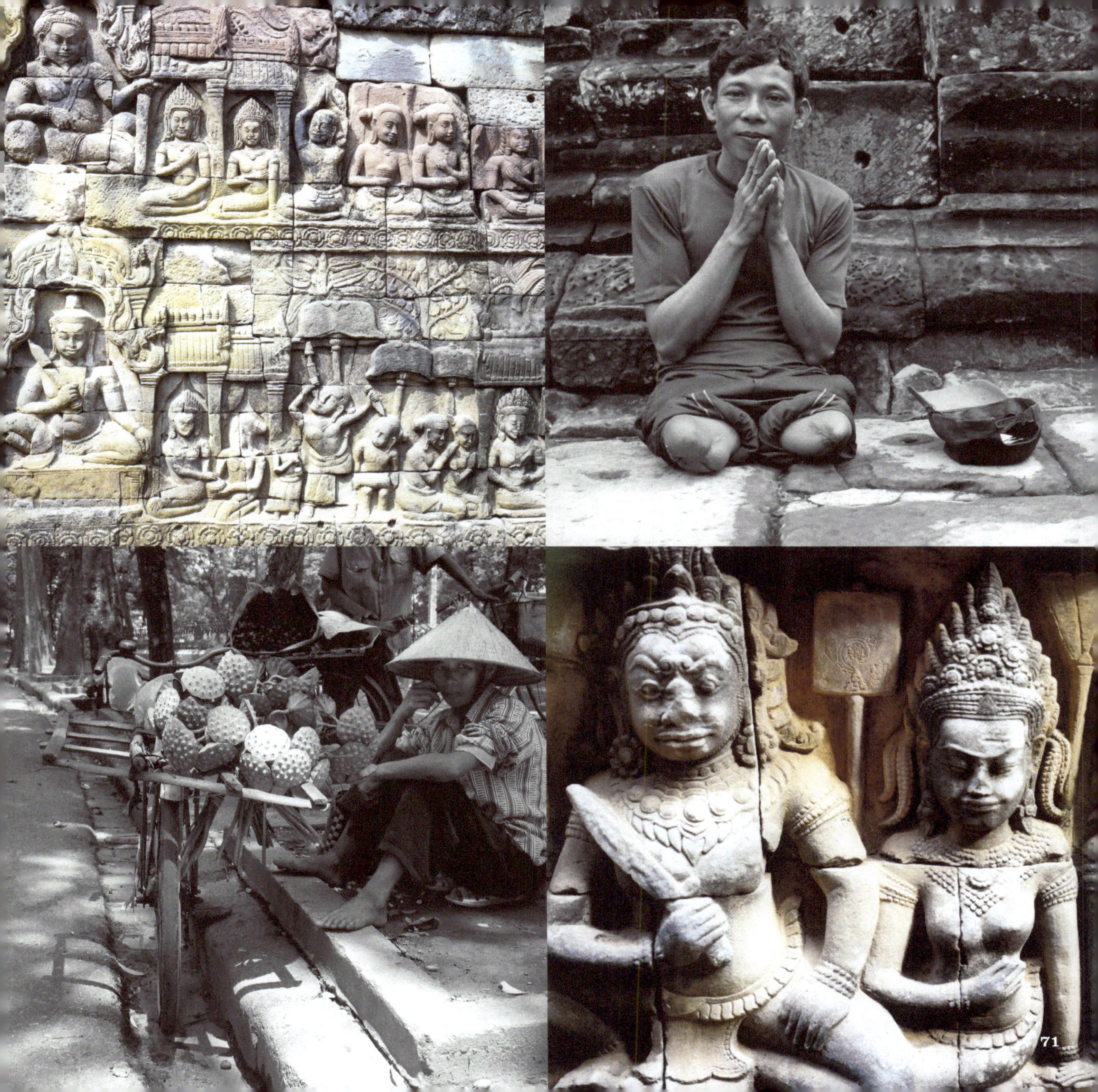

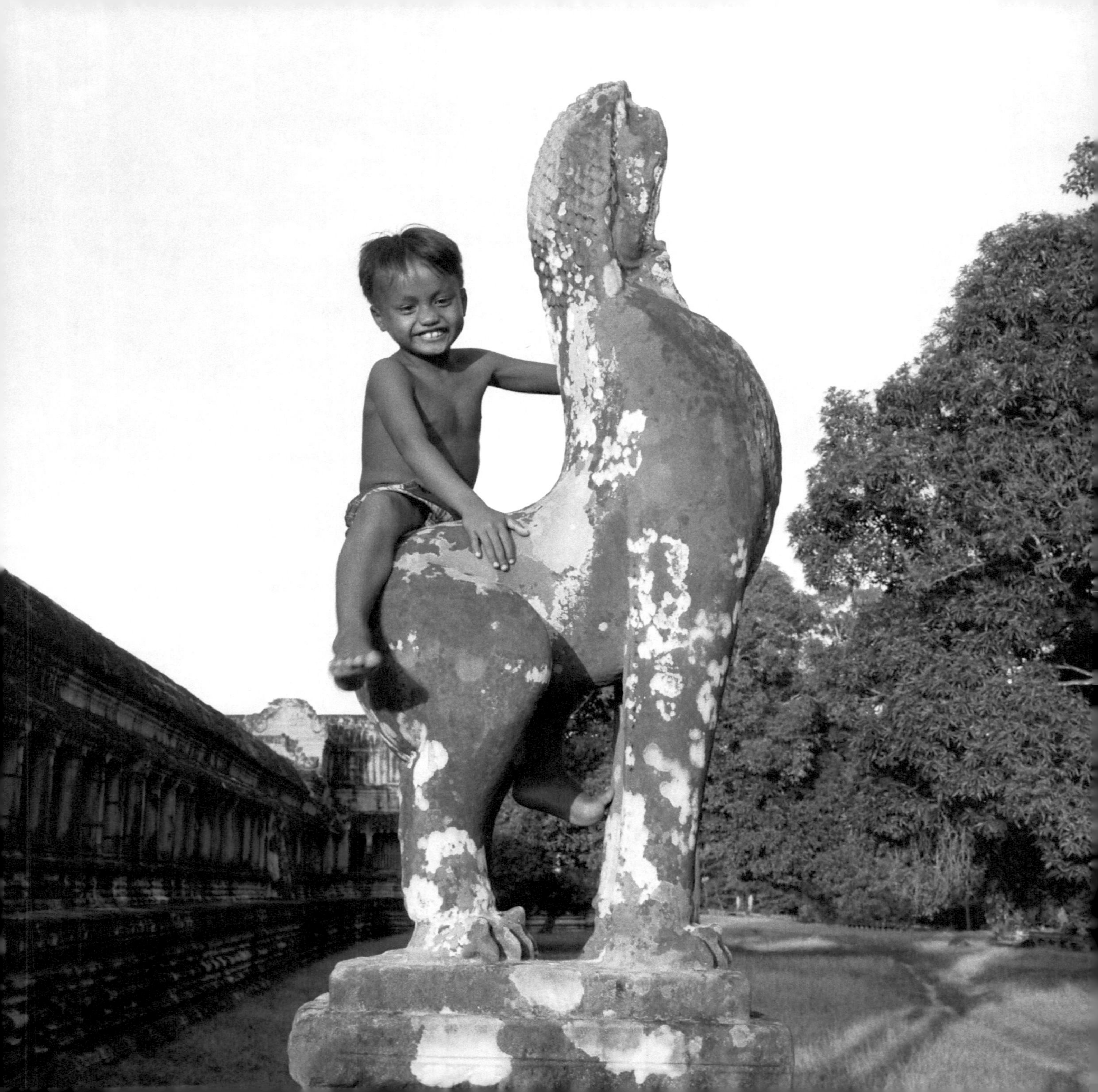

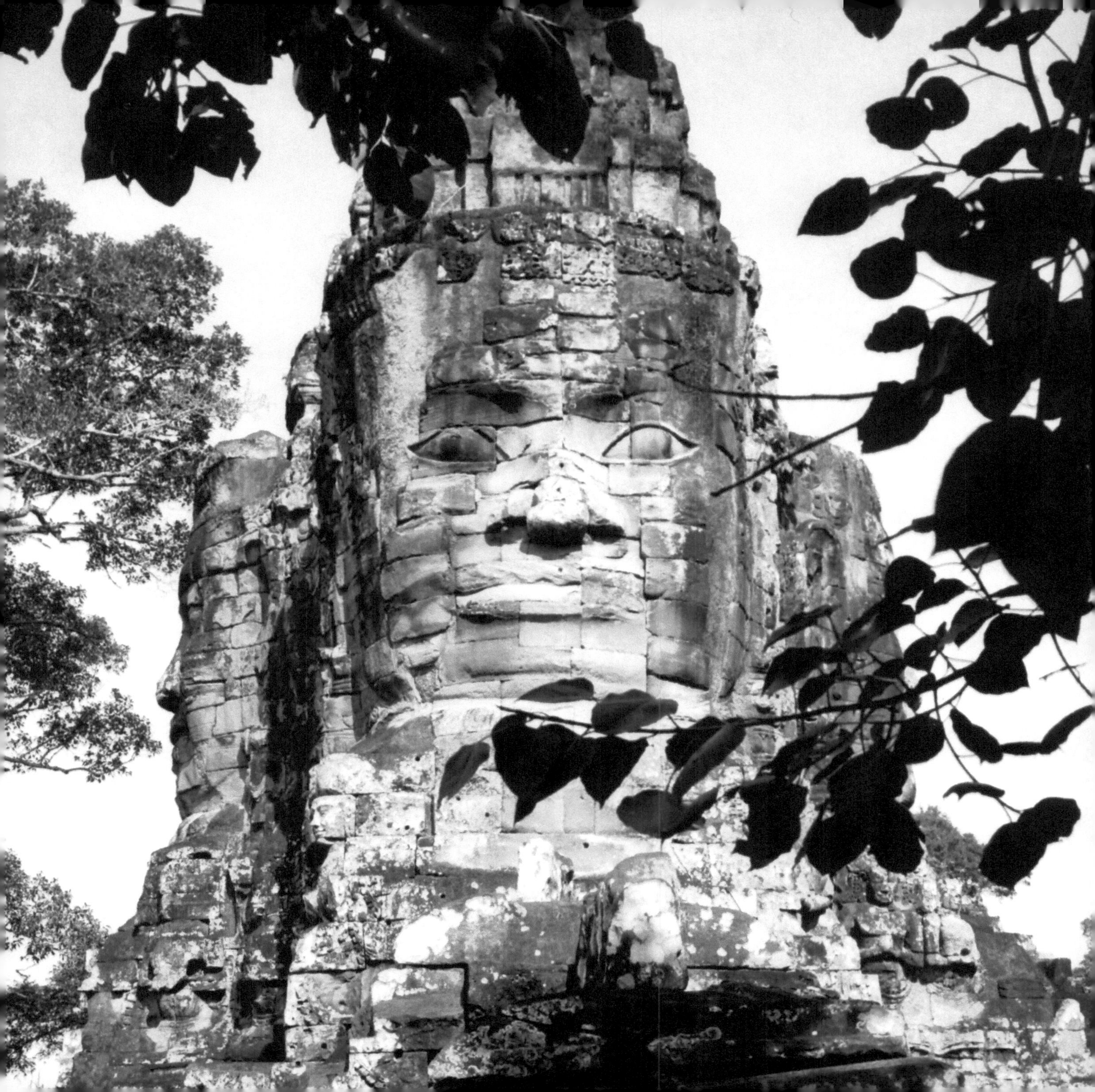

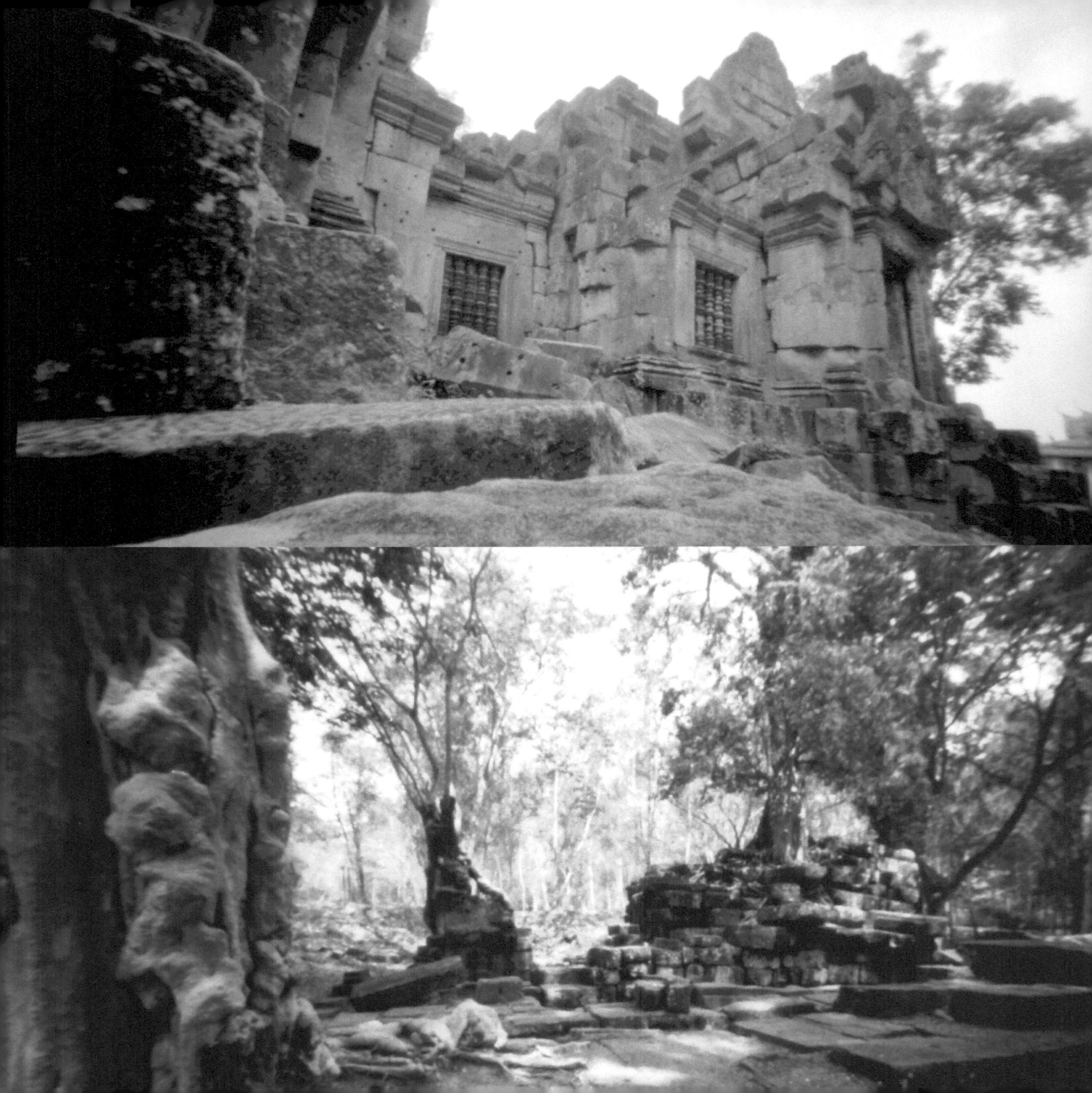

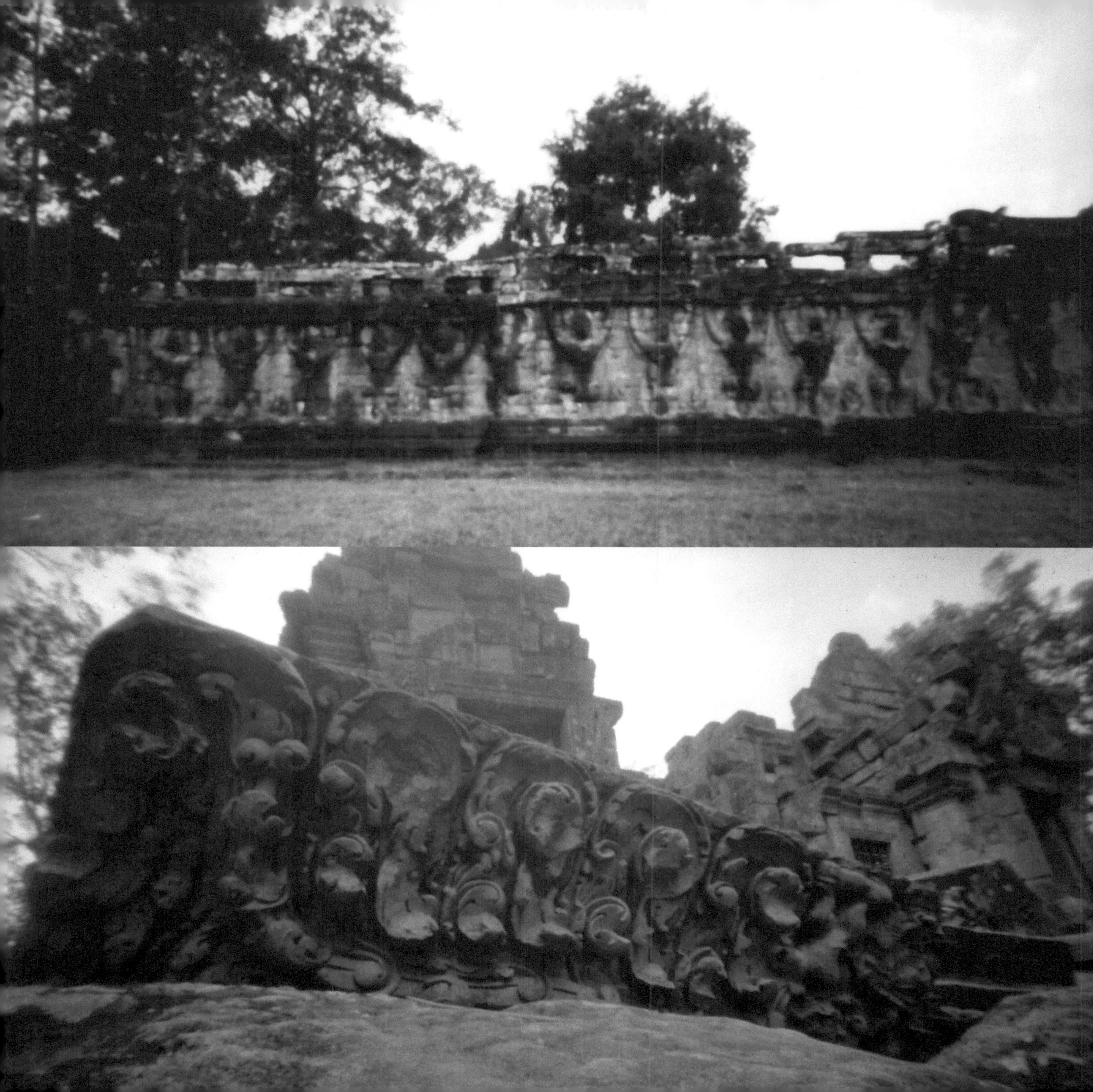

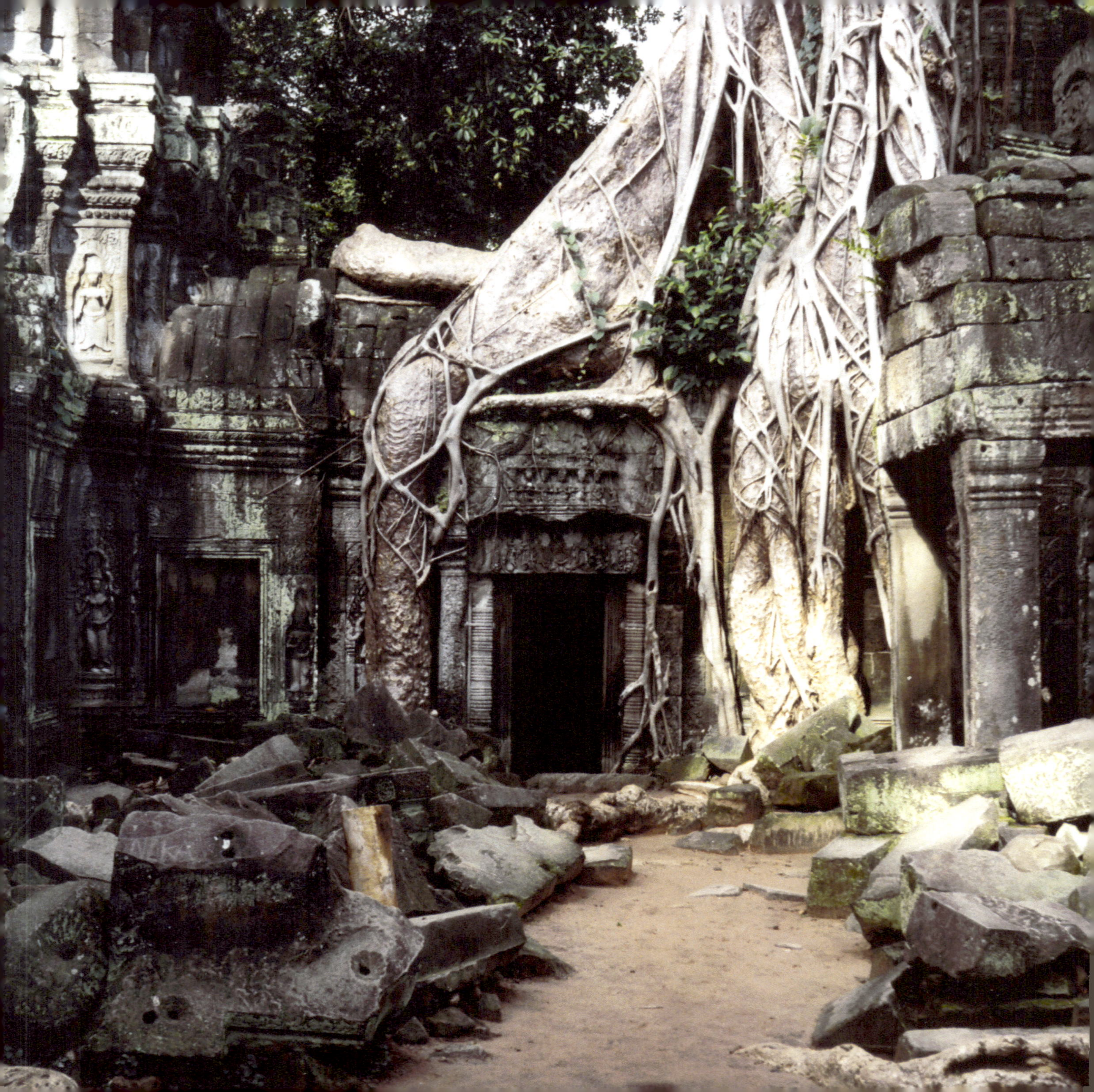

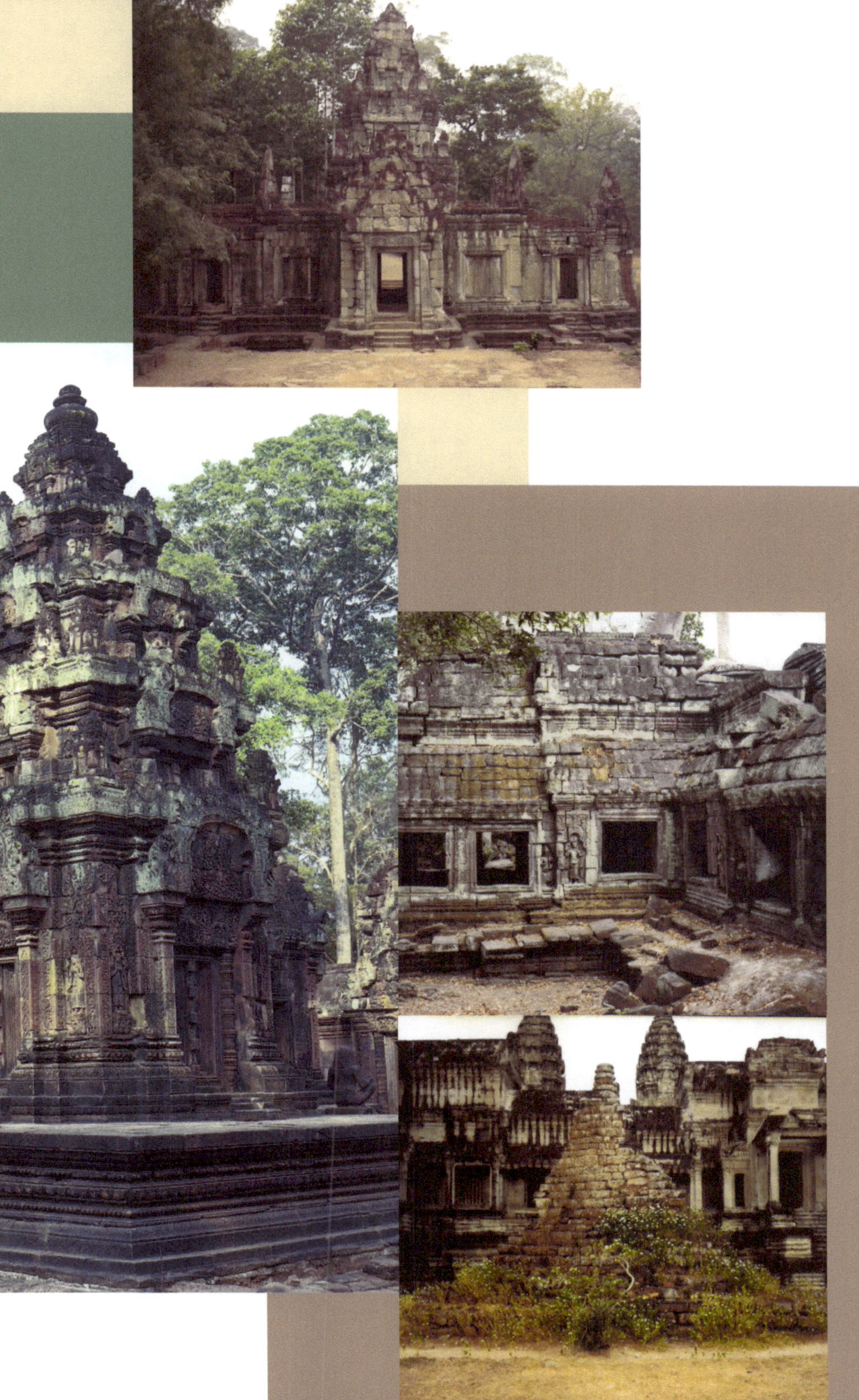

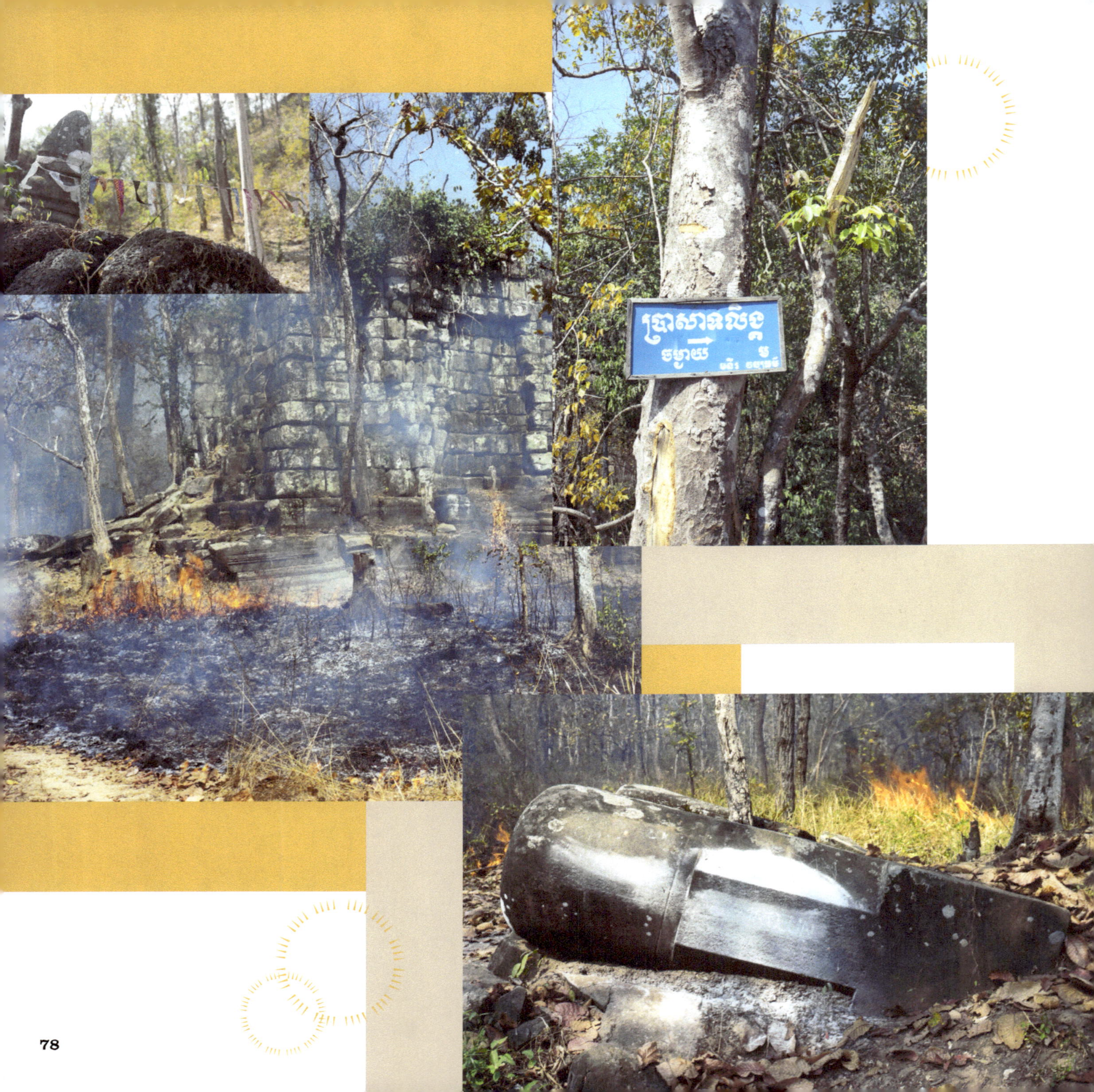
ប្រាសាទលិង្គ
ចម្ងាយ

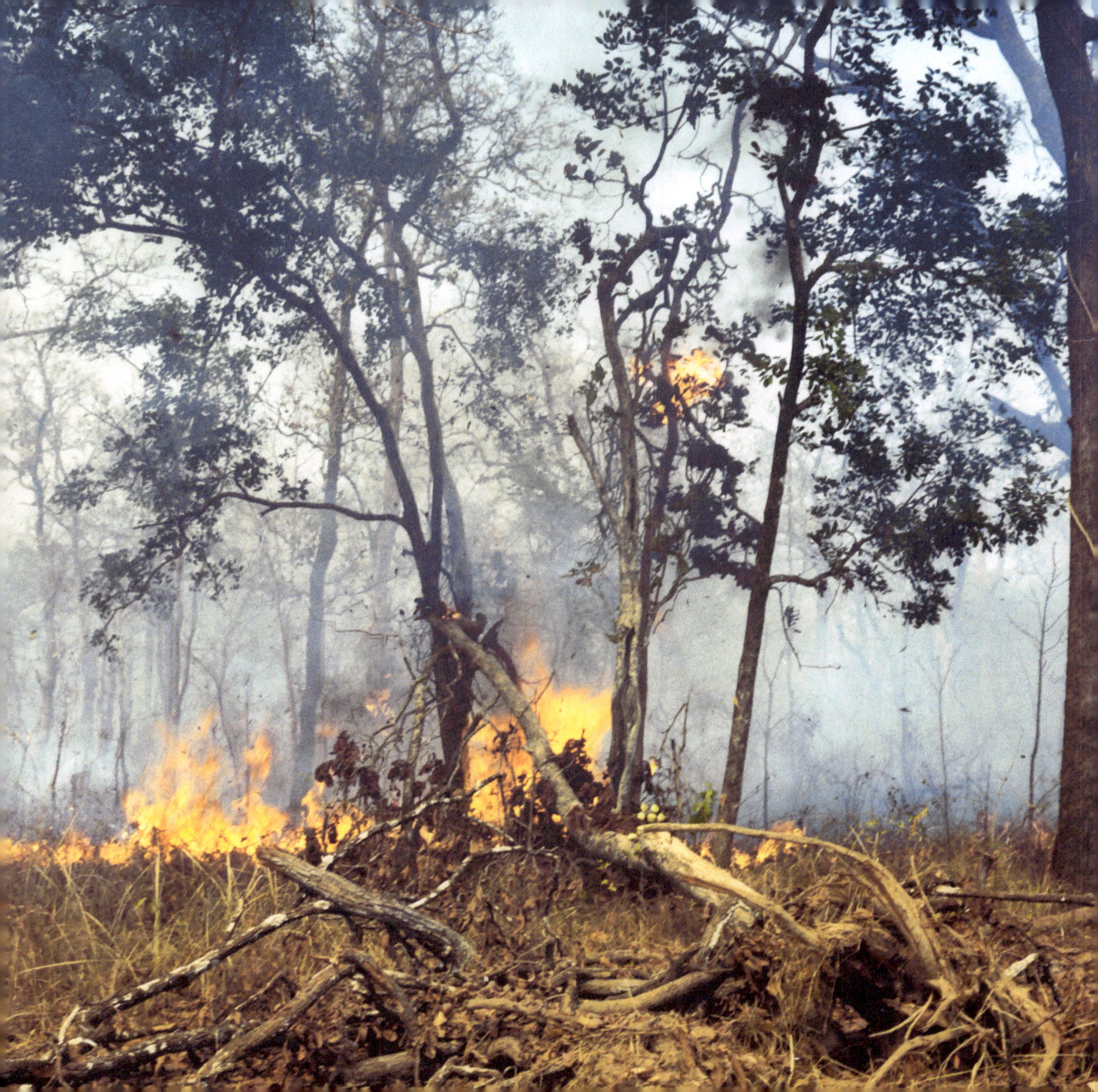

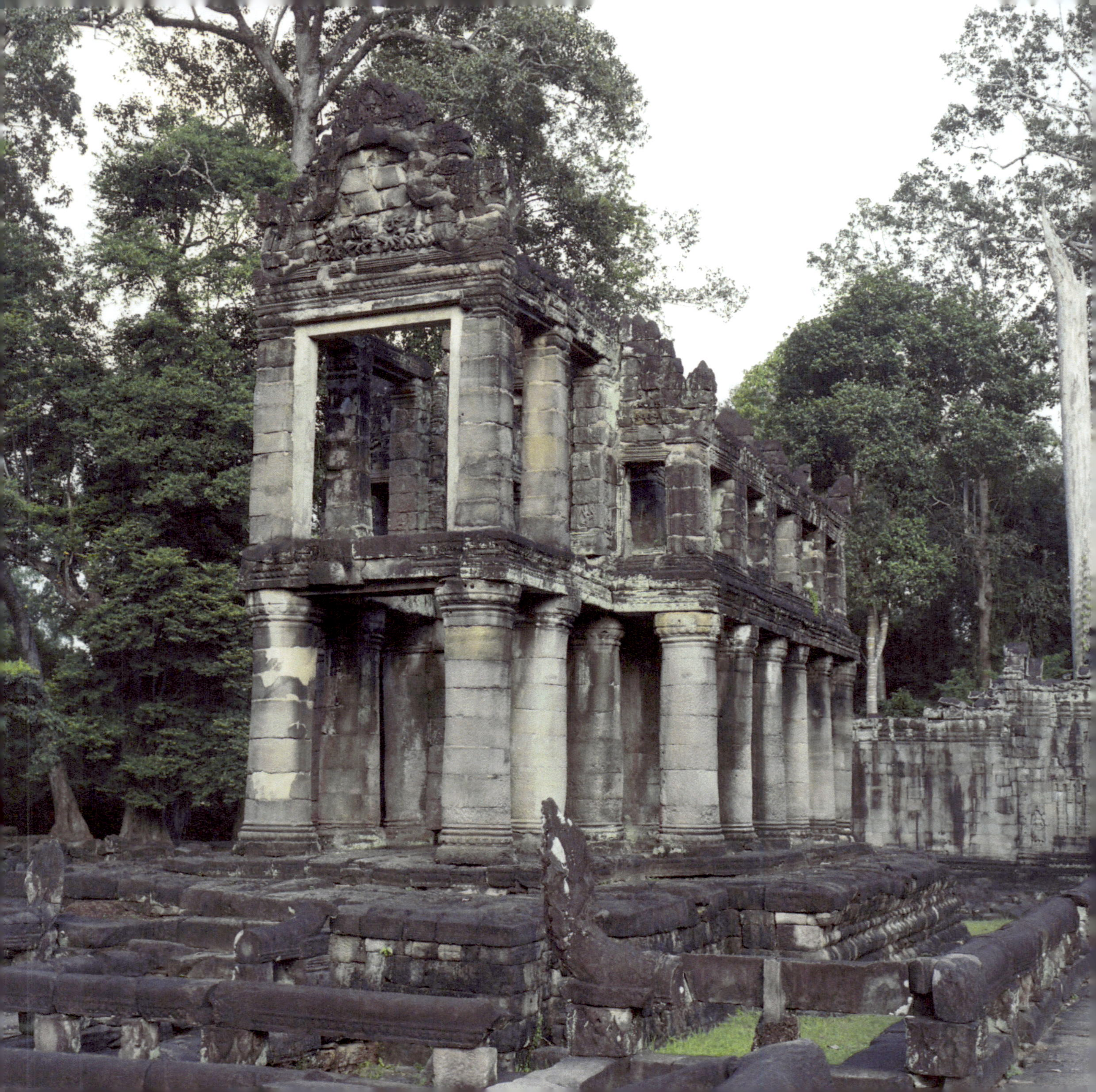

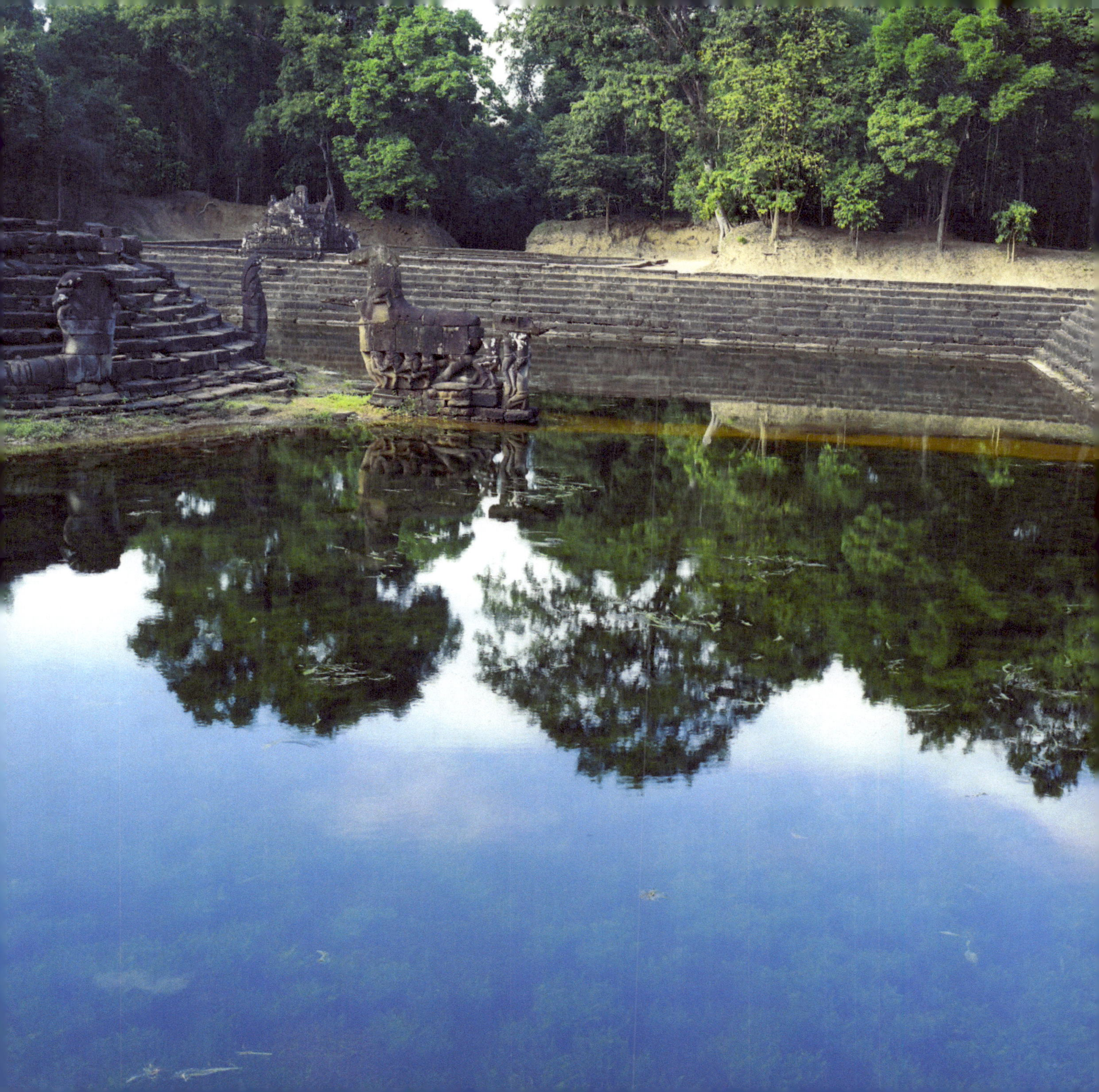

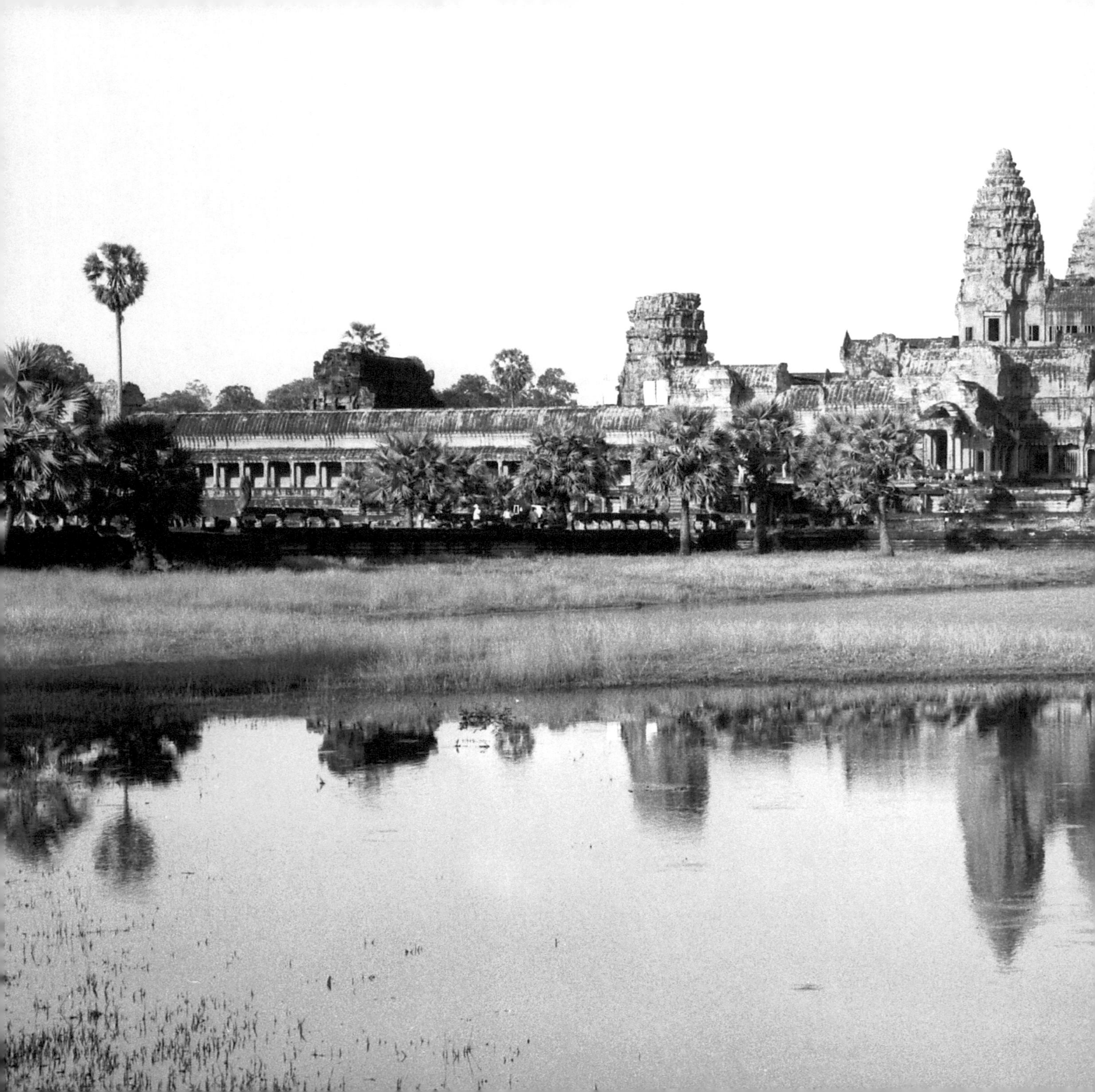

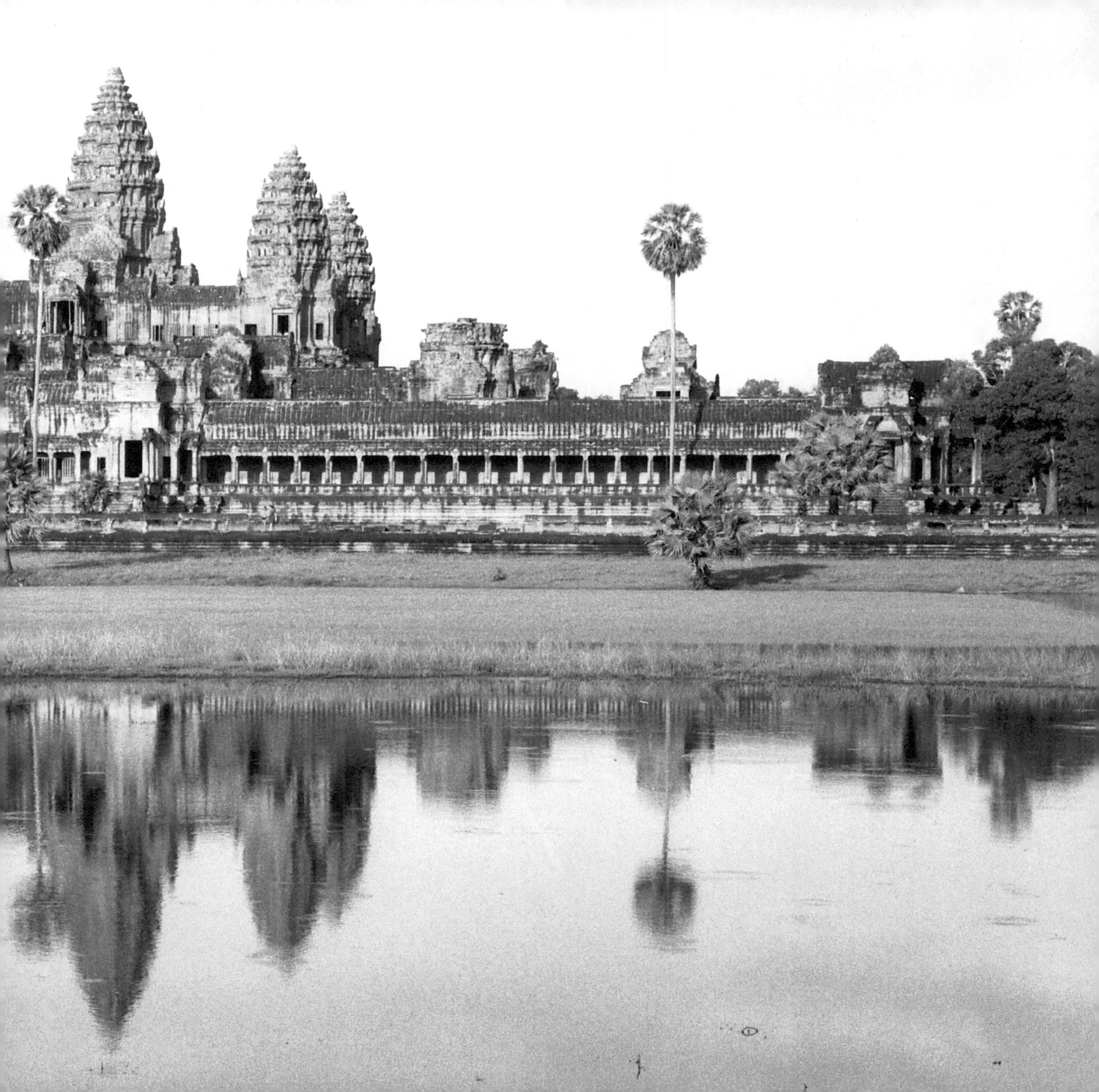

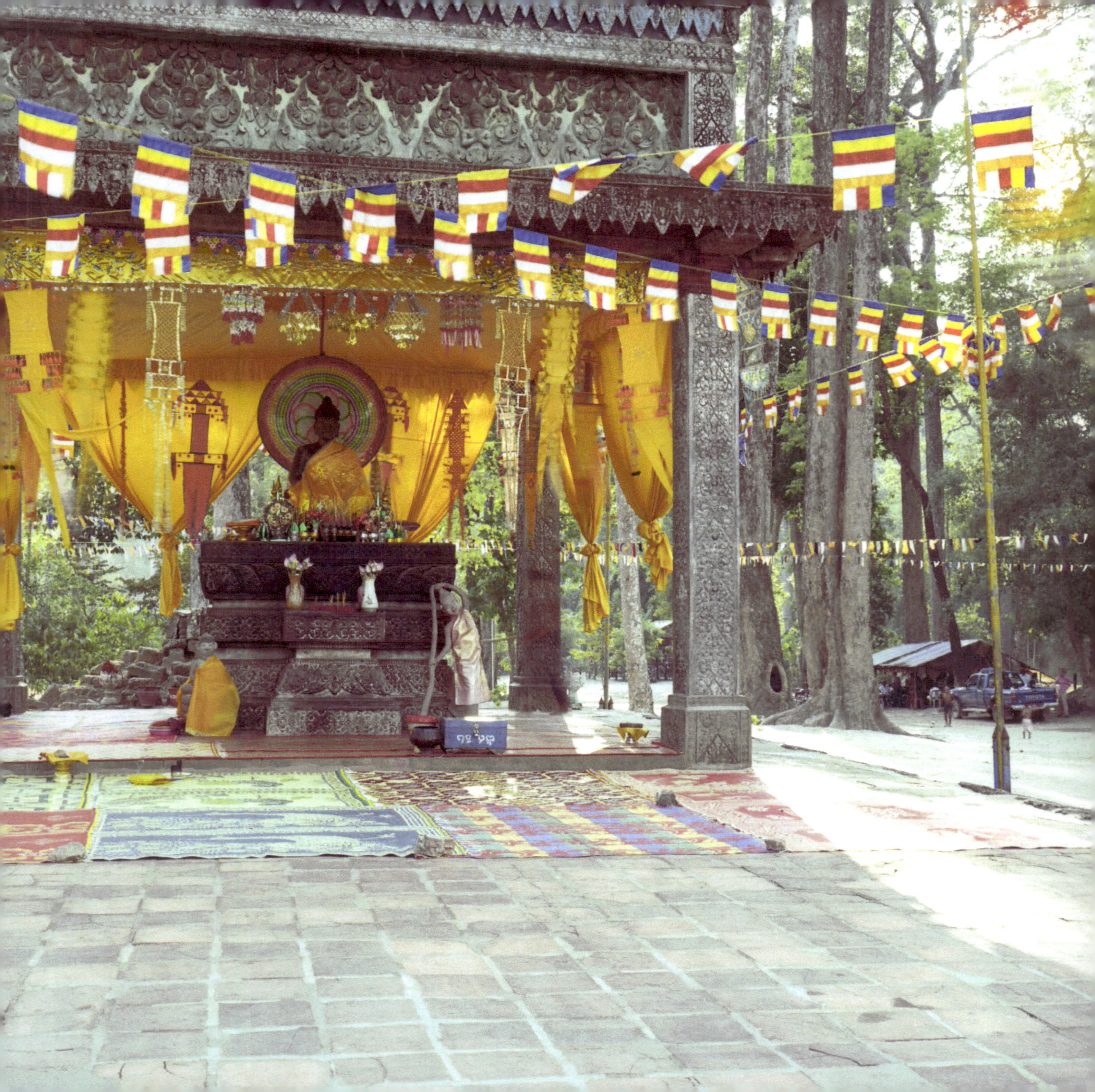

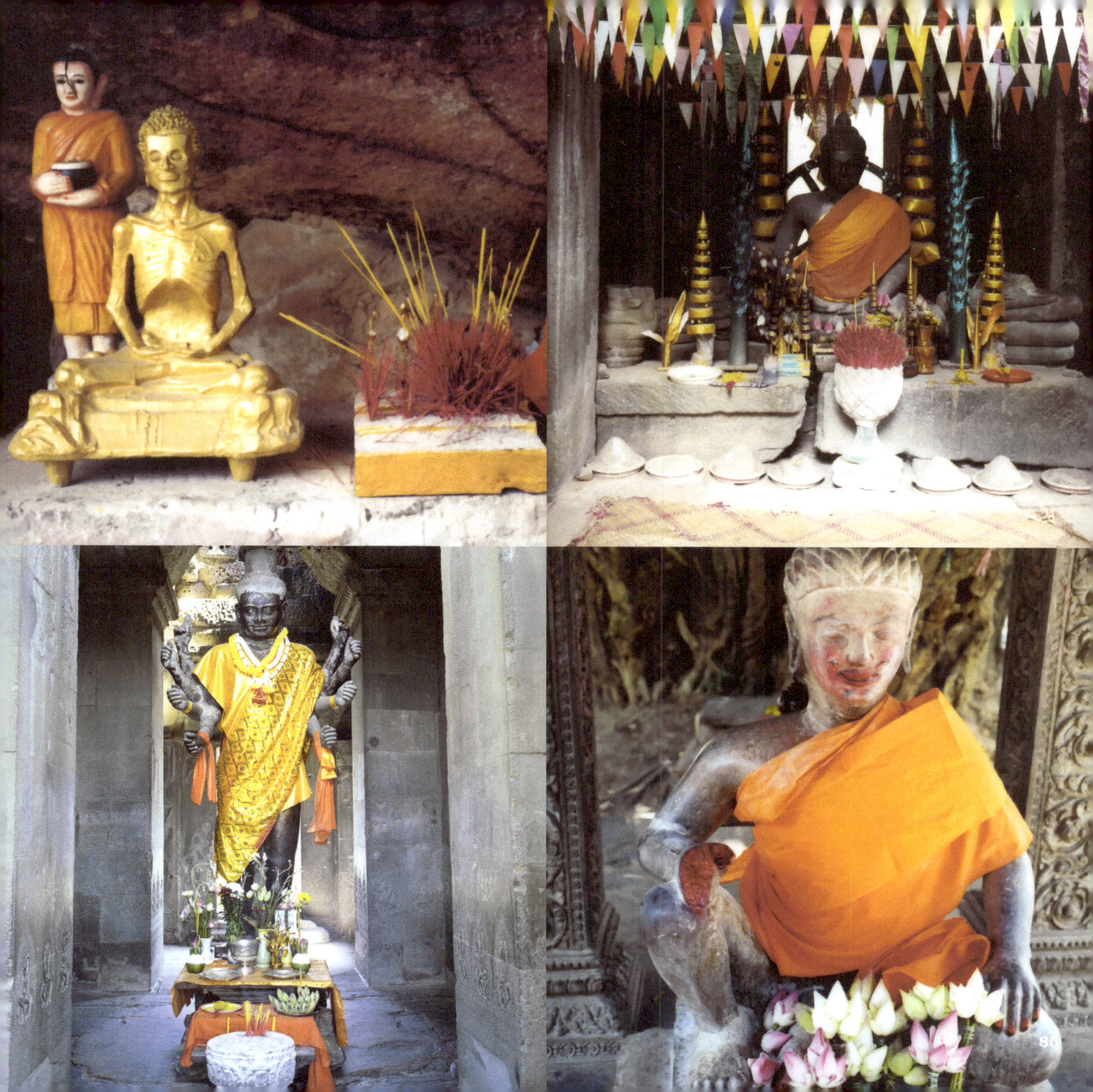

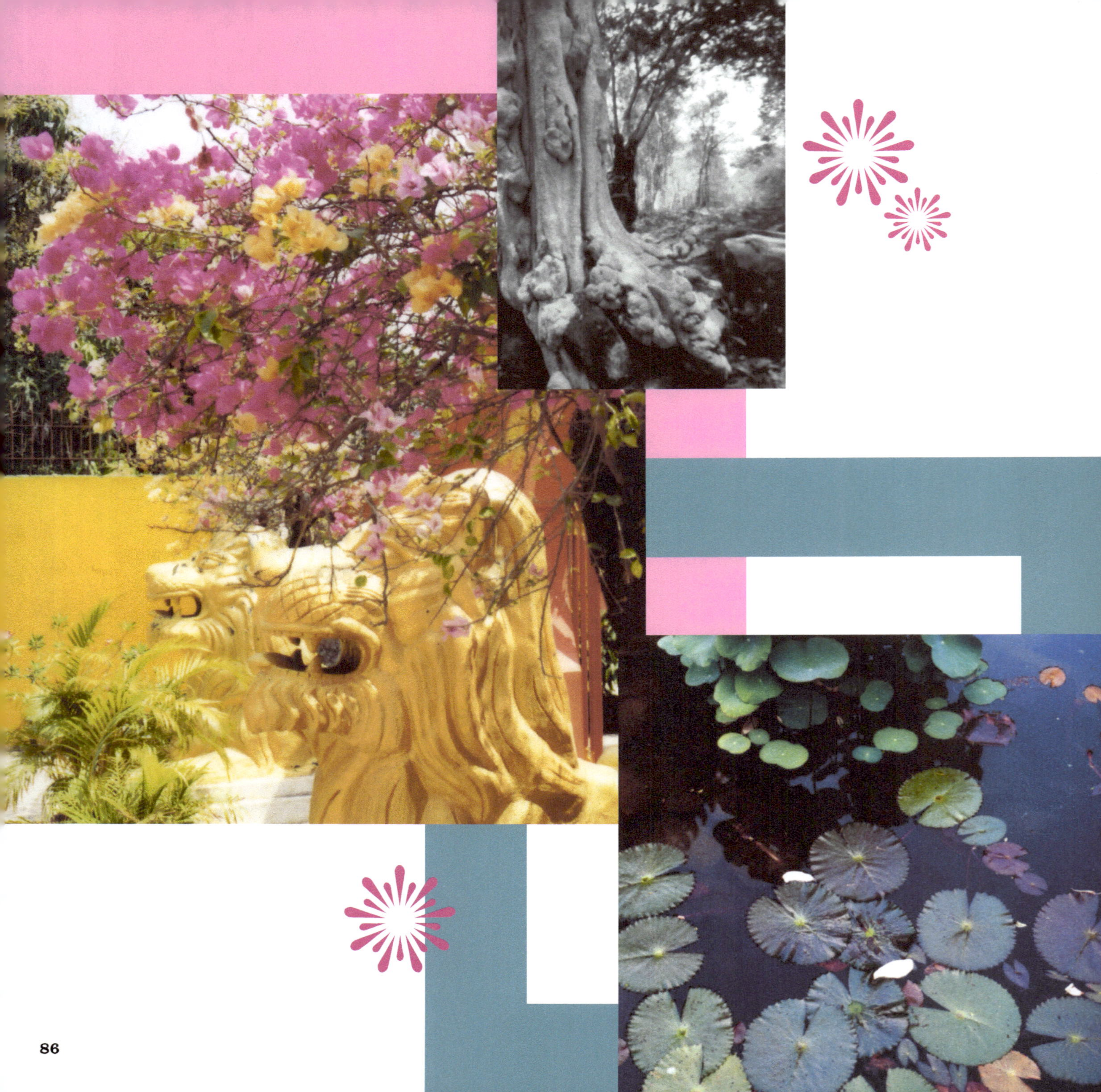

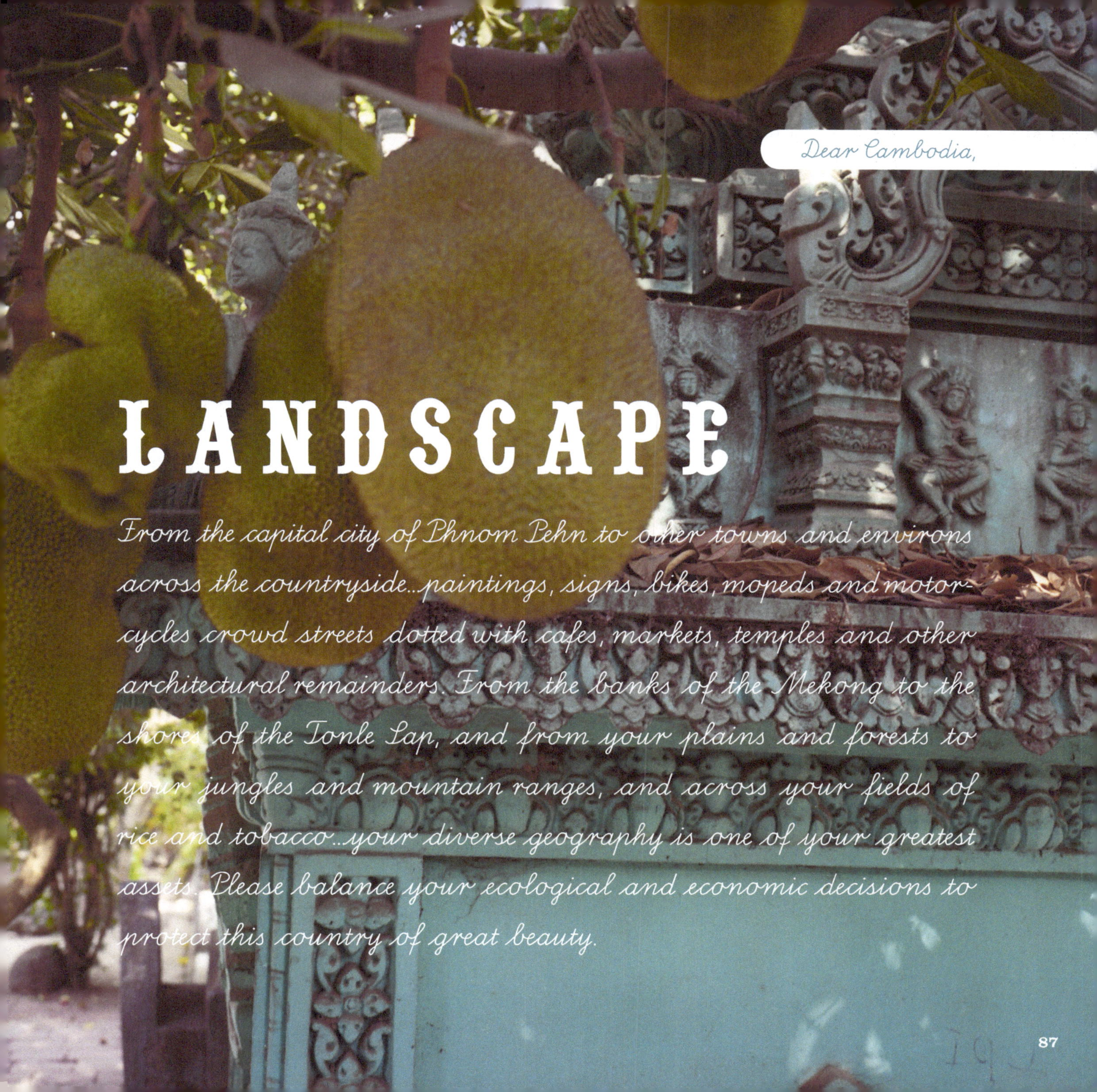

Dear Cambodia,

LANDSCAPE

From the capital city of Phnom Pehn to other towns and environs across the countryside...paintings, signs, bikes, mopeds and motorcycles crowd streets dotted with cafes, markets, temples and other architectural remainders. From the banks of the Mekong to the shores of the Tonle Sap, and from your plains and forests to your jungles and mountain ranges, and across your fields of rice and tobacco...your diverse geography is one of your greatest assets. Please balance your ecological and economic decisions to protect this country of great beauty.

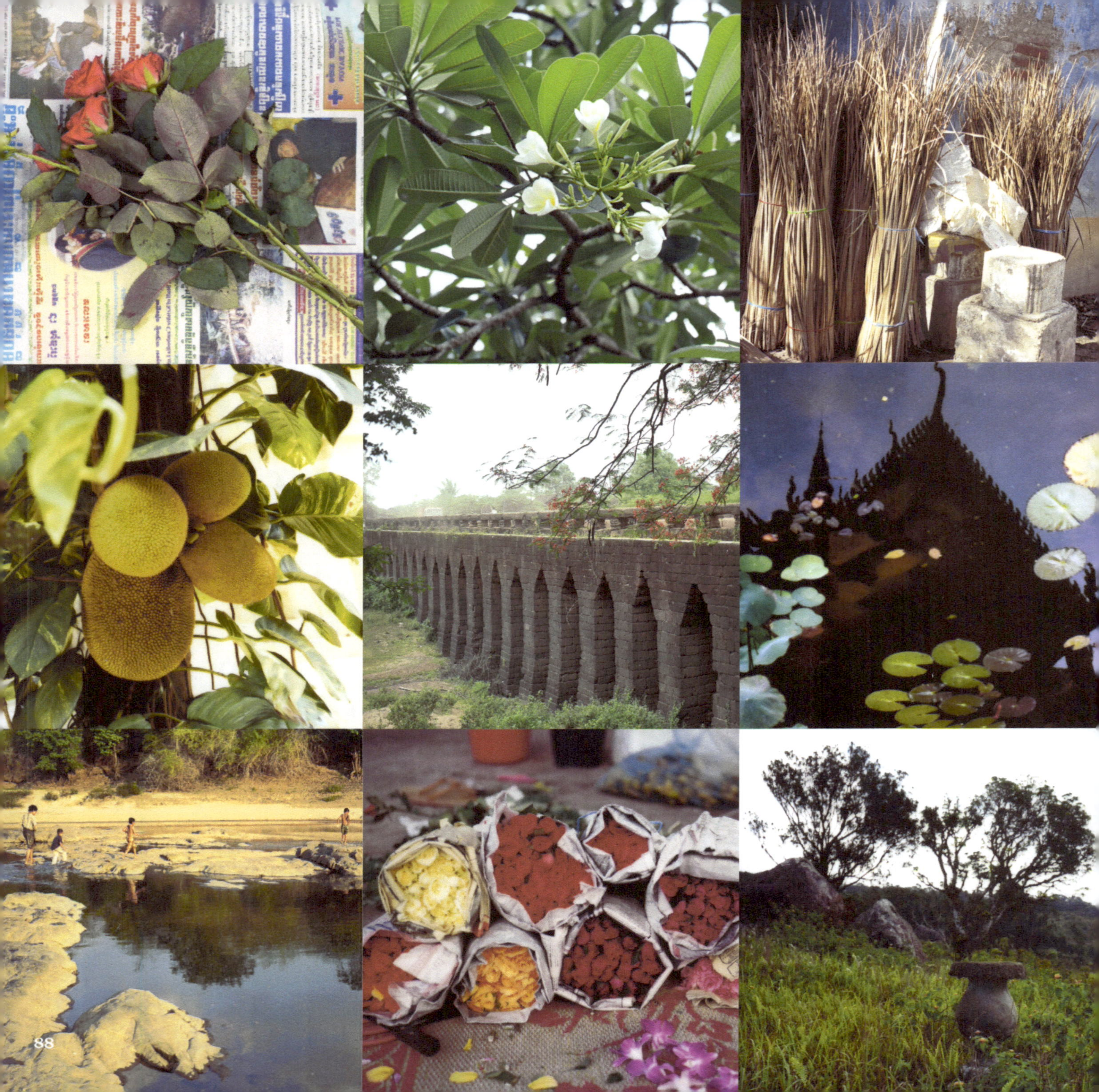

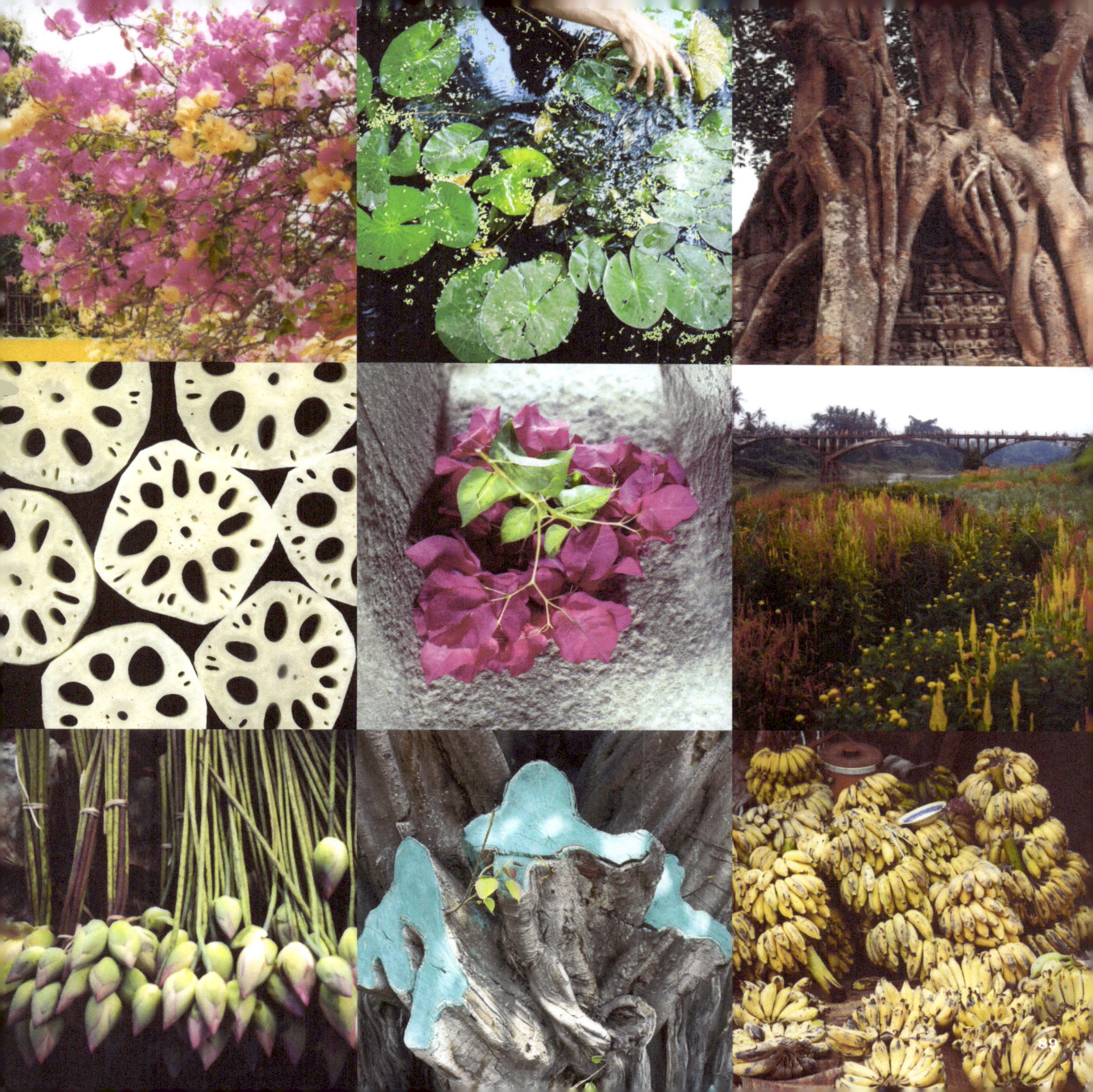

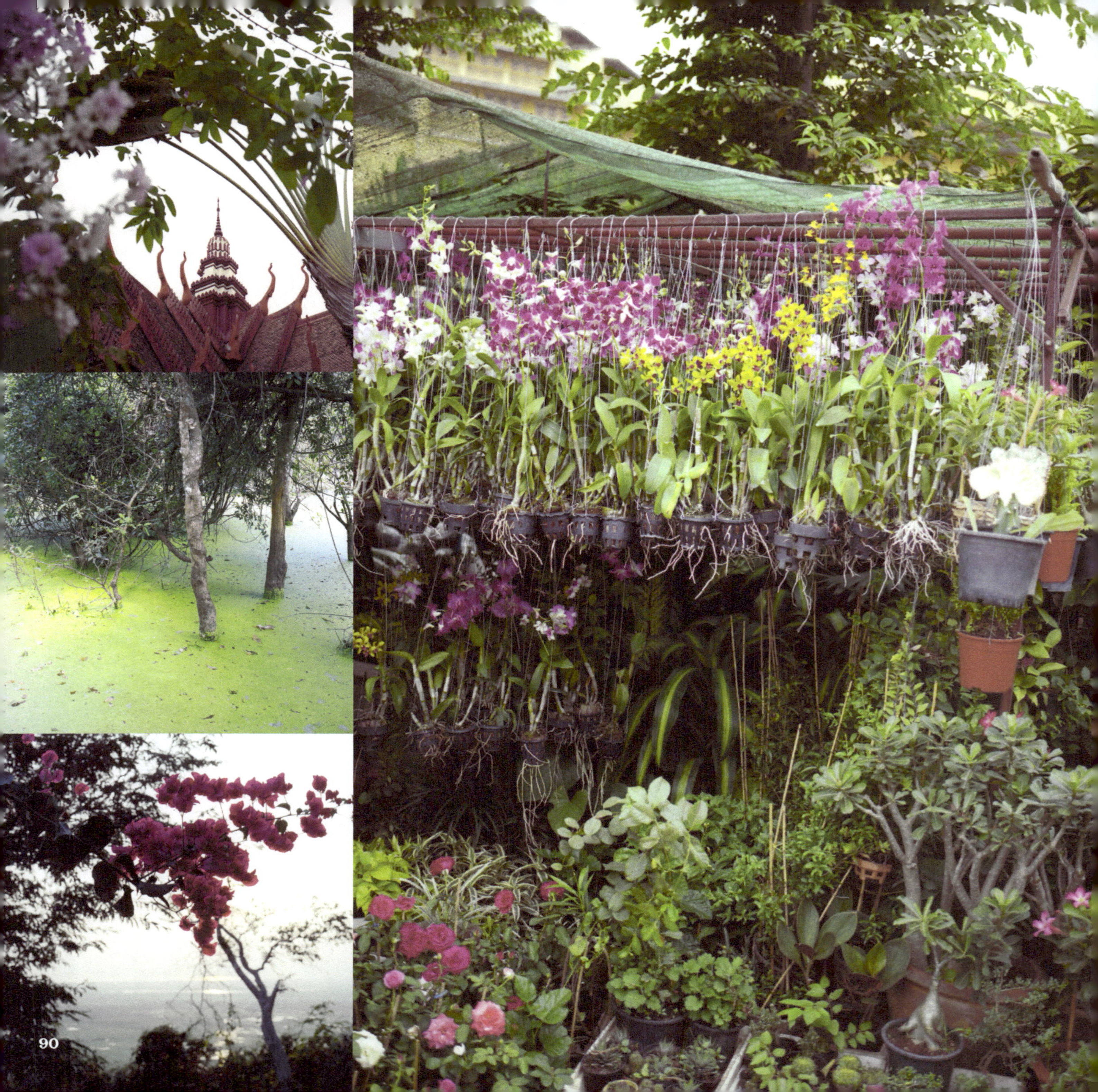

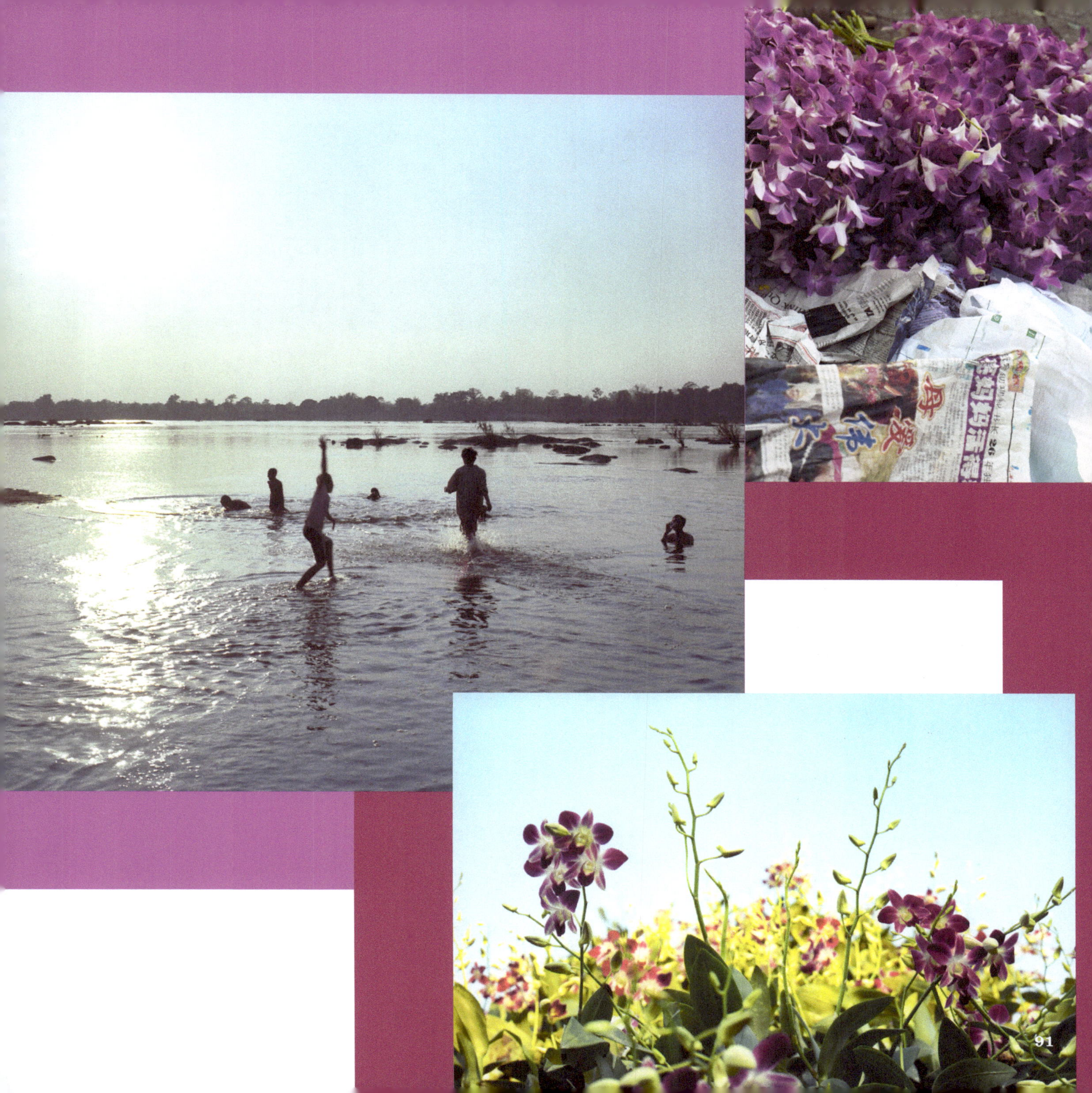

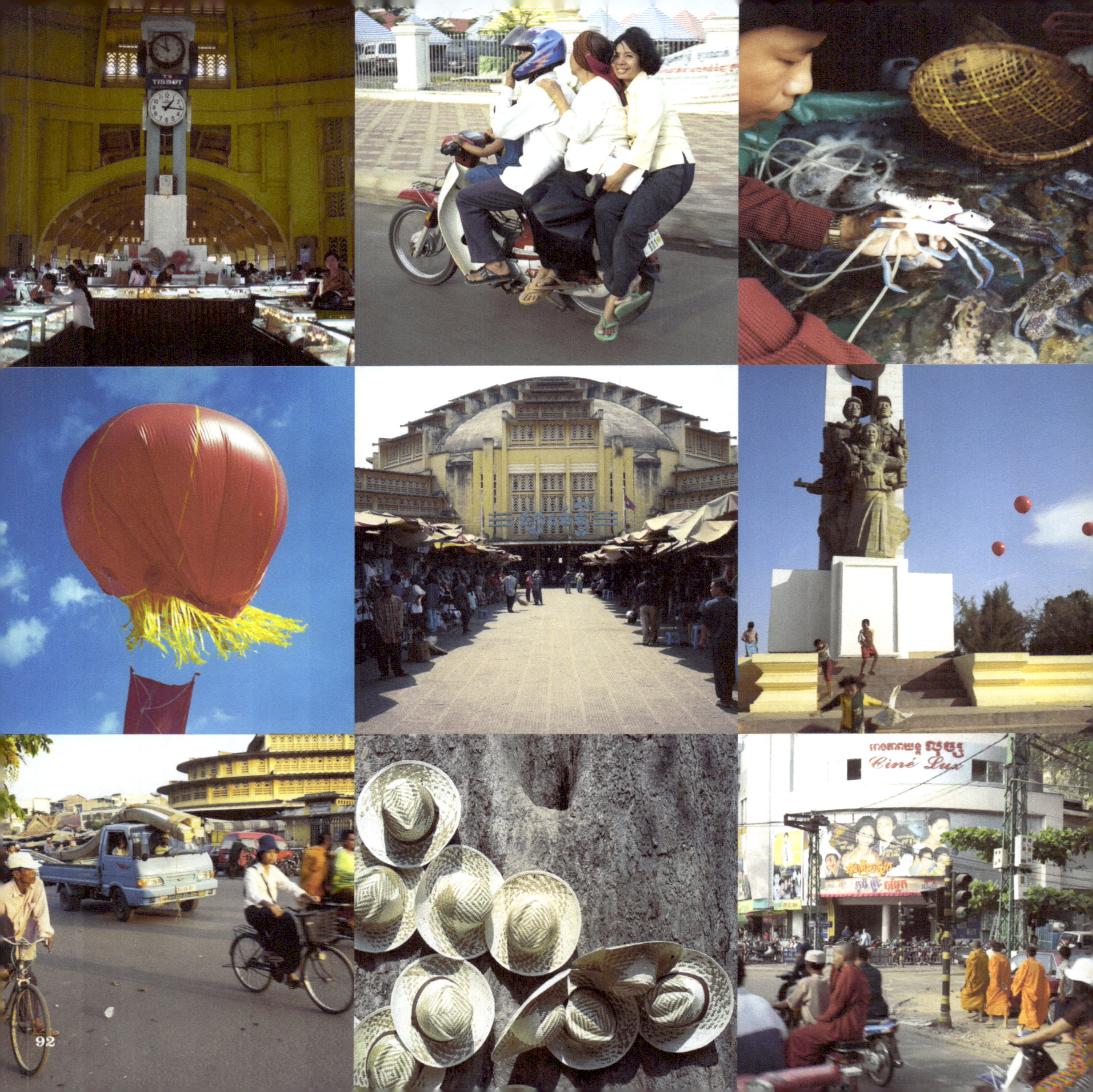
TISSOT
Ciné Lux

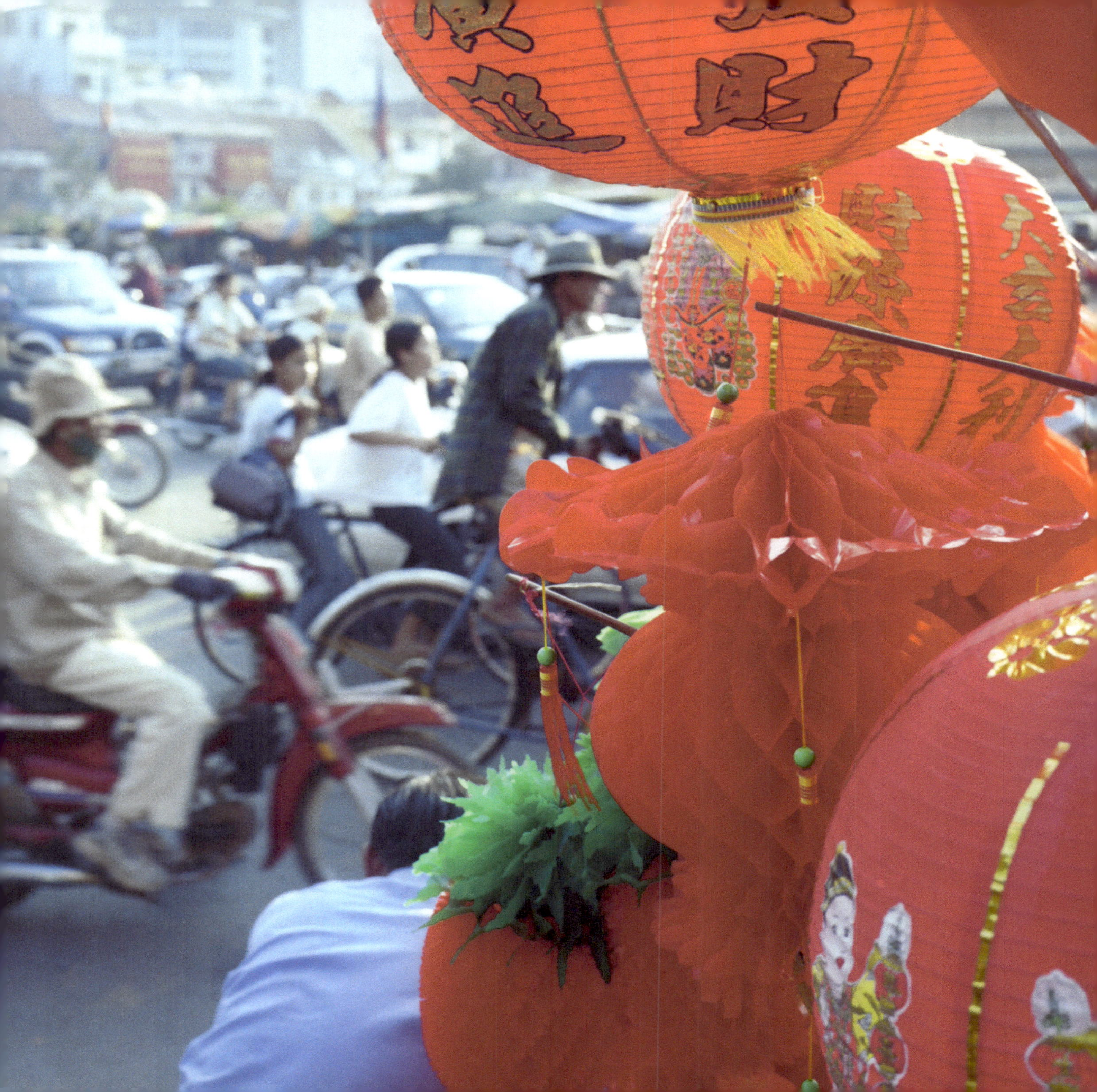
財

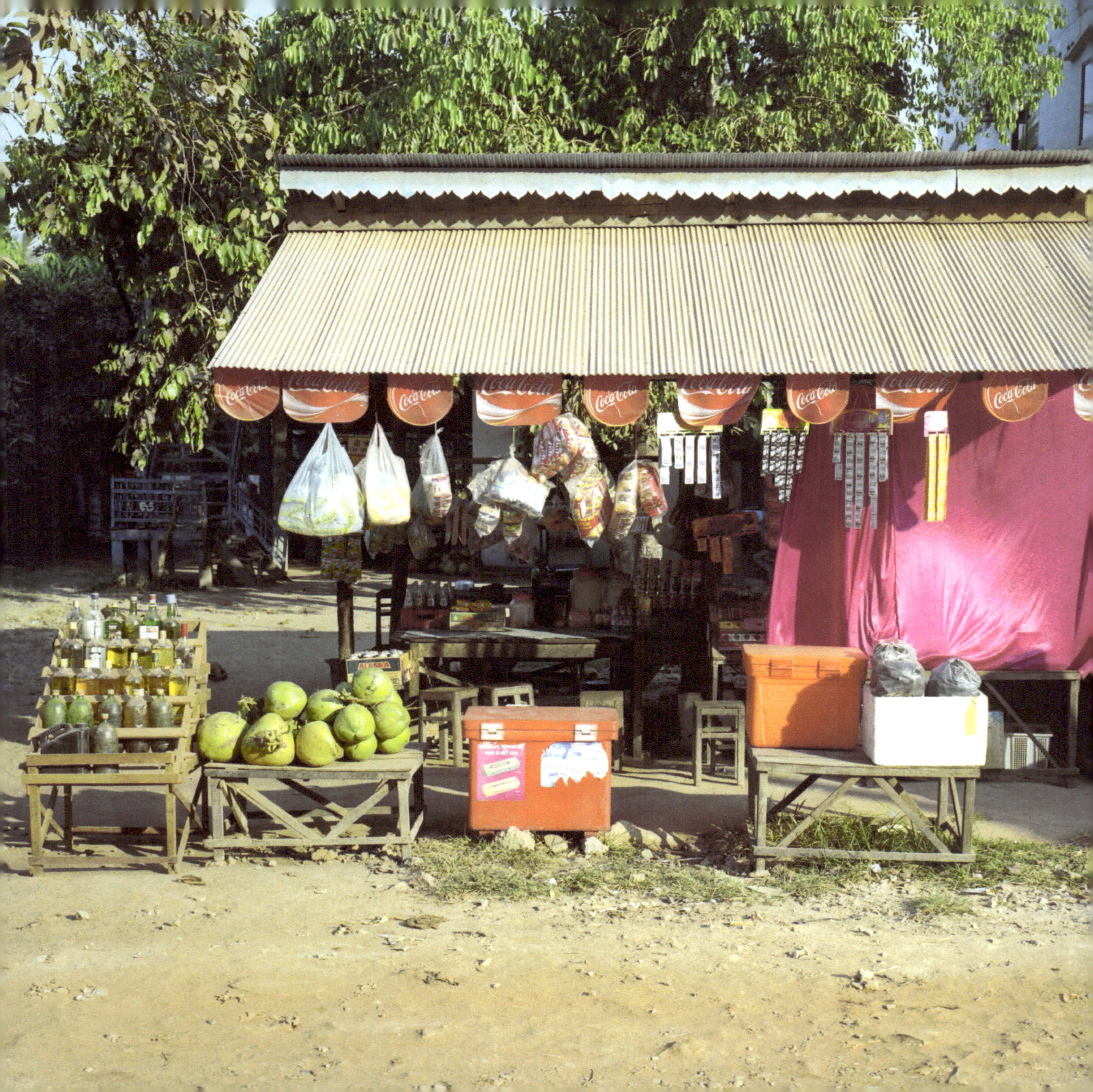
Coca-Cola
ALASKA

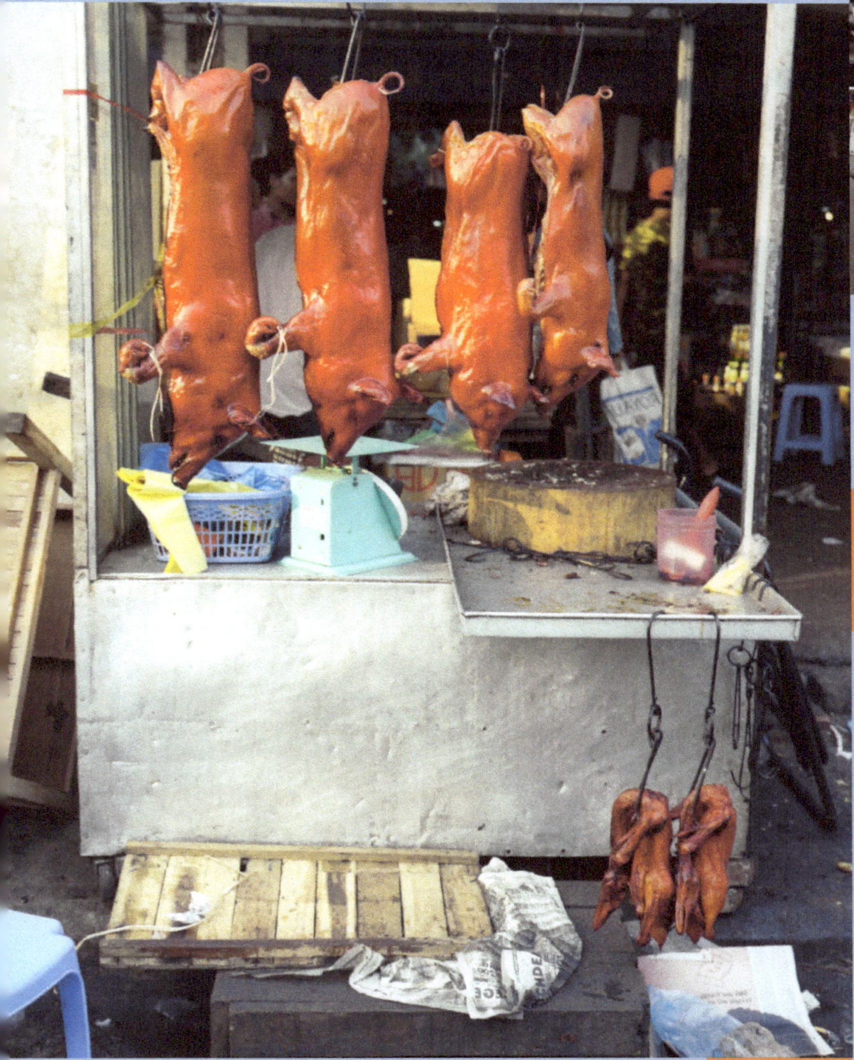

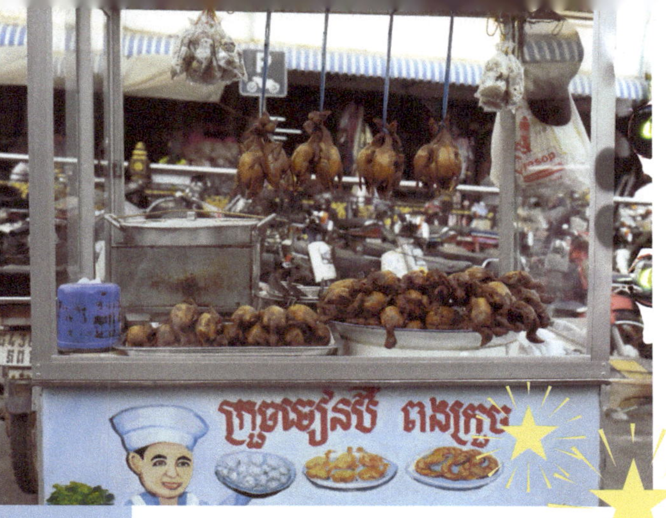

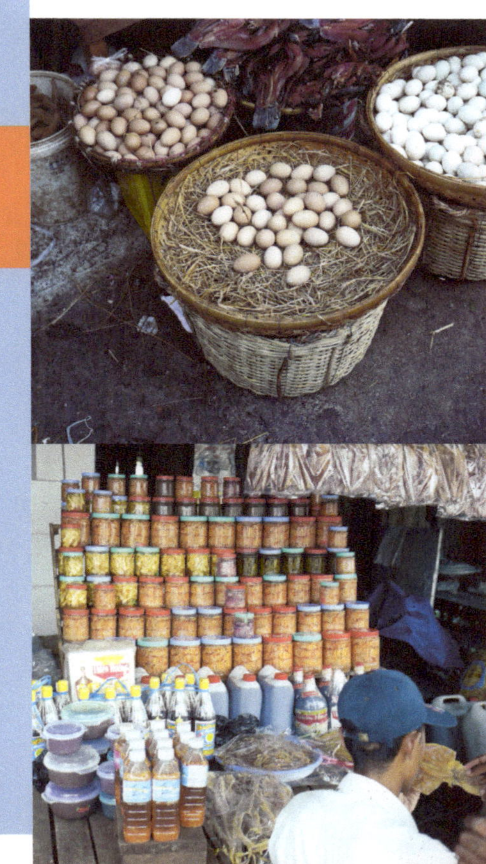

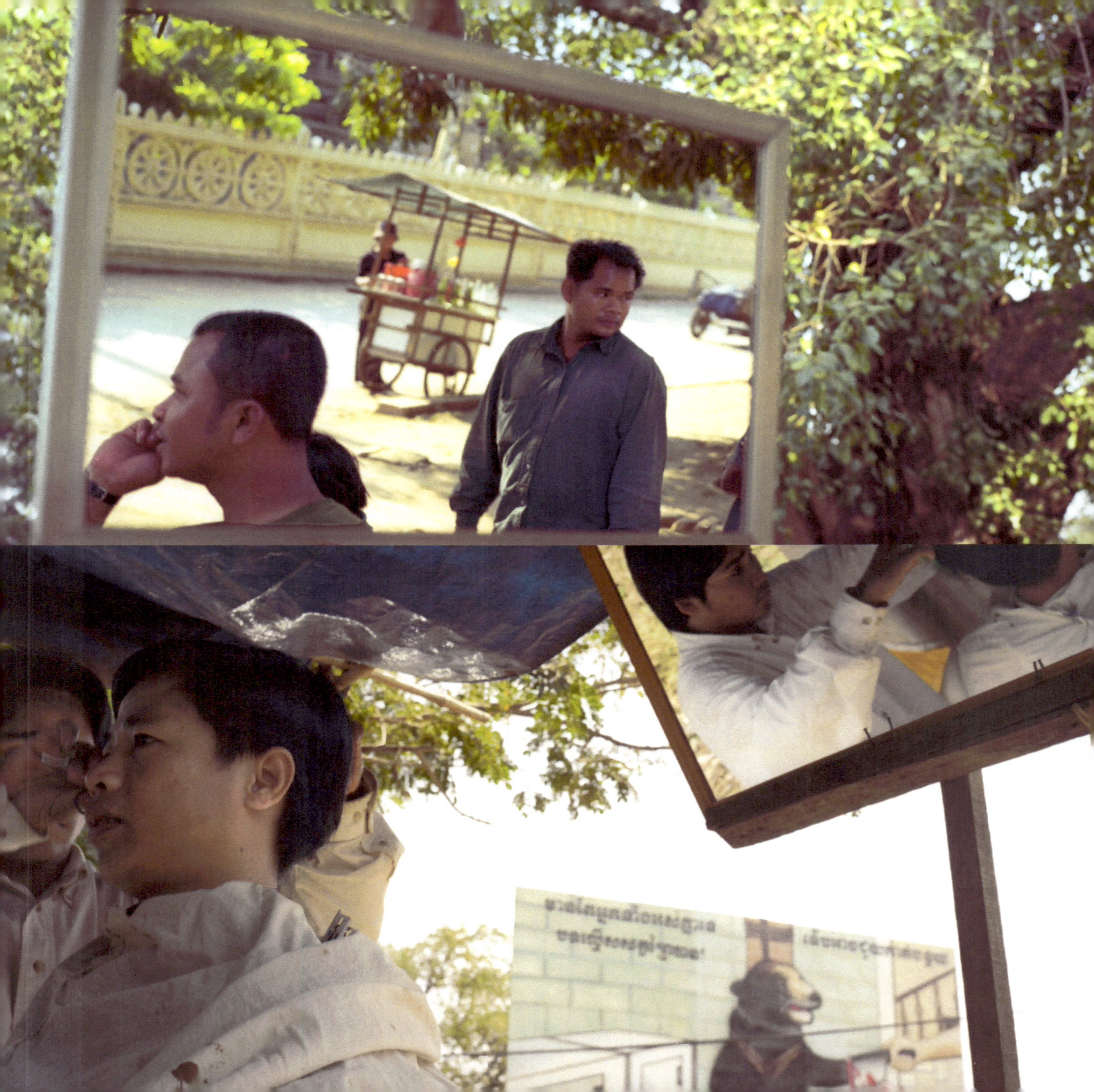

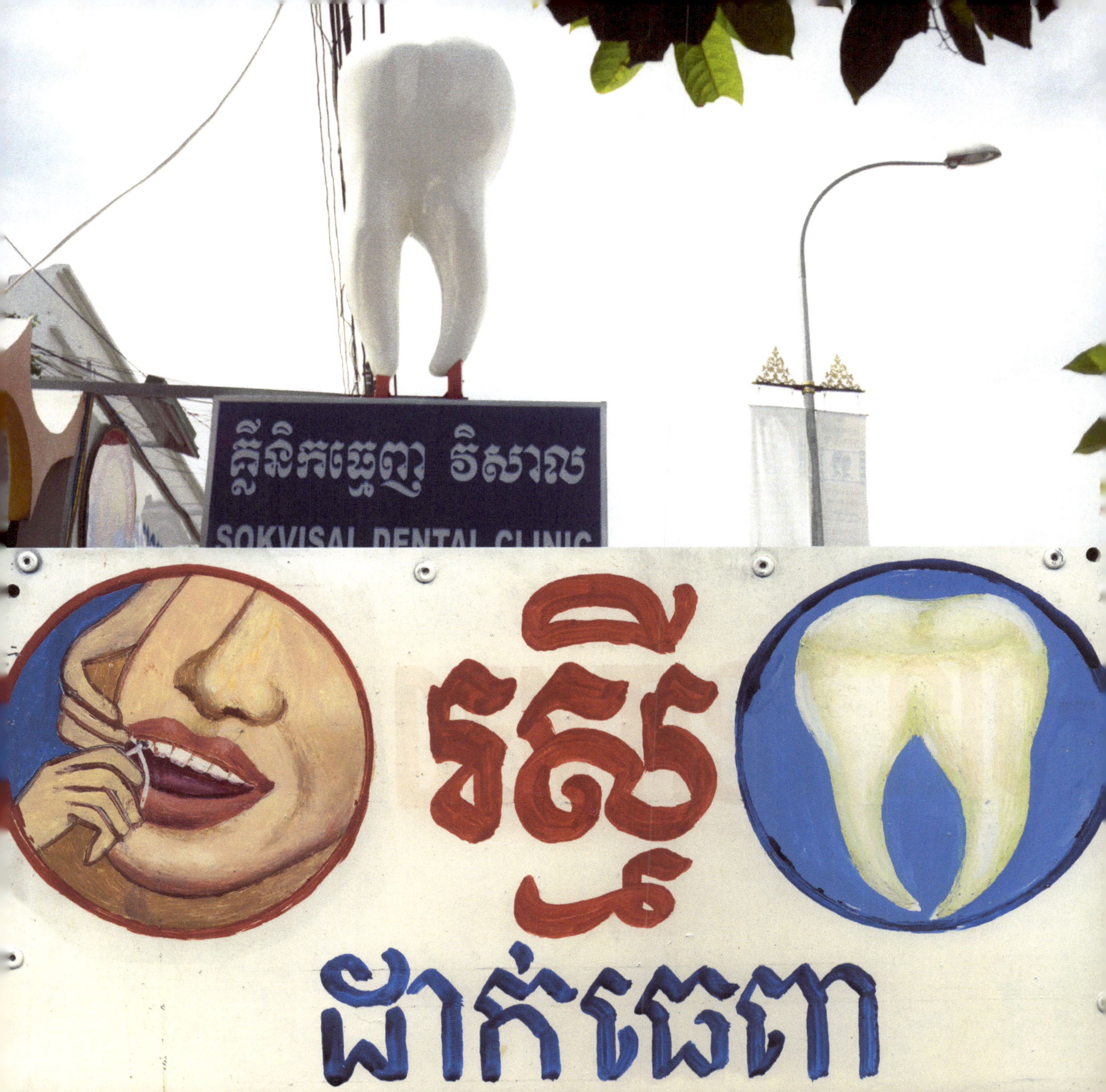
គ្លីនិកធ្មេញ វិសាល
SOKVISAL DENTAL CLINIC

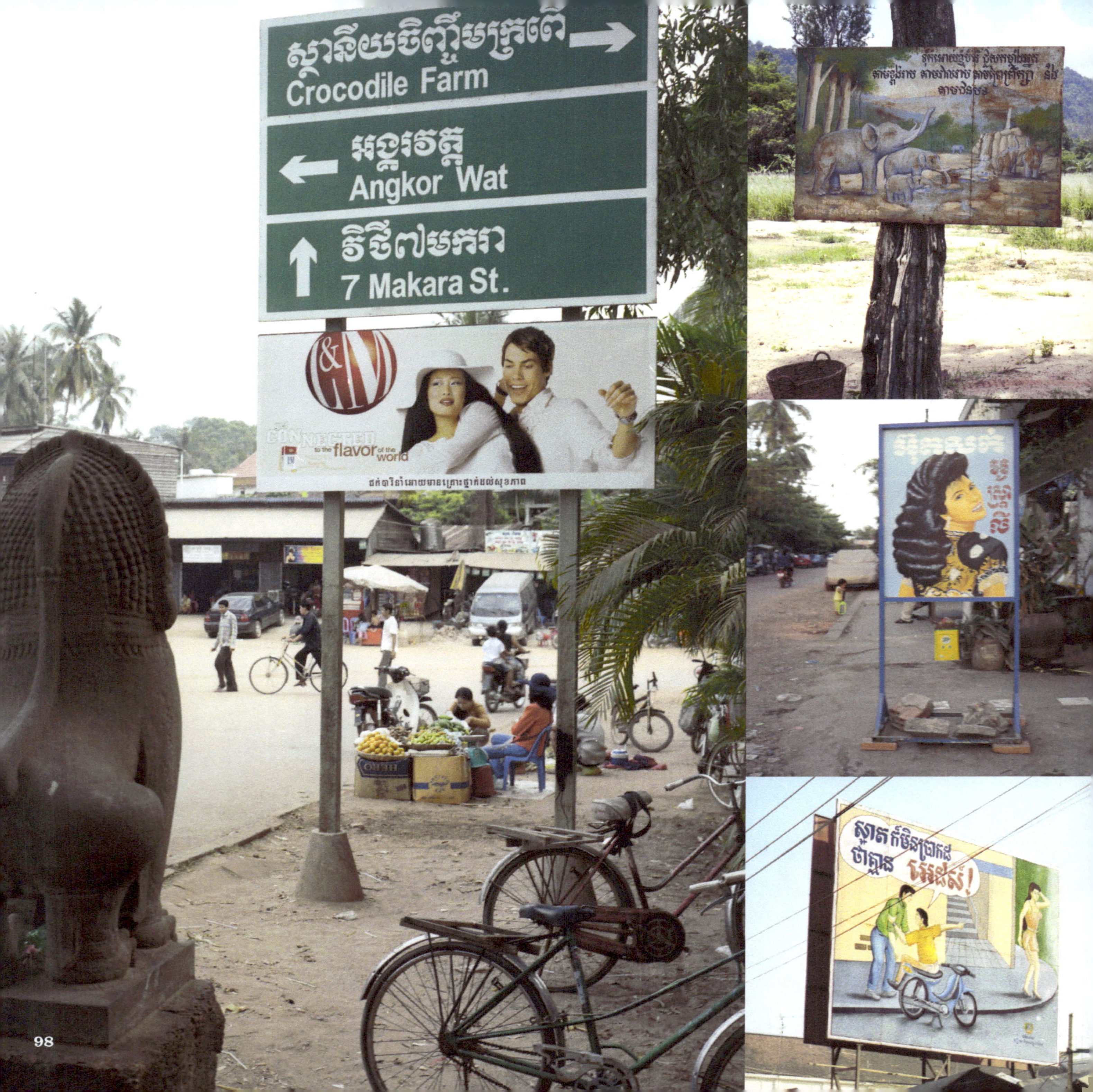
ស្ថានីយចិញ្ចឹមក្រពើ
Crocodile Farm
អង្គរវត្ត
Angkor Wat
វិថី៧មករា
7 Makara St.
CONNECTED to the flavor of the world

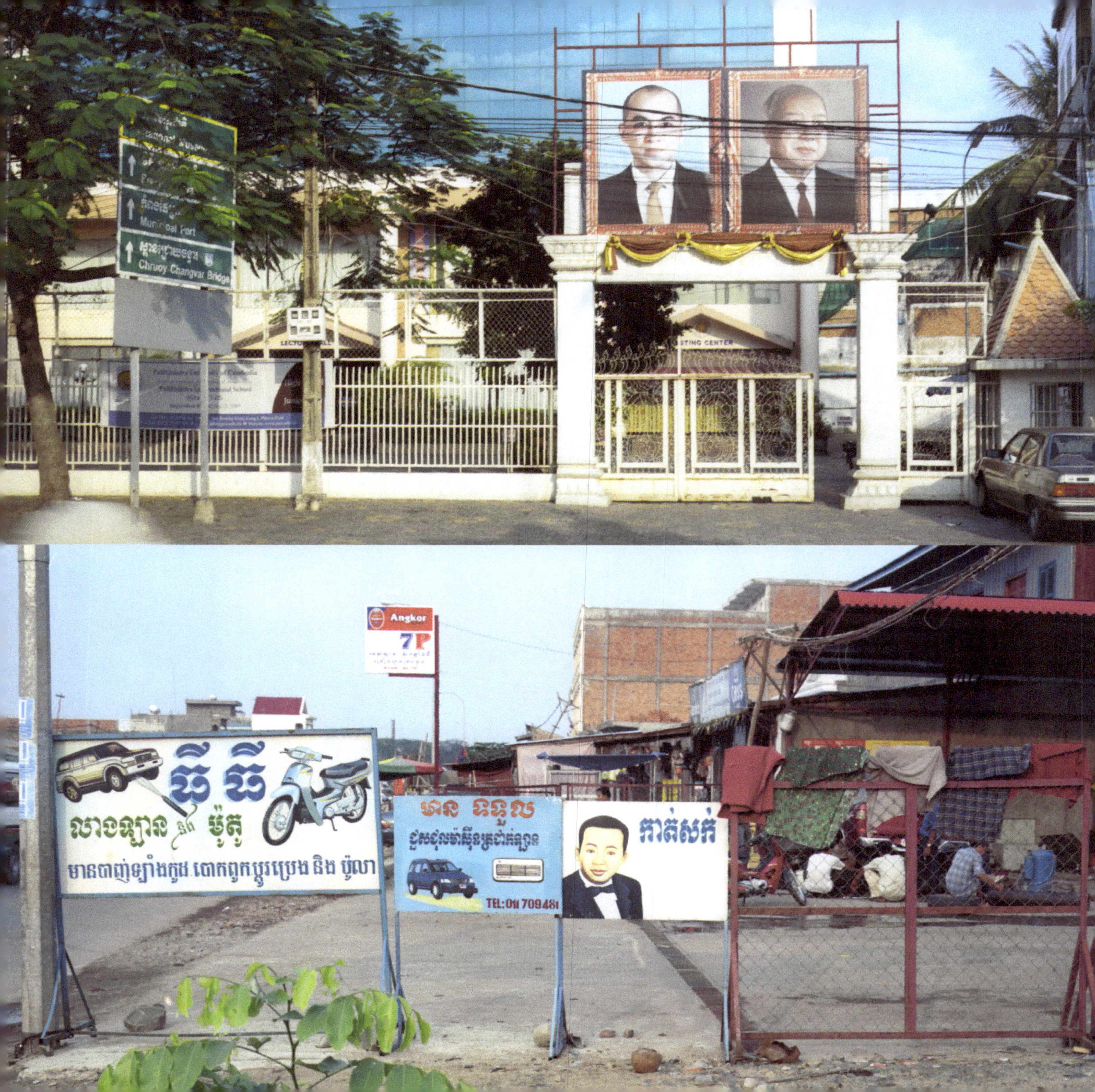

Municipal Port
Chruoy Changvar Bridge
Angkor
7P
TEL:011 709481

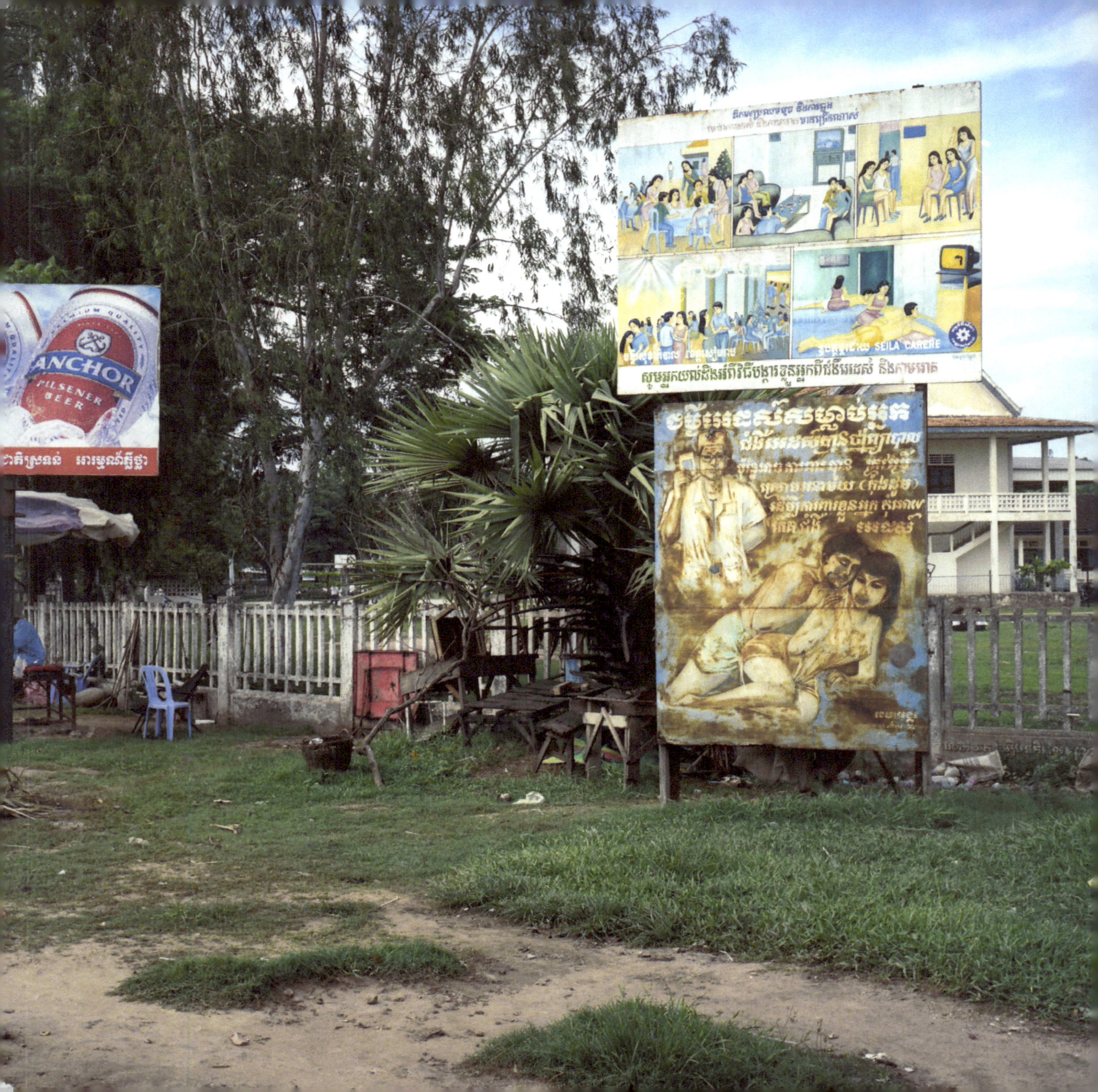
ANCHOR
PILSENER BEER

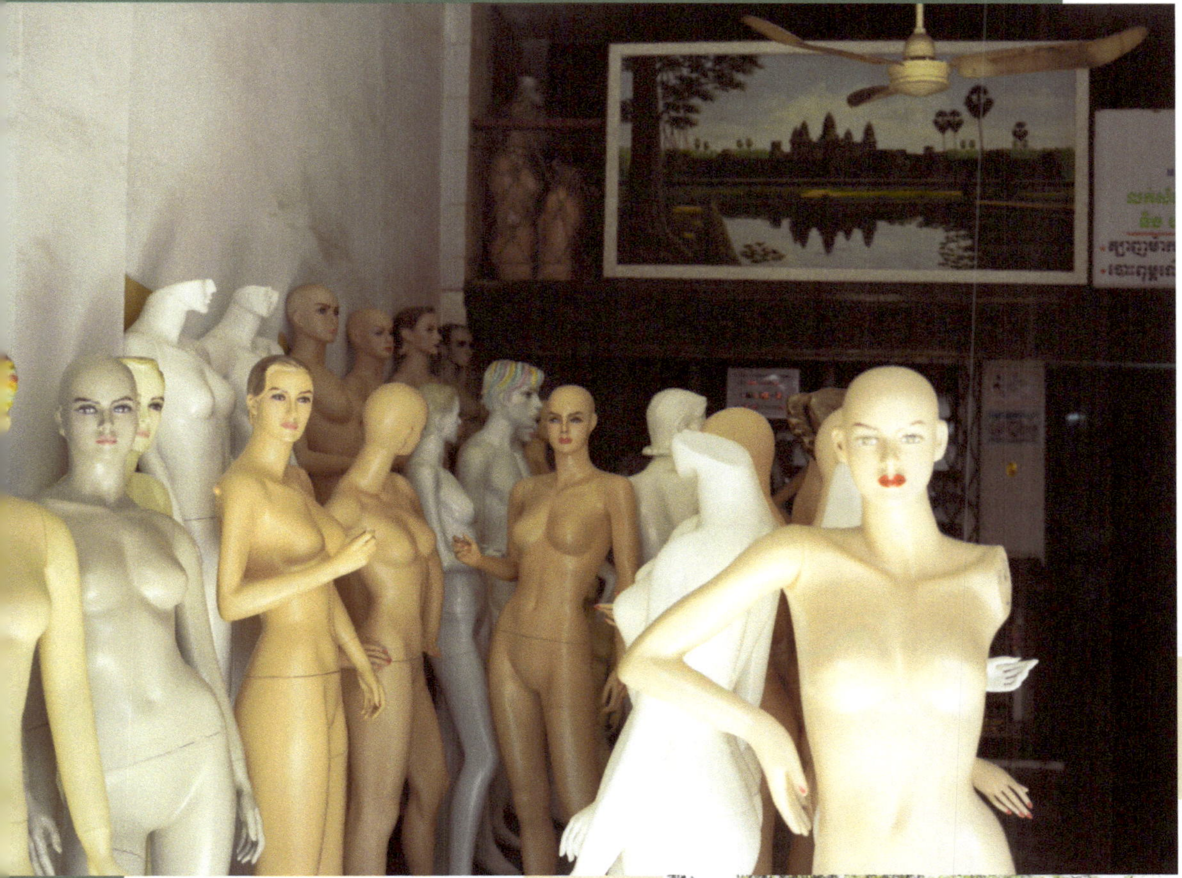

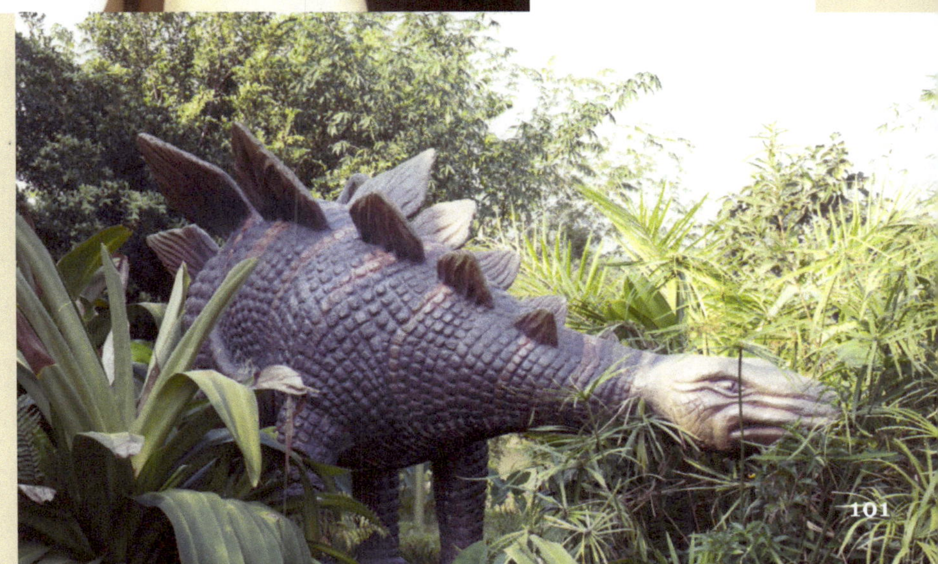

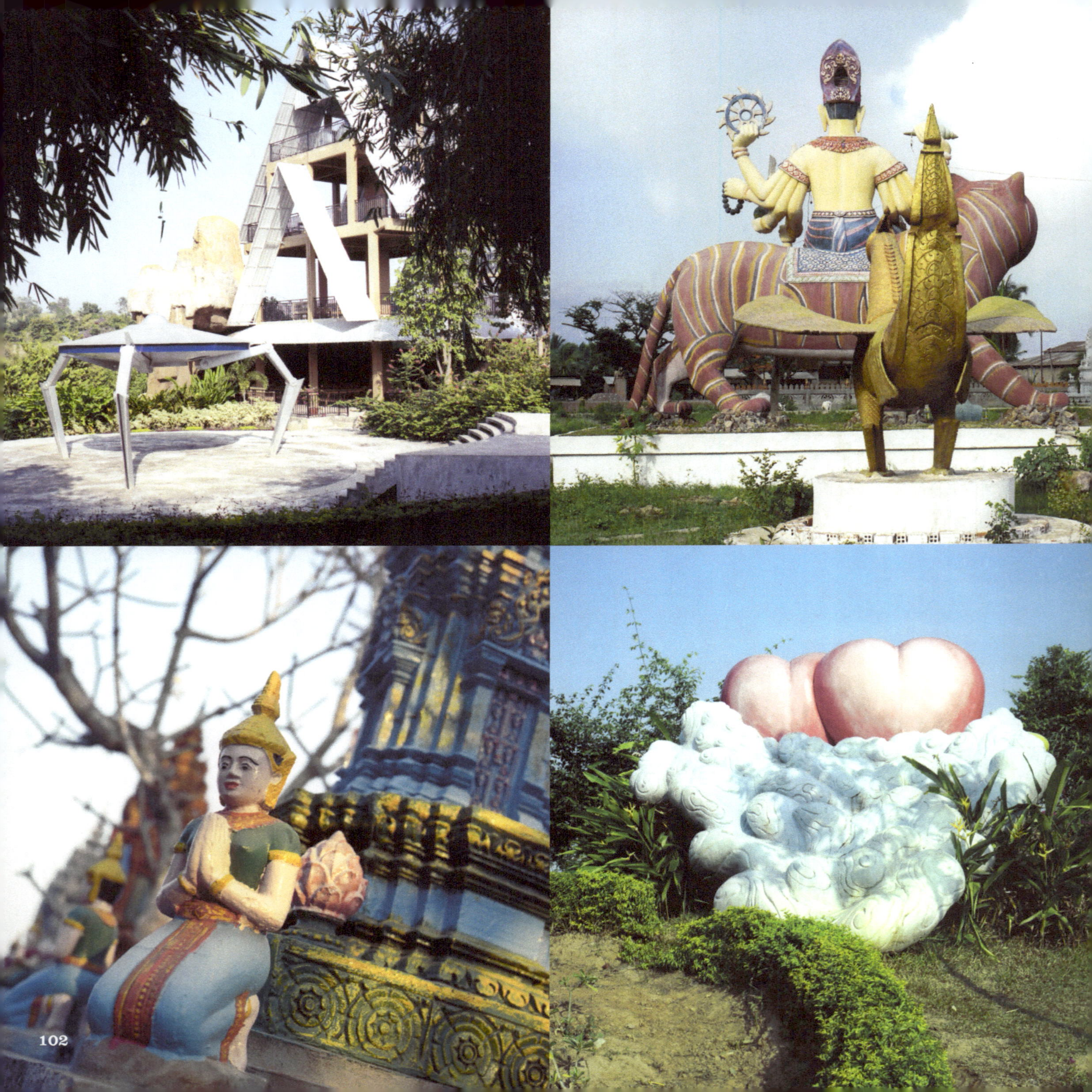

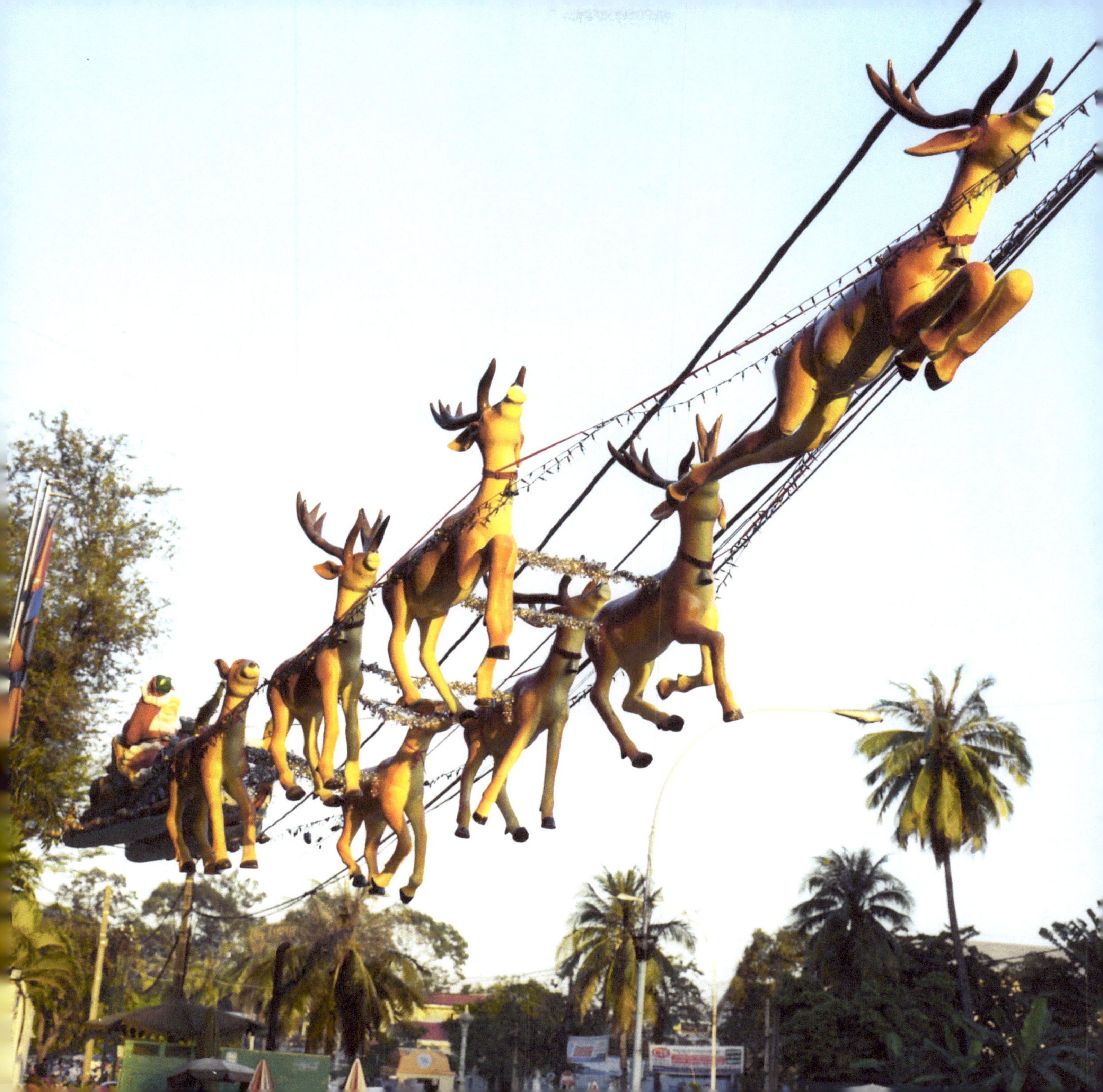

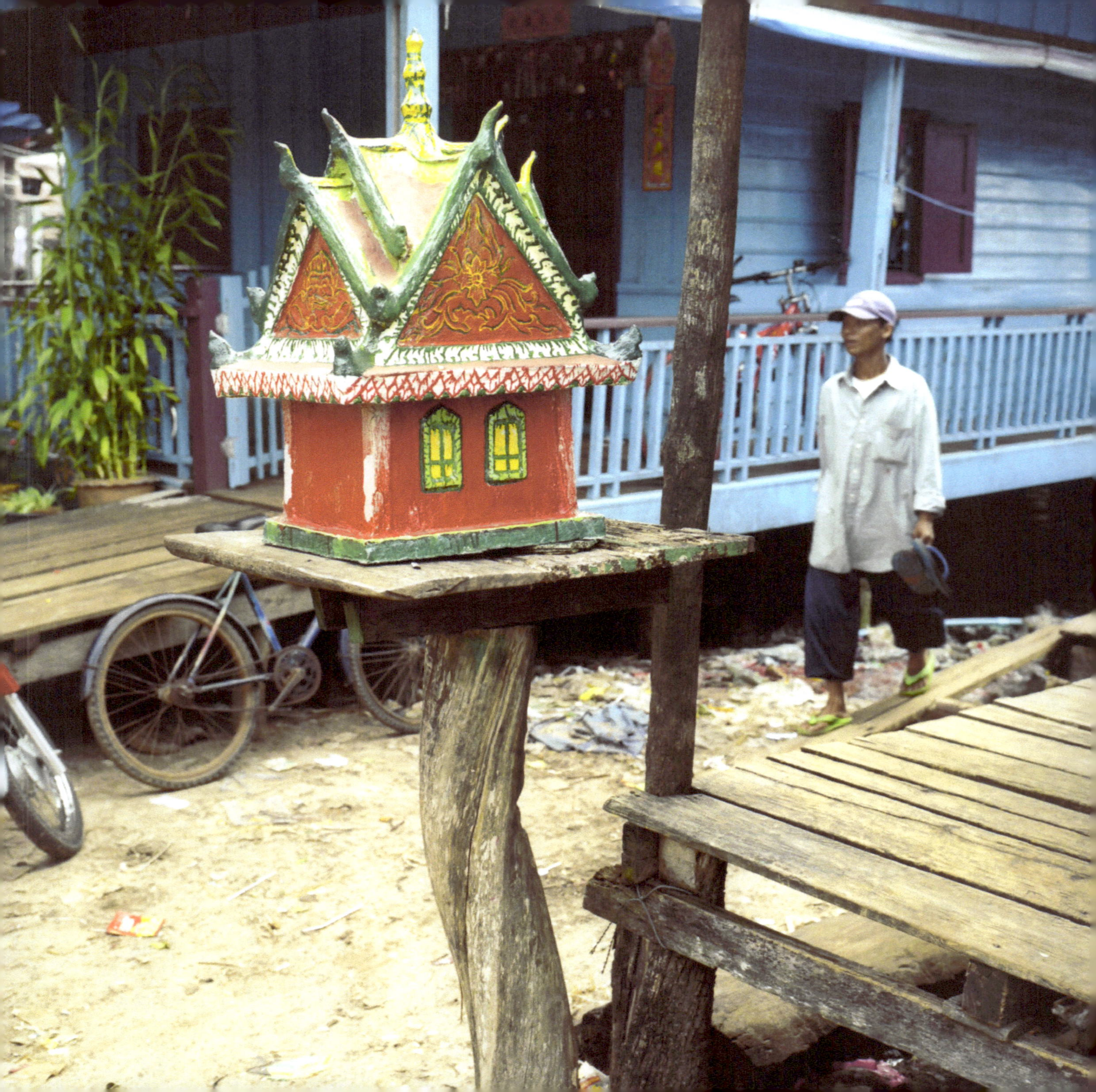

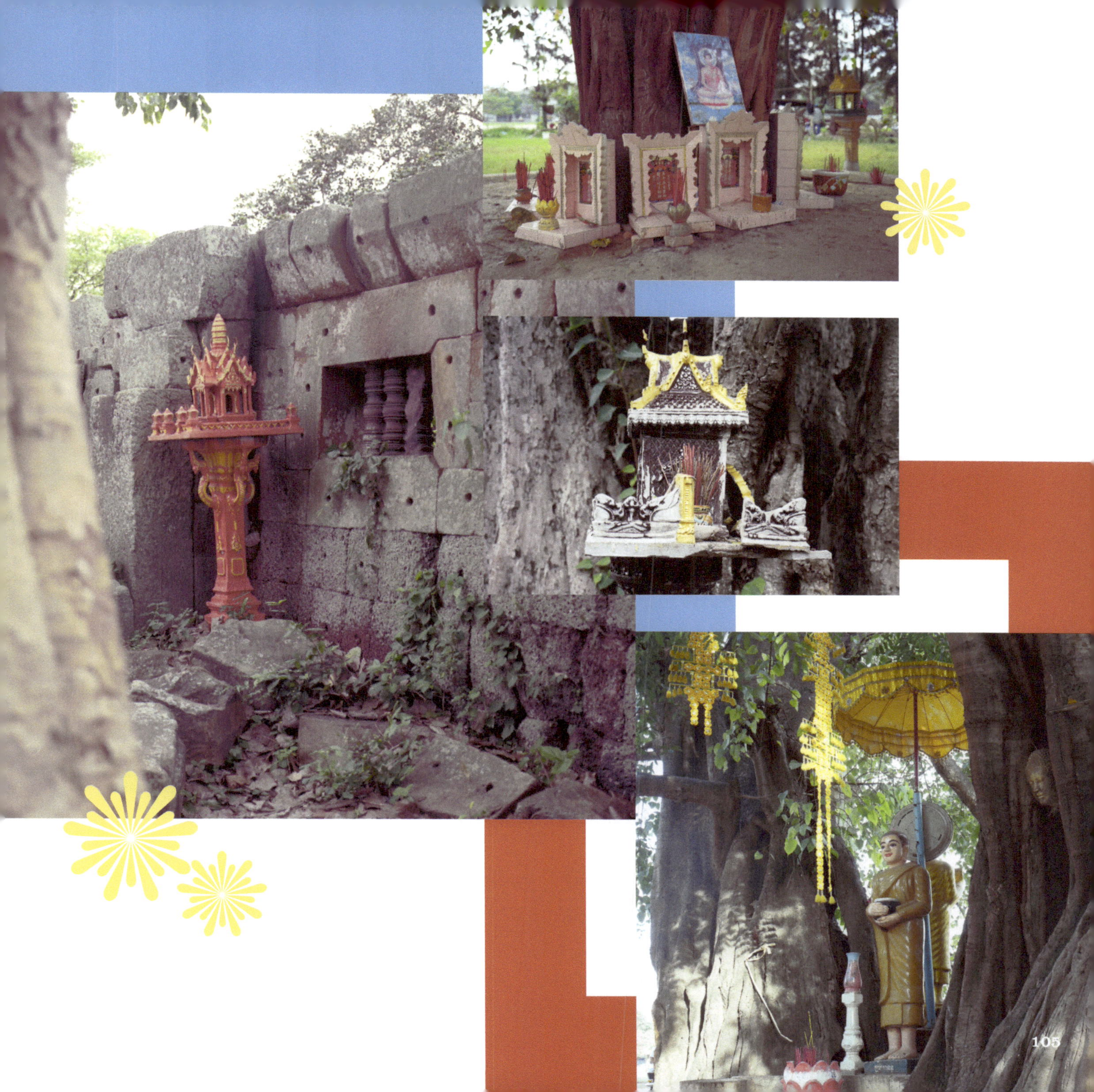

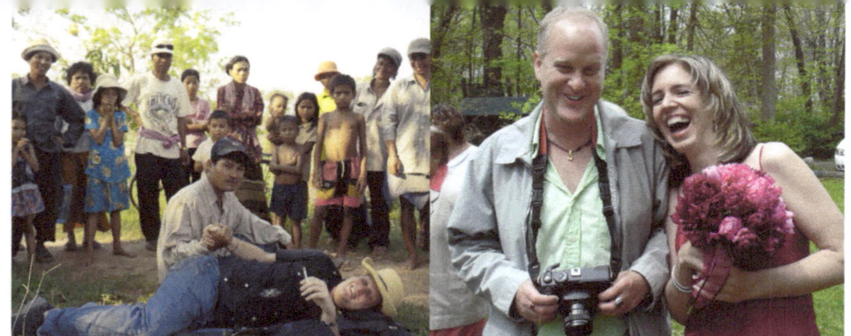

Down but not out, Mat takes a "break" after a motorcycle accident that left him with a compound fracture of the tibia and fibula, and some interesting tales of hospital care in Cambodia.
DECEMBER 2002

The photographer and his designer, laughing again, at her sister's wedding.
MAY 2005

Dear Cambodia,

LOVE,

Photographer Mat Roe's many journeys to Cambodia serve as testimony to the uniqueness of the country and its people. His first visit was in 1998 shortly after the death of Khmer Rouge leader Pol Pot, and in the 10 years since, he has traveled back nearly a dozen times. His images include important and unique monuments, spectacular views of the countryside, glorious landscapes, and details of city and daily life that few have ever seen. This book is full of photographs detailing the fact that life goes on, despite numerous attempts through the years to destroy this country known as the Kingdom of Cambodia.

Jennifer Moody graduated with a degree in graphic design from Western Michigan University in the 1980's alongside Roe. She worked professionally in Chicago for a number of years before moving to California for graduate school and more work in design. Remaining friends over the years, she relocated back to Chicago in 1999, and began collaborating with Roe once again.

Anxious to show the world just a portion of Roe's images collected through the years, they sat down to produce this book. They hope it gives you a glimpse into the amazing world of Cambodia and it's people. Enjoy!